So Far...

So Far...

Kelsey Grammer

HAMISH HAMILTON · LONDON

HAMISH HAMILTON LTD

Published by the Penguin Group
Penguin Books Ltd, 27 Wrights Lane, London W8 5TZ, England
Penguin Books USA Inc., 375 Hudson Street, New York, New York 10014, USA
Penguin Books Australia Ltd, Ringwood, Victoria, Australia
Penguin Books Canada Ltd, 10 Alcorn Avenue, Toronto, Ontario, Canada M4V 3B2
Penguin Books (NZ) Ltd, 182–190 Wairau Road, Auckland 10, New Zealand

Penguin Books Ltd, Registered Offices: Harmondsworth, Middlesex, England

First published in the United States of America by Dutton 1995
First published in Great Britain by Hamish Hamilton Ltd 1996
10 9 8 7 6 5 4 3 2 1

Grateful acknowledgement is made for the following:
"Atlantis" by W. H. Auden. From *W. H. Auden: Collected Poems*.
Copyright © 1945 by W. H. Auden. Reprinted by permission of Random House.
"Moon Landing" by W. H. Auden. From *W. H. Auden: Collected Poems*.
Copyright © 1969 by W. H. Auden. Reprinted by permission of Random House.

Printed in England by Clays Ltd, St Ives plc

A CIP catalogue record for this book is available from the British Library

ISBN 0-241-13671-7

Years after my sister had died, a friend of hers told me this story: One night she and Karen had been talking of life and family and where we all were going. Karen stopped and thought for a moment, and then said, "I'm not so sure about myself, but I do know this—Kelsey's going to do it all."

And so, I dedicate this book to Karen Elisa Grammer.

Karen, if I haven't done it all, I promise I will still keep trying.

Acknowledgments

I'd like to thank everyone I've ever met; whether good or bad, you probably had something to do with how my life turned out, and consequently with this book.

And special thanks to the following: my mother and father and W. H. Auden for obvious reasons; all the teachers who really did make a difference: Mrs. Webb, Ms. Risutto, Ms. Scherer, Mr. Mann, Mrs. Edgar, Mr. Rowett, Richard Mitten, Ron Krikac, Diana Spradling, Mario Peña, Leon Bryant, Larry Pedicord, Edith Skinner, Elizabeth Smith, Robert Williams, Judy Leibowitz, James Kozminsky, and also Peggy, whose last name kept changing, so simply Peggy.

To Leon Bennett for his tireless efforts on my behalf, and to Donald Miod and Father Ken Deasy for being such wonderful friends.

Acknowledgments

In memory of Gary Provost, who convinced me I should write this book but sadly died before its finish; to Jesse Kornbluth, who forced me to write the book I really wanted to; and to Audrey LaFehr, the best of the best in publishing today.

Last but not least, I'd like to say how much I love my daughters, Greer and Spencer. I celebrate your souls. And Tammi, my own, you are a glorious human being, the love of my life, and a wonderful friend.

Contents

Contents

Contents

Assuming you beach at last
    Near Atlantis, and begin
The terrible trek inland
    Through squalid woods and frozen
Tundras where all are soon lost:
If, forsaken then, you stand,
    Dismissal everywhere,
    Stone and snow, silence and air,
Remember the noble dead
    And honour the fate you are,
Travelling and tormented,
    Dialectic and bizarre.

Stagger onward rejoicing;
    And even then if, perhaps
Having actually got
    To the last col, you collapse
With all Atlantis gleaming
Below you yet you cannot
    Descend, you should still be proud
    Even to have been allowed
Just to peep at Atlantis
    In a poetic vision:
Give thanks and lie down in peace,
    Having seen your salvation.

                —from "Atlantis" by W. H. Auden

Author's Note

Although it is implied in autobiography, I would like to emphasize that everything in this book is told from my perspective and my own memories, and of course there are always at least two sides to a story. Many of these memories are painful, but I have endeavored to include only the events in my life that have had a significant impact on my growth as an actor and a man. In some cases I have changed the names of people who played a role in my past, but in all cases I have taken care to recount my experiences fairly and accurately.

Introduction

Two years into "Cheers," the producers decided to add a new character, an uptight intellectual psychiatrist who knew exactly what was wrong with everybody else but not what was screwing him up. They looked at a great many actors in Los Angeles. No one was right. So they started looking in New York. They looked at stand-up comics, and they looked at actors, and then they found me.

They found me because every moment of my life led to them finding me. But on the surface level, where the strands of causality are most visible, they found me because I had been in a Stephen Sondheim musical called *Sunday in the Park with George*.

And that was weird.

Kelsey Grammer

I use this word advisedly—to that point, my life had included such weirdness as the murder of my father, the rape and murder of my beloved and only sister, the drowning deaths of my two half brothers, and a marriage that went south even before the ceremony. But it was definitely weird that I ever got to sing on stage in New York. Because the thing of it was, when I was chosen for that musical, I was in my late twenties—and I hadn't sung since I was in high school.

"I can't get you an audition for the Sondheim show," my agent said. "You have no credits in a musical."

"Jeffrey, you are not a casting director, you are an agent," I said. "You get me the audition, and I'll take care of the rest."

"Kels, this is *Sondheim*. . . ."

"I know, trust me. I can sing. And I'd like to work with the man."

I got the audition.

"Sing 'Oh, What a Beautiful Morning,' " Sondheim said.

I did.

"Sing a little higher."

I did.

"Great," he said. "Thanks."

I got the part. Which put me back in the company of the show's star, Mandy Patinkin. I had

4

known Mandy back at Juilliard. In fact, Mandy and Robin Williams and Chris Reeve and I were all there at the same time, although we weren't close friends. Ten years later, they had made it. I was still waiting. But though neither of us could have guessed it, Mandy was destined to play a part in the process of turning this classically trained theater actor into the star of his own television sitcom.

The show closed. I moved on to understudy Bill Hurt and Christopher Walken in the Mike Nichols production of *Hurly Burly*. And Mandy happened to have lunch with Gretchen Rennell, who was then the New York casting director for Paramount. Gretchen asked Mandy if he knew any funny leading-man types.

"Yes," Mandy said. "Kelsey Grammer."

So Gretchen called me. "Kelsey? Are you interested in doing television?"

Well, just a few weeks earlier, I had been sitting on a friend's couch watching TV. He and I had known each other for a long time and had a remarkable kind of sixth sense about knowing what was going on in each other's lives. He came in and looked at me, and said, very quietly, "You're going to do TV, aren't you?" And, still looking at the screen, I said, "Yes."

So I didn't have to think long and hard.

"Yes. I'm interested," I told Gretchen. "What is it?"

"They've got this new role on 'Cheers.' It's very hush-hush."

Apparently "Cheers" would close out the season with some cliffhanger ending, and then they were going to introduce a new character, and the role was to be kept a secret.

I gave them my assurances that it would remain so.

"Come over and get the scenes," she said. "And remember—you'll have to sign for them. And promise you won't show them to anybody."

I hustled uptown, signed for the envelope, and immediately brought the scenes to Stanley, my old friend from Juilliard. We read the material together and sketched an outline for this kind of upper-crust, well-educated character. A little out of touch, but sincere.

Which is, in a nutshell, a pretty exact description of Frasier Crane, then and now.

As for "Cheers," I'd never seen it. That was probably helpful; I had no preconceived notions going in.

On the way home from Stanley's, I remembered a pair of yellow pants I had in my closet. They were very preppy. Very East Coast. And they had never been hemmed. My mother had given them to me in a classic Christmas faux pas, and I'd never worn them. But they were what I wanted to be seen in when I went to read for Gretchen. In the Grammer theory of auditions, perhaps the most important thing is to show them something they haven't thought of.

So I took out a needle and thread and did my best cross-stitch hem, a skill I perfected during my years in regional theater, and I felt assured that I was now properly armed to get the job. I put on a white shirt and a blazer and loafers. No socks. But of course that was mandatory—I was wearing the summer uniform of the East Coast gentry. I looked as if I was going to spend the day yachting and then have cocktails after. Correction: as if I was a tightly wired WASP who was going to spend the day posing before a sail-filled seascape and then discuss the virtues of a well-rounded portfolio over a martini or three.

I read for Gretchen and she had me talk about myself on tape, and the following Sunday, after the last performance of *Hurly Burly* for the week, I flew to Los Angeles to meet the creators of "Cheers." I read for Glenn and Les Charles, the producers, and James Burrows, who was a frequent director, and I went back to New York. And I got a call to go out to L.A. again and meet the Paramount executives and some of the cast.

This was the big one.

The next Monday morning, I was off to the Paramount lot to read with Ted Danson and Shelley Long. He was warm and easy. So was she. . . .

Everything was going well until, characteristically, I chose this critical moment to say that I had only two problems with Frasier Nye (as he was then called). First: the name. I said, "Do I look like a Frasier Nye to you? It just reminds me of Louis Nye, and it drives me crazy." And second, I didn't like the way Diane and Frasier met. "It seems wrong to me," I offered. "The way you have it, he's her psychiatrist. And he starts dating her while she's his patient. But the thing is, this guy is a *good* psychiatrist. You want him to be credible, right? Then he can't date her while he's treating her. That's just unprofessional and unethical."

Perhaps it was brazen, but I knew that if I was going to play this character, I would have to defend him.

Silence. Then someone said, "Right . . . good point. Let's go."

We walked across the street and up some stairs to a room with the longest table I had ever seen in my entire life. And sitting around the table were the executives. The suits. Any one of whom could say no, and that would be it for me.

Shelley, Ted, and I read a few scenes for them.

Not a laugh in the house.

I said, "Thank you very much. Thank you all," and put the scripts down.

I turned to the room and said, "You know, I'm going to go down to the street now. See if I can get any laughs out there."

And that was that. I disappeared. Literally. I thought I'd make the trip to L.A. worthwhile, so I called my friend Lois, a dear, dear friend from my years in the theater in San Diego, and proposed that we head south. She was game, so we jumped in my little rental Mustang and drove to San Diego, where we had dinner with our friend Craig Noel, who used to run the Old Globe Theater there.

The next day, I returned to the hotel room they had gotten me at the Holiday Inn on Hollywood Boulevard and Vine—a lovely area. And there, on the table, was a mysterious green box. Never before had I seen such a box—I opened it and found my first bottle of Dom Perignon, and a card that read simply, "Welcome to 'Cheers.' "

This was cool.

I popped the cork and sipped the champagne as if to toast the opening of a new chapter in my life.

M y agent asked Mike Nichols if I could get out of the production of *Hurly Burly* for one week—because I had been hired on a trial basis. I was going to do a two-part episode on "Cheers." A kind of public audition.

Mike Nichols told my agent no. I was absolutely flabbergasted. I was making four hundred bucks a week working for this guy. And now I had a shot at making more money in a year than I'd made in my whole life.

Push came to shove. All the "Cheers" producers called Nichols. Half of Hollywood was calling him, it seemed, saying, "Let this kid out."

Nichols had one answer: "No. It's stupid."

Finally, somebody told me that Nichols was staying at the Carlyle Hotel. I hustled over. I called his room. And he got very upset.

"How dare you!" he said. "What are you doing?"

"Look, I'm in the hotel," I replied. "I'm downstairs. And I'm calling because we're talking about my career."

Nichols said something about being busy with his own career, which obviously had nothing to do with mine.

"I'm sorry, Kelsey, but a television show does not a person's career make," Nichols declared, with the hauteur that the world finds so charming.

That was when it hit me. Maybe he didn't know

that this was more than one show. Maybe he didn't know the point of this was potentially a long run of shows.

So I said, "Mike, do you realize that this is not just one guest spot?"

"What do you mean?"

"This is about a *season*. On a *hit show*."

"I have to go to dinner now," he replied. "Please leave me alone."

I went away. And the call came in the next day. It was over. I was out of *Hurly Burly*—but I had to sit with my replacement for a week and a half and cram with him. And I had to pay five thousand dollars for my release.

Did I have five thousand dollars?

Not nearly.

But I got it—I plundered it from the money I got from "Cheers" to relocate.

_____

To an outsider, that moment was the start of the Kelsey Grammer story. From there, we flash back to the obstacles I had to overcome—a sad childhood, family tragedy, and struggling early days—before I got the big break. From there, it's been a lot of success but with a peculiar dark side: more than a decade playing one of the best-loved

11

characters on television, with detours for drugs and screwed-up relationships and a whiff of scandal.

In short, Kelsey Grammer became "Kelsey Grammer."

And as I sit here and look back to the moment when my life—as almost all of you know it—really started, I see how seductive the form of the memoir can be. You start telling your story, and it takes you over. Memories flood in, and you share them. Along the way, you forget that there are other people involved.

I can't forget that. For all the years since I've known there was a difference between right and wrong, personal confidences have died with me. I'm a loyal friend, and I value my loyal friends. And that means this book won't be an egocentric ride through the seven deadly sins, with celebrities as my fellow passengers, and my redemption occurring, right on cue, in the last chapter.

Yes, I will tell stories involving people whose names you'll recognize—and some of those stories may well strike you as "sensational." But I'm not telling those tales to titillate. Or because I've retroactively decided that these folks said what they said and did what they did so that they could read about it later in my book. I have a higher purpose in mind. Those stories are, for me, stones on the pathway, measures of my growth as an actor and as a man.

So Far...

So I've tried to be as careful as I've been candid. If there's anyone who's not spared, it's your narrator. Not because I want to bleed in public. Not because I still take pleasure in being a bad boy. Rather, I've been open here about my failings and my mistakes because that's all they are—failures and mistakes. Apologies are pointless, regrets come too late. What matters is that you can move on, you can grow, you can do better in the future.

So I'm looking back in order to step forward. I know there are holes I'll never be able to patch—nothing I ever achieve will make up for the loss of my sister. And some of the patchwork may be temporary—my present success in overcoming patterns of destructive behavior that go back to my relationships with my mother and grandmother and sister is the result of painful therapy, the love of a good woman, and a share of divine good luck. I've been known to backslide; if I'm not vigilant, it could happen again.

But you know very little of that internal story. Mostly, you know the actor with the starring role on a hit show. The celebrity who makes grossly exaggerated sums of money. That's a good story, perhaps. But not the best. The best story is of my journey, if you will, and it is why "Kelsey Grammer" and Kelsey Grammer have invited you here.

13

1

An All-Too-Brief Childhood

My father was a big brawling wild man. My grandmother told me he had three fistfights on the way to the hospital to see his wife and firstborn child. He didn't start out that way. My parents met at the David Mannes School of Music in New York. Sally was studying voice. Allen was studying music theory. They were initially attracted because of the similarity of their names: Sally Cranmer, Allen Grammer. And when they met, Sally thought Allen was "studious, different from everybody else."

He finished school and the army, started a dance band, played in parades. My mother appeared in summer stock for two years with a traveling tent show, sang with my father's band, then married him. A year later, on February 21, 1955, I was born in the Virgin Islands. Another eighteen months, and along came Karen. And right about then, the marriage ended.

My mom thinks the marriage failed because they were both too young to get married. And because she married for the wrong reason. "I married Allen because I wanted to get away from my mother," she told me. "And Allen had wanted to go to St. Thomas, and I said I couldn't go unless we're married, so we got married."

In St. Thomas, Allen bought into the airport coffee shop and newsstand to keep himself going while he developed his music. He was always opinionated, but his views sharpened the more he lived in the Islands. He tried to change old island ways, and they didn't want to change.

When Mom was pregnant with Karen, my dad and a friend and a crewman went to New Jersey to pick up a sailboat to bring down to the Islands. They had problems almost from the moment they set sail. They got caught in a storm, and the captain died on board and was buried at sea, and then the boat sank. Dad and the crewman were rescued by a freighter that took them to Germany.

While Dad was gone, he lost the lease on the airport coffee shop. Not because it expired, but because he was as likely to pick a fight with a business associate as with a Neanderthal on a bar stool. That was a wake-up call to my mother, who realized that if she continued to live with this man, they'd either kill each other or go insane. So she went back to her parents' home in Colonia, New Jersey, to have Karen—a decision that Dad didn't oppose, perhaps because he was enamored of another woman on St. Thomas.

That wasn't the reason that seemed uppermost at the time, though. The big motivator was an incident that occurred at the bar and grill we owned downtown. A few months into my mother's pregnancy, somebody came in and started to bust the place up. He had a knife and cut up a couple of customers. My father came home and said, "I think you should go home and make your mother happy, and have the baby. Take Kelsey and have the baby up there."

He said he was having "Mau Mau trouble." That is, it seemed pretty obvious to him that he was annoying the local powers, and that someone in that group was trying to get him to leave. At that time he took precautions—he rode around in our truck with a machete in the back. Carried it with him all the time.

After Karen was born, my mom brought us back to the Virgin Islands for a few months, but it didn't take. Where to go? She didn't have any money, and

19

in those days women with young children didn't generally leave them to go to work. So, once again, she went home.

We flew to New York. It was quite a trip. On my first night on the mainland, there was a blizzard, and my grandfather made a call to a friend who ran the Roosevelt Hotel at the time. So the very first night I ever spent in the United States was at the Roosevelt, just above Grand Central Station.

And so, in its way, was Colonia, New Jersey, a small town about halfway between New York and Princeton. My grandparents lived there because my grandfather worked as a sales manager for Chevron Oil, which was headquartered in Perth Amboy. Gordon was a big man, about six foot one. As he got advanced in years, he added some pounds, but when he was at the University of California at Berkeley, he was captain of the rowing crew. He served two and a half years in the South Pacific during World War II, and he never lost his affection for the military or his military bearing.

My grandmother was more of an exotic. She had been a sixteen-year-old at Miss Head's School in San Francisco when she met Gordon, this golden twenty-one-year-old. The "flapper" thing was big then, and she went for it. One night two of their friends wanted to get married. She and Gordon drove with them to Las Vegas to be their witnesses, and, on the spur of the moment, they also decided to tie the knot. Gordon's dad basically disowned him, but they stayed married.

For all his tough-guy masculinity, Gordon was delighted to have his daughter and her two young children in the house. Particularly Karen. He just idolized her. He loved me too, but he was much harder on me. Unlike Karen, I could—and did—do wrong.

But then, Gordon had a clear vision of my future: I was going to Annapolis and then I'd start a career as a navy officer. Gordon knew the admiral of admissions to Annapolis. When I was twelve, I met him. He said, "If you keep your math up, you'll get in." And I was a very good student, at that point, particularly in math, so my future path looked clear—to Gordon, anyway.

My grandmother, though pleased to see Karen and me, was less delighted to have my mother on the premises. Basically, my mother felt that my grandmother never really liked her, that she wasn't what Gam wanted in a child. Mom thought Gam dreamed that her daughter would become a debutante; instead, she got a budding artist who caused a lot of trouble when she was young.

It says something about my mother that one of the first things she did when we moved back to New Jersey was to put my name on the waiting list for Leonard Bernstein's youth concerts. I was two! By the time my sixth birthday rolled around, we had made it to the subscription list, and we began to go to Lincoln Center every few weeks for the next four years. I remember coming out of a performance of *Fanfare for the Common Man* and looking at the fountain outside the theater and thinking, Wow! I'd love to do something here someday.

We also went to plays and musicals. For my eighth birthday, my mother took me to Broadway to see Carol Channing in *Hello, Dolly!* And then there was the rodeo. The ballet. The circus. If it had any artistic merit, my mother wanted to expose me to it. But beyond that first ill-defined urge to "do something" in theater, I had no fantasy of performing.

.My grandparents lived in a colonial-style house. It was one of the first ones built in that neighborhood, and it was—like almost everything about our life with our grandparents—really comfortable. The house had a beautiful living room we used only at Christmas, when we would spend the entire day in it. I remember trying to stay up all night, waiting for Santa Claus to come and also to beat my grandfather up. What I didn't realize until years later was that Gordon was also staying up the whole night. He never let on. I'd rush in on Christmas morning, and he'd be standing by the tree, usually bent over some toy that he had probably just finished putting together moments before. I had a great love for Gordon, and Christmas did seem to be his favorite day of the year, when he was cheerful and always smiling.

I was raised as a Christian Scientist. At the Christian Science Sunday school, they taught us that man was made in God's own image and likeness. I liked that idea. It led me to a youthful affection for Abstract Thinking.

That's how, at the ripe age of six, I found myself sitting on a rock in the woods with my next-door neighbor, Little Al, discoursing on the nature of sin. Little Al was having a more conventional upbringing—he thought sin existed. My view was, If we're made in God's image and likeness, how can we sin? For as I had been taught in Christian Science, "Sin, disease, and death are not real. All is infinite mind and its infinite manifestations."

Al argued mightily, but I didn't budge. And this tenet of Christian Science became one of the foundation stones of my faith. I still believe our minds and our sense of God can get us through almost anything, and that sin, disease, and death are all transitory, material, earthbound impressions of life that don't match up with the truth. But the point isn't so much that I believed anything in particular. It's that, at an early age, I began contemplating my place in the universe, the universe's place inside me, and my sense of God.

This became as real as rain for me that same winter. There had been a huge snowstorm, and I was out playing in the snow. I did a flip in the snow and ended up lying on my back, looking up. The sky was incredibly blue. My eye also took in the tip of a telephone pole. And I looked past the tip of the telephone pole into the sky and somehow sensed the movement of the earth, and that I was a part of it, and that I was a part of God, and a voice came to me at that point, and said, "This is who you are, Kelsey. This is who you'll always be." (If this sounds familiar, it is; I placed it in the middle of *The Innocent,* a television film I did a few years ago.) And from that point on, I had a great sense of trust that God was with me.

In those years, I had the perfect younger sister-older brother relationship with Karen. Sure, there were times when I thought it was an imposition that she would always have to come with me, and that I had to stick up for her, fight for her, and defend her. Mostly, though, I was proud to be responsible for her. If I saw somebody hurt my sister, I was going to hurt him.

I remember the very first moment I realized I loved Karen. I was seven, and it was the first snowfall of the year. I was walking up the hill with my sled; Karen was on her way down the hill in one of those saucerlike aluminum dishes with the handles on the inside. She went trundling by, and had the most enchantingly silly look on her face—a look that was half joy and half dismay that she could not get down that damn hill any faster. And then something amazing happened. As she slid past me I caught her eye. I was struck by a sudden overwhelming sense of how much I cared for her. I realized then that I loved my sister, loved her in a way I would never love anyone else. It was just a simple truth that would always be there—no matter what, Karen and I would always be together.

At my grandparents' house, I had a bedroom with a little window that opened onto the porch roof. My bed was right under the window; at night, I'd slide the window open, step out there, and look up at the stars. But the best view was from Karen's room. She had two windows that came down almost to the floor, and there was a gentle slope to the roof just outside. When everyone thought we were asleep, we would pull our little rocking chairs outside her window. We didn't talk much. We just watched the peaceful stars and the moon. We just listened to the breeze. But we especially loved thunder storms, witnessing the extremes of nature and somehow finding comfort in its contradictions. Bound to Karen, I believed that the evening's song would come to us, bringing sweet messages from a world beyond this one.

School, oddly enough, drove me to seek elsewhere for anything of interest. Let me give some of the credit for that to my first-grade teacher. About four weeks into the school year, nature called at an inopportune moment. I raised my hand.

"May I be excused?" I asked, just as I had been taught at home.

"Do you have to go Number One or Number Two?" was her reply.

"I have no idea what you're asking," I said. And I didn't—in our home, these euphemisms for human functions were not used.

"Well, if you're going to be smart with me, you'll just sit there," she snapped.

I waited a few minutes, then asked again to be excused.

"Are you going to answer my question this time?"

"I don't know how," I said.

"Then you'll sit."

Which I did. Until I pissed my pants. The class rocked with laughter. Except for the teacher. She sent me to the principal, who called my grandmother.

My grandmother was not upset with me. Or contrite with the principal. She gave him holy hell for tolerating vulgarity—and urged him to reprimand the teacher.

She took her revenge a few months later, when our first report cards came out. My mother didn't seem to care that my grades weren't very good. Her attitude, then and later, was "As long as he's happy . . ." But Jack Todd cared.

Jack Todd was our neighbor and a great influence, a great guy. Karen and I would cross the street almost every day after school and visit with him for hours. Jack had one of those electric chairs on his staircase and would let us ride it up and down to our hearts' content.

Jack would sit there, his hand shaking from Parkinson's Disease or maybe from the scotch on the rocks that he drank from a laminated plastic cup

27

with fishnets and starfish and other nautical stuff inside. But Jack was sharp. When I showed him my report card, he said, "This won't do. You are an extraordinary young boy. You don't want to have an average report card. Do you think of yourself as a C person? From now on, I want to see you on the honor roll."

And from the next report on, I was.

I was just seven when one of the themes of my life was revealed to me. I came to it through reading—or just looking at—an illustrated book about the lost, mythical island of Atlantis. And it sparked something, a kind of time travel that only occurred when I was asleep.

The trip began with a young girl coming to my bedside as I was sleeping. She would take my hand, and then we would walk down to the shore together. Right into the water. Right under the water—because as long as I held her hand, I could breathe under water.

And she would take me to Atlantis, and we would talk about the world, about weather, and about God. I remember Atlantis as a place where there were different sexes, but everyone was equal. And thinking was what they did better than anything else.

So Far...

I had this recurring dream for a long time. At least a year. And even when it stopped, it stayed in my mind. And just when it started to fade, it would return.

When I was twelve, my grandparents returned from a trip to Florida and announced, "We've bought a house in Florida near the ocean."

Something in me said, *I'm going home.*

But just as everything seemed so right, something went wrong. My grandfather, who was my friend, my guide, my ally in a house full of women, seemed to change. As I was entering adolescence, he started to have a shorter and shorter fuse when it came to me. He seemed to want more and better than I could deliver, and when I failed him, he snarled.

I felt constantly now as I had felt one day years before. A horrible day. I was eight years old and competing in a Punt, Pass and Kick contest that Gordon fully expected me to win. And I wasn't even close. I totally clutched.

As we walked to the car, Gordon gave me a look of withering disapproval. On the way home, he didn't speak. When we reached home, still silent, I knew I was in for it.

"Come with me," Gordon snapped.

He picked up a football, and we went to the backyard.

"Pass one to me," he ordered.

I did. He moved farther back and tossed the ball to me.

"Again," he said.

I hit him right in the numbers. He threw it to me, then moved farther back.

"All the way," he called.

And I shot him another perfect spiral. He flipped the ball to me again.

"Drop back and punt it," he said.

I punted the hell out of it. And again he returned it to me.

"Now put it on a tee and whack it," he commanded.

And I lofted one farther than any kick I'd seen at the contest.

"Very good," Gordon called. "So what the hell was wrong with you out there today?"

I didn't know. But worse, I didn't know why for the first time he wanted to make me feel so small.

———————

T he drive to Pompano Beach, Florida, was horrendous. We had two cars. My mother drove one, my grandmother drove the other. Gordon rode with my grandmother, and Karen and I would alternate between the two cars.

Gordon really wasn't up to driving a long distance, so we never drove more than five to six hours a day. We'd leave at nine in the morning and stop at four in the afternoon, so the trip seemed to take forever.

One night in a Virginia motel, Gordon delivered a monologue that seemed out of character at the time: awkwardly honest. He spoke to me of something he had never shared, for it was about his days at Guadalcanal, and men of his generation rarely permitted themselves to reminisce about their wartime experiences.

But on this night he was full of stories of men he knew—boys, really—who had been killed there. And what a bloody waste it all was. I had no idea he had these feelings and no way to process his resentment of the folly and unfairness of war. I just sat there and listened, aware for the first time of the extraordinary pain he had known in his life. It rekindled my belief in his extraordinary kindness, the side of himself he had shown me in younger days. In 1965 we moved to Atlantic Highlands, near the New Jersey shore. It had been a difficult move for me because I wasn't particularly fond of the new school I was attending, nor was the new

31

school particularly fond of me. The only pleasant times I spent that year were on occasional walks with Gordon down to the yacht club. I enjoyed the club because it provided me with the rare opportunity to please my grandfather.

He would give me a handful of quarters and send me off to the pool tables while he had a couple of drinks at the bar. After a few months of this, I got pretty good. Good enough, in fact, that Gordon would take delight in challenging an unsuspecting member to try me in a game. And as I proceeded to run the table, I felt exhilarated by his obvious pride in me.

Yes, there had been better days, simpler days. We would water the lawn together, and talk. Gordon taught me how to draw, to chop wood, to count to a hundred in Spanish. How to listen, how to think.

And he taught me one great lesson about character and trust.

It happened while Gordon and my grandmother were on vacation. I snuck into their bedroom, curious, looking through drawers. And came across his gun. I pulled the clip out, took a bullet from the clip, and slipped it into my pocket. I don't know why; I was a boy. An eight-year-old. And now the only eight-year-old with a bullet in his pocket. Somehow it made a difference.

A few months later, sitting across the breakfast

table, Gordon cleared his throat and said, "Kelsey? I went to clean my gun yesterday and noticed that a bullet was missing. Do you have any idea what happened to it?"

I hesitated for a beat, looked him right in the eye, and said, "No."

Had I left it at that, I might have gotten away with it. But the lie seemed so baldly naked out there all alone. A simple no was not enough. I would have to think of something better, something more. A plausible explanation . . . a possible perpetrator.

"You know, Gordon, Little Al was over a while back. Maybe he took it."

The crime was now complete.

Gordon got on the phone to Big Al, and minutes later Little Al stood beside me, crossing himself and swearing his innocence on his mother's grave.

The jig was up.

I said, "Gordon, I took the bullet. I have no idea what happened to it." That was the truth; I had quickly lost track of it.

He looked at me and said, "All right, Kelsey. I'm going to have to spank you. Not because you took the bullet but because you lied." He had never spanked me before, but I knew that he was right. From that day on, Gordon would not spank me, and I would never lie to him again.

At last we arrived in Florida. Six days later Gordon was dead.

Dead? I didn't even know that he was sick. The doctors said his body had been riddled with cancer and he had never told us. I was outraged. Angry with him. If I had known that he was dying, his abuses might have been a little easier to take. Then I might have understood how little time he had to ready me for life without him. A life he knew would not be easy.

He knew that I would have to give up childhood and become, as I became, "Gamma's little man."

In playing that role, I found it hard to grieve. I was too busy taking care of things, being brave. Until one night, months later, I was talking with my grandmother on the porch, speaking of Gordon as we often did then, and I said for the first time, "We were going to have such fun together." That's when I finally broke down. I ran down to the dock and cried until I couldn't cry anymore. And in that moment of quiet I looked up at the stars and I thought, "You know what? You're always going to be alone. That's the deal. That's the deal."

I wasn't sad about it. It was a kind of revelation for me.

So Far...

Shortly after Gordon died, my father invited Karen and me to visit him in St. Thomas for a month. My father had remarried, and in addition to his music, he was publishing and editing *Virgin Island View*, a small monthly for island residents and visitors. It wasn't the usual tourist magazine, with articles that read like advertisements. As ever, he wanted to present a certain viewpoint of the Islands to the tourists who would be coming in. And he wanted his resident readers to be more progressive.

When my sister and I flew to St. Thomas to visit our father, we had no idea who was going to meet us. I had no recollection of him. I hadn't even seen him since I was five years old, and so had no picture of him other than the one my mother gave me. "Oh, you'll know him when you see him," she said. "He looks like Blackbeard the pirate."

That turned out to be an exact description. He stood more than six feet tall, he weighed about three hundred pounds, and he had a big black beard. I saw that figure coming toward us all the way across the airport, and I knew instantly he was my father.

I think that was the only real pull of the heart-strings I ever experienced with him.

Karen and I had a good time that month. I got

to play drums with his pickup band. Not a lot of memories, but I liked the man I met on that visit.

I would see him only one more time when, two years later, Dad visited us in Florida. He'd had business in Miami and took us to dinner before he headed back to the Islands. At one point that evening, he and Mom got up and danced together while Karen and I sat at the table and watched. "You know what?" I said. "I think they really loved each other. You can see it in their eyes."

Later that spring, my mother was late one day picking us up from school. Mom was often late, so we were used to it. But this was a particularly late day. When she finally arrived, I began teasing her about her punctuality, which was my custom. She was silent. It was then that we knew something was wrong.

We got into the car and started home in silence.

Finally, I asked her what was the matter.

"I have some bad news," she said. "Your father was shot last night."

And she began to cry.

It was then that I was certain that no matter what had happened between them, she had truly loved him.

So Far...

My father was killed on April 22, 1968. He was just thirty-eight.

Though tragic, his death was not entirely surprising. He was a very outspoken man, very controversial, and had little room for compromise. He saw and stated things in black and white, a trait that earned him a lot of enemies in the Islands. In addition to the magazine, he had a radio show, and in both he fancied himself a Virgin Islands H. L. Mencken.

That night, his murderer set a circle of fire around his home, and when Dad went out to investigate, he shot him. There were rumors that it was an assassination. But in court the killer was found not guilty by reason of insanity.

My mom was far more upset than my sister and I were. To me, Dad's death was strange and sad, but nothing personal. I didn't really connect with his murder or with him until I too was thirty-eight, and I realized only then how brief a life he'd had.

I can't say that Allen Grammer was a good father. Or that he was my father at all, except genetically. Basically, my father abandoned me. When you look at it right in the face, I didn't have a dad. And my not having a dad was part of my deal for a long, long time before he died. That's why I say, in terms of being there and caring and guiding, my father was Gordon.

But for whatever reasons it played out that way, I don't blame my father. His absence went into the shaping of who I became, and no amount of re-crimination will unwind that. For me, the real message of his death was that life wasn't to be trusted. You couldn't count on it from one day to the next. And that made me develop a sense of urgency—because I too could disappear.

2

Grammer
Lessons

You may have read somewhere that I was a wild man at an early age. You know, discovered alcohol when I was nine. Moved on to drugs at thirteen. Started seducing my friends' mothers before I could shave. Not true.

In New Jersey, I remember helping Gordon carry cases of Haig and Haig scotch up from the cellar. He did a bottle a night, but he got up and did his job in the morning; his stamina was extraordinary. Although he was my role model, his influence didn't extend to alcohol.

I had my first drink at fourteen. One night my friends John and Ronnie and I found a guy who would buy us some vodka. We each got a bottle of Five Flags vodka, which cost us the staggering sum of four dollars a fifth. And we each drank a bottle over at Ronnie's house. And, of course, just felt like shit the next day. I remember waking up and thinking, Oh, man, I gotta have a Coke. I was walking toward the refrigerator when along came John, saying, "Oh, man, I gotta have a Coke." We all ended up, almost at the same moment, drinking Coca-Cola and saying, "Oh, oh, this is really good."

I didn't drink again much after that. Maybe a beer at most. But you forget, don't you? And so I soon found myself at the home of my friend Bob. His mother had lived in Caracas, Venezuela, for a long time and liked to make really, really hot chili. Smart Kelsey said he liked hot things. So she did her chili challenge.

I suffered through a bowl of chili that was virtually inedible, so hot that there was no taste at all, only fire. Finished with dinner, Bob and I went out for a walk on the beach. There by the sea Bob produced a pint of Dewar's scotch that he had pilfered from the liquor cabinet. He took a swig, then offered it to me. I choked down a manly swallow, walked on a step or two, then—projectile vomited the chili, scotch, and all that was within me. So explosive was the stream that not a drop touched me or anything within ten feet of us. As if I had done nothing more than simply paused for a thought, I turned to Bob and said, "Hmm, that was rather interesting, wasn't it?"

As for drugs, not my style (then).

And sex: I was a lot less aggressive than I care to remember. This will come as a surprise to those who think of me as a loose cannon when it comes to the female population, but as a teenager I was shy with girls. That wasn't a condition; it was a decision. When I moved to Florida, the first words I heard out of a girl's mouth were, "What a queer, what a jerk, what an asshole—so ugly."

That was so ruthless, so cruel, so utterly condemning that I immediately lost any interest in ingratiating myself with the local females of my generation. It wasn't that I didn't like women. I just didn't think it was worth it to play a game that was rigged against me. And so I turned my attention to more spiritual longings—I began to meditate every night. And soon I was so removed from most student activities I was like a mystery guest at school.

It was at this point that I became a devout surfer. I started when I was thirteen, the spring after Gordon died. It was the most casual thing. A friend at school asked, "Want to go surfing?" I tried it and

I loved it. My friend said, "Kels, if you do this every day for six months, you'll be a surfer." So I did. I would put my board in my little boat, go up the cut to a break I knew, drop anchor, dive in, and start paddling. Whether it was a big wave day or a small one didn't matter. Any way the waves broke, they had something to teach me about surfing.

I surfed every day from five to seven in the morning and again from four to seven at night. School became an interlude, an interruption between sessions of surfing. At night I would race through my homework, do whatever my mom and grandmother and sister needed, and then go to my bedroom and meditate for an hour or two. And that was my day, from ages thirteen to seventeen. It may seem an odd existence for a teenage boy, but to me it was perfectly normal. I knew of no other.

I started getting really good when I was fifteen. At sixteen, I got my driver's license, which gave me the opportunity to surf better, more distant breaks. On weekends we'd drive up coast to Coco and Sebastian, where the waves were always bigger, and surfing became my passion in a life otherwise filled with a host of obligations. Through surfing I found a connection to the sea and, through the sea, a connection to the deepest part of myself. And to God.

The greatest religious experience of my life took place on a surfboard. It was midsummer, a really hot day, and the water was even warmer than the air. I'd been surfing for about an hour—a southeast chop off one of the jetties along Palm Beach. I dropped into my next ride, and was suddenly surrounded by the wave. I looked up through a wall of water and saw the sun, and at that moment I vanished. There was only peace. I felt I was at one with the universe. There was no ego, no pain—only light.

"God," I thought, "if this is death, then take me now."

Yes, those were days of constant grace with God.

Still, in the nights, there were times of doubt, and question, and fear. I didn't know where I belonged, or what I was meant to be. I would pray for guidance: what was I to do? I was a young man, terribly sensitive, and, perhaps because of the tragedy in my own family, very aware of all the pain and suffering in the world. It occurred to me, and I know this may sound strange, that I might be Jesus. And I prayed that God would let me know. I didn't mind the idea of having to die for mankind; I was just sick and tired of not knowing.

After a while it became painfully clear that I was not Jesus. That this was not exactly what He had in mind for me. Still, it was that same desire to do good, to serve mankind if you will, that led me to become an actor.

After our grandfather's death, Karen and I entered Pine Crest Preparatory School. It wasn't the kind of school you may think of when private education comes to mind—it wasn't guys in blazers and khakis and girls in crisp white blouses and sensible shoes. It was, all in all, a pretty reasonable place, run by people who weren't terminally uptight.

Although my relationship with school was rather ambiguous, it did manage to introduce me to what became the most important thing in my life: language.

In the seventh grade, I read my first Shakespeare play, *Julius Caesar.* The teacher explained that the Brutus character lived a philosophy of stoicism, a belief that life, though painful, still afforded us a choice not to become its victim, that we could rise above its contradictions and injustices and live by a code of our own making.

Given my confusion and inability to deal with Gordon's recent death, it was as if I'd been thrown a lifeline. I threw myself into the world of Shakespeare. I felt I had discovered a brave new world, a world of poetry and thought, and most of all, extraordinary language. This inspired me to start writing on my own, to use language as a tool for self-discovery.

So Far...

One night I was sitting in my room, searching for a phrase to capture life's imperative. A motto, if you will. This is what I wrote: "Stagger onward, rejoicing." That sounded right. "Stagger onward, rejoicing." Exactly right.

One day I staggered into the office of Richard Mitten. Richard was the new head of the music department at Pine Crest, and he started recruiting all kinds of kids—jocks, heads, nerds—to sing in the choir. He had an enthusiasm that was contagious, and people started saying that he was doing some very exciting things. So I decided to check it out. Which is exactly what I told him.

"What can I do for you?" he asked.

"I've heard good things; I thought I'd check it out."

"Well, sing me a song," Richard said, "any song you'd like."

I sang "Yesterday" by the Beatles. I did about two bars.

"You're a baritone," Richard said. "Great! You want to sing with me?"

"Sure, I'll give it a try," I said.

I was willing to try anything back then.

Richard was very energetic and passionate about music, and made its discovery an exhilarating experience. In retrospect he played a very important role in my life. He got me on the stage, and I liked it. And it was something I was good at.

Around this time the school did an about-face on the "hair code." Above the collar and the ears would now be regulation. As I had spent the better part of three years cultivating my rather ostentatious tresses, this was clearly unacceptable. I would rather die than cut my hair.

I was too young to die, and so I resolved to wear a wig. A "Jane Fonda" wig, in fact, cut to specs for a very reasonable thirty-five dollars.

I wore the wig in bold defiance of authority, refusing to comb it so that it rose a full five inches above my head. I couldn't help thinking how foolish it was of the school to allow one of its students to look so foolish. But if they were willing, so was I.

I even wore it when I sang, imagining whispers in the audience like, "Oh, that poor child. He must have some horrible disease." It looked that horrendous.

I never got embarrassed. I'd leave the stage, pull it off, shake my own hair loose, and toss the wig in the back of my car. Next morning, I would exhume the rat pelt from the backseat graveyard of books and plop it on my head, prepared to face another day wearing my crown of protest.

Through singing Richard and I became very, very close. I learned a lot from him about opening up on stage—exposing myself with a safety valve. Suddenly I was no longer an introverted, introspective kind of enigma; I was a public enigma.

Richard also got me involved in singing with the choirs of various churches. I enjoyed the music, and I enjoyed the exposure to different faiths. I could wear my hair long and get paid twenty-five bucks a Sunday. More important, I enjoyed the knowledge that I was capable of doing something that gave others pleasure.

But more and more I began to realize that I didn't have much in common with my peers. For example, other kids avoided their teachers while I sought out their company. Long after Leon Bryant had been my art teacher, I would still drop by to talk. Larry Pedicord was the basketball coach and ran the camp office. I wasn't on the team, he wasn't my teacher, but we would visit nearly every afternoon. Mario Peña became one of my greatest friends at school. He had taught my sister in the

49

sixth grade, and loved to recount the occasion of our first meeting. As he told it, I walked up to him one day and announced that I was Karen Grammer's big brother, and that I was very good. I guess, underneath it all, I always had a cocky kind of confidence in myself.

And then there was Ron Krikac. He came to Pine Crest my junior year to head the drama department and teach English and coach the debate and speech teams. We first met at a banquet for new teachers shortly before the term began. The school choir sang, and afterward I veered away from the students and took a seat at Ron's table. In my most charming way I welcomed the new arrivals and warned them that it was likely they would have to deal with me.

For Ron these were prophetic words, for he became my English teacher.

After class the first day, Ron pulled me aside and reminded me that we had met the week before. "You're very interesting," he said. "Do you know how to smoke a cigar?"

"I don't know," I said. "Sometimes I smoke a pipe."

"Well, my first play is going to be *The Little Foxes* by Lillian Hellman. You might be good as Ben Hubbard. He's fifty and smokes a cigar. Would you be interested?"

"Sure," I said. "What the hell."

A few weeks later, rehearsals were about to begin. Ron repeated his offer, but added: "There's just one thing. I've heard some bad things about you."

"What?" I asked.

"I hear that you're a little flaky. You don't show up, and when you do, you don't apply yourself."

"That's absolutely true," I said. "I've got some problems at home. But don't worry, I'm interested in this. I'll be there. I'll show up, I promise."

"Rehearsals begin next Saturday at one o'clock sharp."

Well, I went up coast with some friends that morning, surfed a few hours, and on the way home a rainstorm hit. I was driving, we caught a dip in the road, and hydroplaned. Four or five spins later, we slammed into a cement canal barrier.

I missed the first rehearsal.

Ron called my mother, furious. "Where is he?"

"Well, he's had an accident."

"Oh, Jesus."

I showed up for the second rehearsal, graciously accepted Ron's apologies, and took my first step toward life as an actor.

When I'd told Ron that there were problems at home, it was a masterpiece of understatement. The truth is, life at home was awful. It seemed that my grandmother and mother, and even my sister at times, were members of a bizarre conspiracy, its sole purpose to ensure that I fulfill their needs.

No matter what I was doing, they could call at any time and make me stop. Not because there was a big problem, but maybe just because they were having a fight. I was the glue, the man of the family.

The bottom line on my mother, you see, was that she basically never left home. She got away for a couple of years with my father, didn't like it very much, brought her kids back to Mom and Dad, and she stuck with that. I remember her going to work sometimes. It was never a career thing, though; after Gordon died, she had part-time jobs. But my grandmother held the purse strings. And my mother was pretty much under her thumb. Not what my mother wanted, really, but she knew it was the key to the comfort of her children.

What my mother didn't immediately see was that my grandmother thought I was supposed to replace Gordon. She leaned on me hard. And I never seemed to give her as much support as she needed.

Actually, that was true for my mother and sister as well. Kelsey was supposed to take care of everything—in essence, I was supposed to be father and mother. So I was responsible for running errands, cleaning and cooking, as well as peace-keeping. But Kelsey never did any of it well enough. I felt like I was trapped in a game I could never win.

I didn't ask for this domestic drama, but it was the deal. In the Bible, Matthew says, "Do what is given unto you." I tried to find solace in that. What I mostly found, though, was an unhealthy definition of love—to me, love meant not being good enough.

This couldn't be all that I was meant to do. I tried to fulfill their needs, but always sought the course away from them and toward myself. So I found friends in wildly disparate circles—all ages, all backgrounds. Some stand out to this day as lessons in my life, and as gifts.

Ray, for example. We met in Driver's Ed at Pompano Beach High School the summer we were fifteen. At first I thought, nice kid. Maybe a little stuck on himself. He probably thought the same thing about me. We devised a little contest: who could get the VW into third gear going around the track? This was frowned on by the teacher. Also there was an old Le Mans that had a bit more oomph. When the teacher wasn't looking, we'd stand on the accelerator, drop it into drive, and squeal across the dirt. Left a nice patch on the track. And this was how we bonded. Through these shenanigans we became the best of friends. But there was something in Ray that bothered me. Even frightened me in a way I couldn't grasp. There was pain in him I couldn't fathom.

But I gained some insight the first time I called his home. A woman answered, and I asked for Ray. She responded, "Ray Senior? Or do you want Butch?" That said a world of things about his constant need to be the strongest, the toughest guy around.

That helped me to understand why, when we got our licenses, Ray began to acquire speeding tickets at an alarming rate. Every time I'd see him, he was getting pulled over for something. Sometimes we'd be going to the same place and I'd see him on the road—there he'd be, a cop behind him. With reason. Ray drove like a wild man, hellbent to be the first to get wherever we were going.

I left Florida after high school, but I was home when Ray had his twenty-first birthday. His dad's present was a gun. I guess Ray was doing some drugs, and driving, of course, and he started shoot-ing at stop signs. When the cops picked him up, he had a bottle of booze in his car and a knife tucked into his boot and a big bag of yellows and stuff. And the first question the cops asked him was, "Is somebody after you?"

There was no one. Only Ray after Ray.

Ray called me to bail him out. When I saw him, he had a big cut across his face, the result of having slammed into a telephone pole when the cops chased him. He ended up going to jail for eight or nine months.

A few years later, when I was working in San Diego, Ray called—he had completely straightened out. He was holding down a job, and had met a wonderful girl, and they were getting married, and he wanted me to be the best man.

I told him I wasn't sure if I could make it, but would do my best. He asked his fiancée's brother to be the best man instead. But as so often in my life, events unfolded in a way that made it possible for me to be there. And everything he said was true. She was a lovely girl, and he was finally on track. And in my eyes, the wedding consecrated more than just their love. It consecrated Ray.

I returned to California. Two days later, Ray's mother phoned. There had been a car accident. Ray's wife was dead. I tried desperately to reach him, knowing he could not express his pain except in violence, and certain he would turn it on himself. For three days I begged him, knowing he could hear me, listening to his machine, unwilling to accept my argument to go on living.

Finally, his sister called. Ray had been found burned to death, after slamming his car into a tree.

It's difficult to call his death a lesson, but I did discover that I envied Ray. Envied how deeply he could love.

Harry was another.

He was the father of Jay, one of my better friends in school. In tenth grade, Harry moved his family to Rhode Island. But Jay and I kept in touch, and when I was eighteen and studying acting at Juilliard, I went to visit them for Thanksgiving.

Thanksgiving morning Harry and I were sitting together enjoying a Bloody Mary when he did something so extraordinary it took my breath away. It was time to leave for the midday feast. Harry rose and hollered up the stairs: "Where's my bride?" And again I envied a man who could love someone so much that after all those years together he still thought of his wife as his bride.

Three years later, Harry's bride left him. And it destroyed him. Two years later, he died.

These stories did not teach me but confirmed a simple truth: loss and death were givens and therefore cause to make uncommon choices, reasons to take risks in life.

Perhaps that was why, in spite of everyone's advice to the contrary, I chose to honor Ron's assessment that if I wanted it enough, I had the talent to become an actor. I had made my decision, and that decision became firmer every time another unsolicited opinion told me I had no idea how hard it would be. The truth is, it would be harder than anything they could imagine.

 As for the idea of having "something to fall back on"—if I'd had something to fall back on, I probably would have. So instead of college it was off to New York to become an actor—now, that was mammoth, that was beyond.

3

Portrait of the Actor as a Young Man

When I applied to Juilliard, the acting program was just six years old, but it was already the most prestigious school of its kind. John Houseman, who was its director, had run the Mercury Theater with Orson Welles, produced the movie version of *Julius Caesar* with Marlon Brando—he was one of the kings of the stage and screen.

And when I applied, I was a seventeen-year-old surfer.

My attitude was: I'll check it out, see what I can do.

So I went to my interview as myself. I had my hair in a ponytail. I did the pieces I'd prepared: a bit of Bottom from *A Midsummer Night's Dream* and a snippet of Willie Loman from *Death of a Sales-man*—not exactly choices a seventeen-year-old might normally make.

When I finished, I heard a voice from the back of the theater.

"Oh, Mr. Grammer," the voice began, and I knew it was the voice of John Houseman, because it was very cultured, a little like what God would sound like if he'd made the world during the golden age of twentieth-century theater.

"Yes?"

"Tell me, do you intend to make acting your career?"

"Well, I flew up here from Fort Lauderdale. What do you think?"

There was a silence.

"Do you have any questions?" the cultured voice asked.

"Yeah, how did I do?"

"It was a good audition, we'll let you know."

A few weeks later, they did. And I was overjoyed, overjoyed but also overwhelmed. Manhattan loomed before me—exciting, terrifying, inviting, yet foreboding. Impossible and inevitable at the same time. The hope of an uncertain future.

In the fall of 1973 I moved to New York. With 760 dollars. Money I had earned that summer. Money that had to see me through the year. I'd taken two jobs: from seven a.m. to three in the afternoon I worked construction; from nine p.m. to three in the morning I was the houseman at a hotel on the beach. I gave up surfing. It was one of the first of many sacrifices I would have to make in the coming years.

I was given a full scholarship to Juilliard, but the word *full* was misleading—cavalier in some respects. It did not include the cost of housing, electricity, or food. This would rest upon the puny shoulders of my 760 dollars. My grandmother couldn't help me out financially, because the money Gordon left us had dwindled to at best a comfortable subsistence level. So I was on my own.

Clearly I would need a budget that would meet my longterm goals: shelter, warmth, and sustenance. I concluded warmth and shelter were expendable until at least the middle of November; sustenance, however, was a priority. This was a good first step. I had decided it was critical to eat.

So, I'd taken care of the essentials, and now was ready to begin my education.

B ut all kidding aside, let me briefly tell you how I did it. The first month in Manhattan I spent with my old friend Bob and his mother, Gigi, of chili-challenge fame. They had moved to New York a few years earlier, after a divorce, and Gigi was now working for the American Cancer Society. Their hospitality was an enormous help because it meant I wouldn't have to spend my money for at least a month. So it was in October, when I sensed my welcome had been worn extremely thin, that it was time for me to go. Go where? I thought. The Park. It was still warm enough to sleep outdoors, so I found a little spot on the West Side a few blocks from the school. I could shower there, attend my classes, and then at night jump back over the wall to my secret home.

Idyllic as this may sound, it really wasn't that much fun. So a few weeks later, as the weather started turning, I looked for an apartment. The good news was, in seven weeks I'd spent only eighty-two dollars. If I was prudent, and could find a cheap enough apartment, I was convinced that I could make it through the winter.

S chool was monstrous. On the first day I had arrived in sandals, cutoff shorts, and a Hawaiian shirt, bright-eyed and bushy-tailed, thrilled to be there. The novelty wore off very quickly. The common philosophy in acting schools is to begin the curriculum with humiliation and a commitment to convince each student they are absolutely worthless. So you go around feeling pretty small for the better part of a year. You do nothing well. Walk, talk, sit down, stand up, think—and most definitely—act. In fact, you do not act at all.

Still, I found it fascinating. There were several teachers I adored. Pierre LeFevre, who had been the voice of the Free French during World War II, taught a class using masks to illustrate archetypes in drama from the Juvenile to the Elder. Robert Williams and Elizabeth Smith had very different ways of teaching voice production. Each I liked, for very different reasons. And speech class was with Edith Skinner, who had helped invent the phonetic alphabet, and knew more about how the English language should be spoken than any person alive.

But there was an enormous pressure to conform—not one of my strong suits. So even when I knew the information might be helpful, I resisted it with all my might because of its delivery. This was a problem. And I felt desperately unhappy.

As a result I looked forward to the coming summer more than I could say. I dumped my apartment and headed south to warmth, and waves, and work I could enjoy.

I took a job with Big Chief, a demolition company owned by my friend Dean's father. Dean ran the job, and I'd be beating walls doing a remodeling project in Palm Beach. In the beginning it didn't look as if I'd have much of a connection with my co-workers, Jimmy and Jesse. I was a young white middle-class kid studying acting in New York; they were seasoned laborers and would be all their lives. They were also black. I mention this only as a point of interest in the upcoming story.

As you know, I liked to sing. And had always been particularly fond of gospel music. Some of my favorites were "Go Down, Moses," "March Down to Jordan," "Swing Low, Sweet Chariot," to name a few. Anyway, I especially liked to sing when I worked.

Jimmy and Jesse thought I was out of my fucking mind. Perhaps I was, but they came to like me. And I them.

And they taught me.

One great thing about kicking around in life is the variety of experiences. You discover a kind of perfection in every person you meet, and in what they do. Jesse and Jimmy taught me how to walk into any building, anywhere, and know how to knock it down. That's a great feeling, very powerful. I got so I'd make a cut in a wall, leave it standing, poised to fall, then push it over with a finger.

And they taught me something golden.

Pacing. To see a beginning, a middle, and an end. How to accomplish something without rushing it. Trusting that the patience and good work would lead inevitably to a good ending. A big lesson in terms of my career. Particularly when you're nobody. Because you can't panic, you can't make it happen through effort alone—you have to trust that you'll get there.

It's a marathon, not a sprint.

I returned to New York for my second year at Juilliard. Unfortunately, my acting teacher and I didn't get along very well, and since acting was my reason for being there, I began to see the writing on the wall. My interest waned, I started skipping classes. It was clear to me and to the faculty my enthusiasm for school was gone.

Outside of school, things were a lot better. Because of the year I'd spent away from home, I was now legally independent, and therefore eligible for education grants and my father's Social Security survivor benefits. Also, I had fallen in love with a wonderful girl, a dancer at school named Jill. I was devoted to her; we even spoke of marriage.

I met her parents and liked them. I think they liked me too. They didn't like my motorcycle, or the uncertainty of an acting career, but they didn't dismiss me out of hand. They were willing, it seemed, to welcome me into the family, if that was what their daughter wanted. I really was impressed by both of them.

So my focus was elsewhere on that spring day when I found a pink slip in my box at school: *Please come to the office on the fourth floor*. And that was it.

Upstairs, Liz and Robert, Pierre and Gene, told me that though some of my work that year had been exquisite, they nevertheless thought the time had come for me to go.

"Okay, then. I'm gone."

We hugged and smiled, said our goodbyes, agreeing it was for the best.

It never crossed my mind to ask for a second chance—ask to stay. It just wasn't in my nature to beg, or to lie, and the truth was, I was really more excited about *not* being there.

———

To his credit, John Houseman thought it necessary to meet personally with students who were leaving the acting school. I sat down in his office for my second and last encounter with him.

He reassured me that this was not the end of the world, no reflection on my talent, that things had simply not worked out. And that was all.

He also told me something wonderful.

As I was leaving, he said, "Oh, yes, by the way. Read the great novels. That's the only way to learn of worlds outside your own, of lives and manners, customs and relationships, that now are vanished. Without such information you will as an actor never be able to portray those periods with authority and style."

That advice was dead-on.

It was rare for me to take advice, but this was good, perhaps the best I'd heard at Juilliard. This I would take with me.

After the meeting, Edith Skinner approached me in the hall. "Kelsey, I know what's happened, but not to worry. Oh, you have the most wonderful blue eyes. You have a future in acting. Meet me in my office in fifteen minutes. There's something I have to show you."

In her office, Edith showed me a short paragraph, apparently written by a director, on what he looked for most in an audition. "More than anything," he wrote, "I look for a single moment of truth from an actor. Just one phrase or sideways glance that's genuine. And that actor is the one that I will hire."

Wow. Two of the greatest things I'd ever heard all in one day. This leaving thing was looking pretty good.

Until I saw the expression on Jill's face when I told her the news. I said I felt good about it, that things were going to be okay. But it was obvious she didn't think so.

"This upsets you," I said.

"Yeah."

"Why?"

"Well, how are you going to provide for us?"

"I don't know. You still want to be a dancer. How did you expect to provide for yourself?"

"I never thought I'd make a living at it," she said.

Though our relationship would last another year, I feared right then that we would never make it. She was so obviously disappointed in me, and once again someone I loved was telling me I wasn't good enough.

Nothing could hurt me more.

———

But I was wrong. Something could. A heartache lay ahead of me more devastating than anything I could imagine. It would involve my family; that it would involve my sister was a bitter irony, for Karen had done so well those last two years. That hadn't always been the case.

At Pine Crest, Karen had been in trouble because she resented being reduced to "Kelsey Grammer's little sister." I guess she felt that she was living in my shadow. So she acted out, as they say. She was suspended from school for a month for drinking. She also got in trouble for shoplifting.

One night my mother woke me in the early morning. Karen was in jail, she said, and I had to go and get her. So I threw my clothes on, jumped in the Maverick, and drove down to the Ft. Lauderdale police station. She had been arrested for breaking and entering, and possession of marijuana. Apparently she and her friend Momo had snuck into Momo's parents' home. They had gone out of town, and the girls decided it was time to have some fun. As I told Karen, this was where her thinking eluded me. Their home was in a gated community that was privately policed. Naturally, they knew the home was supposed to be vacant. Why, then, would they turn on the lights, crank up the stereo, smoke a little weed, and somehow be surprised when the cops showed up?

Rather than answer the door and explain that everything was fine, they hid in the closet.

"In the closet?" I asked.

"I guess I wasn't thinking very clearly," said Karen.

That much was certain.

I spoke to the arresting officer, and he said he'd give her a break. She wasn't a bad kid, maybe a little confused. As we left the station, Karen turned to him and shouted, "What a pig!"

I went through the roof. I put her in the car and said in no uncertain terms, the only person acting like a pig that night was she.

During the next two years Karen went pretty wild. Dated, stayed out late, and even did some acid. In general drove my mother crazy, and really kept me on my toes.

Then in her junior year she left Pine Crest to attend a school in Hillsboro Beach. After a month they advanced her to the senior class. She was a brilliant student, and she'd made it through her "time" like a champ.

I remember how proud I was at her graduation. It seemed that every other time an award was presented for excellence, it went to Karen Grammer.

She attended Barry College in Georgia on a scholarship, but after a year she decided she would rather wait on college. She moved back to Florida, rented a little apartment, and got a job in the mall where my mother worked. Things were going well, but it was no surprise when that summer she decided to take off with a friend to Colorado.

We both came home for Christmas. It was wonderful. Karen was happy in Colorado Springs and would return there. I would go back to New York City.

I would never see her again.

4

The End of
the Innocence

In the spring of 1975 I left Juilliard and headed to Rhode Island for the summer. I got a job unloading fishing boats. The work wasn't bad. You just jumped down in the hold with a pitchfork and pitched fish. It wasn't steady, but when a boat came in, I'd work for a day and it paid pretty well. I rented a house in Narragansett with a couple of guys and would drive to Connecticut on the bike to visit Jill when I was free. It looked like it was going to be a good summer.

Just as I felt settled in, my mother called.

"Kelsey, you have to come home. Gam's in the hospital, and I think she's going to die."

So I packed my things, hopped on the bike, and left for Florida an hour later. I drove straight through, 1,400 miles, through storms and heat waves, traffic and exhaustion. I got soaked at least eight times, and then would freeze until I was dry again, and then would cook once more beneath the summer sun. A miserable experience.

When I arrived, my grandmother was back at home and feeling fine. A false alarm, I guess. In fact, I had never seen her look so good. I, on the other hand, was in considerably worse shape, and took to my bed for a couple of days.

Once I had recovered, I spoke with Karen on the phone. She told me she was going to leave Colorado and would be home for her birthday, July 15. Great, I thought. Karen's coming home, I'll spend a couple of months in Florida before heading back to New York.

We spoke again, on June 30, just before the holiday weekend. She said she might be going out of town for the Fourth of July, but she would call when she got back and let me know when she'd be leaving for home.

She didn't call.

On July 7, after trying to reach her for several days, we finally got in touch with the police in Colorado Springs. And I was scared. The police said they didn't have anything on a girl named Karen Grammer, but they would check it out.

Two days later, while I was cooking something in the kitchen, I saw two men in suits and ties approaching our front door. Cops. My first thought was, "Oh shit, they finally found me." I had a couple of outstanding speeding tickets, and I assumed that they had come for me.

Hesitantly, I opened the door. They asked my name. I told them. And then they asked if I was alone in the house.

"No," I said. "My grandmother's here."

"Does she have any medical problems?"

"No."

"A heart condition?"

"No," I told them.

They paused a moment. "Perhaps it would be better if you stepped outside."

As I walked behind them to their car, it suddenly hit me. "Is this about my sister?"

They opened a file. Across the top was printed: KAREN ELISA GRAMMER.

"The Colorado Springs police have the body of a murdered girl they think might be your sister. She was classified as a Jane Doe for the last ten days, which is why they didn't call you sooner. They've asked that we send out her dental records as soon as possible so that we can make a positive ID."

I gave them the name of our dentist, but didn't know his number. They said they would take care of it. They seemed upset, and so I thanked them for their kindness in an effort to comfort them somehow. They said they were terribly sorry and then left.

I walked back toward the house in a kind of daze. Karen was dead. I had trouble letting that sink in. It was too much to comprehend. Murdered.

I stood searching helplessly for an appropriate response. I should be crying, I thought. I entered the kitchen and went back to cooking. Yes, I thought, I should be crying, and so I tried. But it didn't work. Something strange was going on. It was as if I were split in two, and one half of me was watching the other. One a victim, and the other an observer, noting from a distance like a stranger what was happening to me.

It's difficult to explain what I was going through. The one who was watching said, What the hell is wrong with you? Your sister's dead. Why aren't you crying? Didn't you love your sister?

Of course I did, the other said, feeling guilty that the tears would just not come, and fearing if they did the watching one would say that they weren't real.

This first response to Karen's death bothered me for quite some time. Several years later, though, I found some insight, and even some comfort, from the book *Death Be Not Proud* by John Gunther, an autobiographical account of the death of his own son. In a certain passage he described a quandary similar to the one I had experienced. He spoke of feeling as if he were two people at the same time: one involved, and one aloof. One in pain, and one recording it. Almost like a writer who would one day want to tell the story.

And there it was, that was the answer.

He explained that this was not a crime, but a condition of the artistic personality. A gift of sorts, of logging all experience for future use. The fact that we record emotions as we feel them doesn't make them any less genuine. It's who we are: actors, writers, painters, musicians, all have this in common. In everything we do, each of us are two. One for life, one to hold the mirror up to life.

I told my grandmother the police were fairly certain that Karen was dead and I would have to go to Colorado. I then called my mother at work and told her to come home. I think she already knew, but I found it hard to tell her. So after a moment of hesitation, my grandmother finally blurted out the words.

"She's dead. Karen's dead."

It was the most awful thing I've ever seen. Almost like a Jack-in-the-box, my mother jumped around the room, thrashing, wailing, crying out, "My baby, my baby!"

I called my friend Spencer. "She's dead," I said.

He said, "I'm coming over."

When he arrived, I walked outside to greet him, and when I looked into his eyes, I started sobbing.

The next morning I flew to Colorado. Karen's dental records had confirmed that it was she, but it was necessary that a family member make a positive ID and arrangements would have to be made for a casket and transportation home.

A detective from the Colorado Springs Police Department met me at the airport. As we drove into town, he filled me in on some of the details. Karen had been killed the night of July 1. She had been found by a stranger, but they couldn't identify her. They had even run a picture in the paper: *Do you know this girl?*

But she remained a Jane Doe until we called, concerned that she was missing. The paramedics said they worked on her for an hour when they got to the scene, trying to bring her back to life. But they could not. Karen had bled to death after being stabbed forty-two times. There were no suspects. I asked if she'd been raped as well, and the detective told me she had not.

So Far...

After that we rode in silence to a funeral home where they had taken her once they found out who she was. The detective, with the funeral director, walked me down a long, long hallway. I could feel my heart pounding, and I trembled as we stood before a door.

The detective said, "I'm sorry that we have to do this now, but I think it's best to get it over quickly. Are you okay?"

"I guess so."

"I should warn you, she's quite dehydrated. She's been dead for ten days, and the body loses a lot of moisture, so she's probably going to look a little different."

He opened the door, and I stepped in.

In the middle of the room was a body. I avoided looking at it for a moment. Then finally I looked up, and it was Karen. Her face was so thin. The bone in her nose seemed to stand out somehow, and her toes looked like sharp little needles underneath the sheet. I guess that's what he meant about dehydration. She did look different, but it was obviously Karen. And yet at the same time it was not.

Standing there alone with her dead body, I got a glimmer of hope and comfort from the fact that her body seemed so empty. And that it was never really Karen, just a shell she didn't need anymore.

I left the room and told the detective I was sure. It was my sister.

Then I bought a casket and booked it as freight on my return flight. As we drove to the Ramada Inn, the detective told me he had lost his best friend just the week before in a helicopter accident. He sympathized with me and I shared his loss with him, and realized that was why he had told me. Because he shared my loss with me. It touched me very deeply, and I was glad he was the one who helped me through this terrible time.

As we said good-bye at the hotel, he assured me that they would find the killer. "I promise," he said.

I shook his hand and checked in for the night.

Then it was home for the funeral. I don't remember the service very well. The chapel was filled with Karen's friends, almost all of them dissolved in tears. Jill came. It was the business of death, and I took care of it. But I have one regret I carry to this day. I had ordered the casket closed, telling my mother that Karen looked so unlike herself, it would be better if she didn't see her.

It didn't occur to me at the time, but perhaps I did my mother a disservice, depriving her of the same realization I had had. There was a finality in seeing her dead body, a kind of closure.

Years later, I apologized to my mother and she said it was all right. And yet it haunts me still.

I t took a while for the Colorado police to solve the murder.

Apparently, on June 30, only a few hours after we spoke, Karen went by the Red Lobster, where she worked in the kitchen, prepping, to pick up her check. As she got there, she saw three men pull up behind the restaurant. She walked up to them and asked what they were doing there. And that's when they grabbed her.

They had planned to rob the place, but once they saw Karen they were afraid they might be caught, so they threw her in their car and drove away. The next few hours are still a mystery, but the police told me they think she got away from them at one point, only to be caught again. And I imagine that was when they raped her—something I didn't know until just recently. When asked, the detective explained he thought it was something I didn't really need to know at the time. Perhaps he was right, but it was difficult to learn of this new horror so many years after the fact.

Those three young men held my sister down and took her, and after that they stabbed her forty-two times, mostly in the back and shoulders. Many of the wounds were superficial, but there were seven, any one of which was deep enough to kill her. They left her for dead, but somehow she had the strength to crawl to a nearby mobile home. She knocked at the door for help, but the stranger who would find her wasn't home. And when he got there, it was too late.

Four months after her death, the three men were arrested. Boys, really: sixteen, seventeen, and nineteen years of age. Karen was the sixth of seven they had killed, apparently for fun. There was a trial. They were convicted, and the eldest boy received a death sentence. I don't know if it was ever carried out, although I understand the families of victims are notified of executions, so I assume he's still in jail.

I rarely think about the boys that killed her, but I think of Karen every day.

5

Facing West

Until Karen's death, I was a believer. Part of it was my Christian Science background. And some of it was the feeling I got from surfing and meditation, the feeling I was in touch with the energy of the universe. I had a constant sense of affirmation in those days that God was everywhere.

When I decided to become an actor, this was my thinking: If I truly do have talent, with some luck I'll be able to do everything I ever wanted to. I was willing to work at it, and I was willing to wait for it, assured that God was on my side.

All that was taken from me with Karen's death.

I felt abandoned and betrayed. I quite consciously said, "All right, God. If you're not going to help me, that's fine. At least keep the hell out of my way."

And I cursed God, and began to listen to darker voices within.

After the funeral I decided I would stay in Florida for a while, pick up a little cash for my eventual return to New York City. So I painted roofs. In Florida the rooftops are made of large slabs that need to be steam-cleaned and then re-painted every few years. I did my grandmother's, Helen's next door, and several others.

The best thing to come out of that summer took place while I was painting Helen's roof. It hadn't been done in some time, so I ran out of paint. To finish the job and to make any money at all, I had to ask her for more.

As Helen wrote out an additional check, I put it to her this way: "Just think, Helen. Someday you'll be able to say, 'You know what? Years ago I helped out that young man and I have never regretted it. Just look at how far he's come.'"

I promised Helen this was going to happen.

It was hard for her to hide her skepticism as she handed me the check, but I am thankful to her to this day. And, I think I got her.

So Far...

I returned to New York to move in with Jill. We found an apartment, and Jill insisted we had two phone lines so her parents wouldn't find out that we were living together. I guess you could say that didn't do a lot for my self-esteem.

I got a job in a restaurant and started buying the theater newspapers, the "trades" as they're called, in which auditions are published for upcoming productions. I auditioned a hundred times in four months, and I didn't get a single job. But I kept slugging away at it; I had no choice (I had nothing to fall back on, as you may recall).

Late at night I paced the city streets. I would go to Central Park or walk along Columbus Avenue behind the Museum of Natural History. Sometimes I'd spot a guy standing in the shadows, waiting. Waiting to rob someone, I guessed, or even worse. I'd let them know I'd seen them, walk toward them as if to invite a confrontation.

But nothing ever happened. Maybe they thought it wasn't worth it, sensing how disturbed and full of rage I was. People on the street have a kind of intuition about others. Whether I was dangerous or not, that I might be was enough to make them wait for easier prey.

It wasn't hard to figure out why I took these

walks. I hadn't been able to protect my sister; I felt guilty, ashamed, and angry, and wanted to make up for it somehow. Maybe even get myself killed.

There were also days when I would sit in our apartment for hours, watching old movies or just gazing out the window. I'd get up and open the fridge for a bite to eat—there was nothing, so I'd close the door. Then I'd realize I had stood there for an hour, staring at the emptiness. I was completely lost in grief.

Jill begged me once, "You've got to stop this."

But I couldn't. I didn't know how.

Had I been into drugs at the time, God knows what would have happened. The only thing I knew for certain was I had to keep on going.

One positive experience that year, curiously, was with my landlord. Possibly the only nice landlord in all New York. Money was scarce, so we were late with the rent. I called him to say that we needed a few more days, and he said, "Hey, I was late with the rent a lot when I was a kid. Look, whether you've got the rent or not, I'd like to drop by in a couple of days to see how you are."

He did. And after looking around, he said, "You guys are doing just fine."

But the truth is, we weren't doing just fine. As desperately as I wanted it to work out with Jill, I was so distraught over Karen's death it had become impossible to make any contact with me. I think Jill really did try, but eventually it killed her love for me.

Christmas was impossible that year, but I went back to Florida to share it briefly with my mother and Gam. In January, I actually began re-hearsing for an off-off Broadway production of *Miss Lonelyhearts* by Tad Mosel. There was no pay, of course, but the director knew someone who needed help remodeling an office space. I went to work for Ellis Raab, a famous actor and director, staining floors and dropping ceilings for his new production company. And as is usually the case with produc-tion companies, there was a casting director.

When I was standing on a ladder one day, he looked up at me and said, "You're an actor, aren't you?"

"Yes."

"Are you good?"

"Yes, I am."

"Well, the San Diego Shakespeare Festival is coming in. Want to audition?"

I read for Jack O'Brien, whom I'd once met at Juilliard.

"We'll hire you, but there's just one problem,"

he said. "We don't fly apprentices out, so you'll have to get to San Diego on your own. Oh, yes, and you'll need to get there by next Friday."

"I'll get there," I said.

I told Jill about the job, and it was almost a relief. This way she wouldn't have to leave me; it made things easier for both of us.

I called my grandmother and asked her for $129—$69 for a plane ticket down to Florida, and $60 to get me to California on my motorcycle. Say what you will about cycles, it's hard to argue with fifty miles a gallon.

I got to Florida the next morning, took the bike in for a tune-up, and organized the bare essentials to put in my backpack. Next day I picked up the bike, strapped on the pack, and headed for Tallahassee. My old friend Spencer was living there then, so I spent the night with him. We drank a bit and stayed up late, talking of the past, but with a focus on the future. A future I would find in San Diego.

The journey ahead of me seemed very romantic in my eyes—you see, I'd never been farther west than Tallahassee.

That morning Spencer, who had a bike of his own, drove along beside me on my way out of town. With each mile came an increasing sense of excitement, because with every moment that

---

passed, I was entering territory that was entirely new to me. What an adventure. And a blessing.

The trip was the first intimation I had had that I would someday heal.

Spence stayed with me all the way to the Alabama state line. He was sorely tempted to keep on going but turned back, knowing there was a life for him in Tallahassee. My life lay ahead of me, and as I drove I got further from my past and closer to my future.

Riding alone in the middle of Alabama, after night had fallen, I was caught in a downpour. Wild crashes of thunder surrounded me, and lightning bolts bounced off the highway in front of me. Suddenly I felt a jolt of energy shooting through my body, and I realized what had happened: I had been hit by lightning. But I seemed okay. The motorcycle must have grounded me, so I wasn't hurt, just a little shook up.

I drove on into the night with images of Greek mythology in my head. Of Zeus and his lightning bolts, and I found significance in what had happened. They say, coincidence is just God covering up his footsteps. Whether you believe that or not, I took that moment as a sign, as God's blessing on my journey. "Kelsey Grammer, I bear you witness. You're going to be all right."

6

The Incredible Lightness of Acting

When life fails you, art can be a salvation. So it was for me. The theater was my outlet, the one place I functioned as a full, healthy human being. There, I could stand up for my choices. I had boundaries I could defend. I had a presence that was worthy of honor. On the stage, where most people feel really threatened and nervous, I felt great. I had finally found a home.

Thoreau went to Walden Pond, he said, because he wanted to live "deliberately." That, in a word, was my approach to my two years at the Old Globe Theater in San Diego. From 1976 to 1978, I completed the education I hadn't quite received at Juilliard. I did Shaw, Shakespeare, Ionesco,

Pinter—the work a young actor craves and needs in order to grow.

In San Diego, I became an actor. A young actor, to be sure, but a professional, an actor who had the right to claim his place on a stage.

And so, in San Diego, I had indeed begun to heal. I no longer felt the same degree of rawness over Karen's murder; the despair and loneliness, though still ever present, had become just muted enough that I could function.

Jill was no longer the woman in my life. After crossing the country in just four days, I called her, said I'd made it safely, and reassured her that though we'd have to be apart for a while, I still loved her and hoped that we might work things out in time.

There was a silence on the other end of the phone. I asked if there was something wrong. That was when she told me that she had slept with Michael last night.

I realized she had made her decision.

I was hurt, and definitely angry. The last thing I told her when I left New York was, "Please, Jill, whatever you do, don't sleep with Michael." Michael had been hanging around with us for the last year or so, and I could tell that he would love to be with Jill. He'd drop by constantly and flirt with her, and even though I knew what he was up to, I opened up my home to this man, fed him, and even shared a glass of wine or two.

So when Jill told me she had succumbed, I was not surprised, but was disgusted. And felt incredibly betrayed. There are few men of whom I hold as low an opinion as I do of Michael.

Finally, a chance to get that off my chest.

The last piece of my past was gone, and I found in that a new clarity and a kind of freedom.

Most of the plays I did in San Diego were Shakespeare. I developed my own style of playing him—my own theory, if you will. Some actors, when they're performing Shakespeare, take on a kind of superior attitude, and self-importantly slow down the language as if to say to the audience, "You're far too dim to get this, so I shall enlighten you. It's better than you can comprehend, and I am smarter than you'll ever be, so listen to me as I beat the language to death, and consequently bore you all to tears."

Obviously I find this approach presumptuous and offensive. It's insulting to the audience, and to the playwright as well.

The way I see it, an actor should drive through the language like a freight train. That way he invites the audience to join him on a fabulous and exciting ride through the greatest stories in the English language. He plays up to them. And when the night is done, the audience should leave the theater buzzing and turned on by what they've seen, not weary and indifferent.

One of the greatest moments in my life, at least as an actor, came one day outside the Winter Garden theater in Manhattan, where I was playing Cassio in *Othello*. It was just after a matinee, and I was on my way to lunch when a young man came up to me and said, "Mr. Grammer, I saw you do *Macbeth* last year, and I wanted you to know that I've been reading Shakespeare ever since. Could I please have your autograph?"

It was one of the most beautiful things I had ever heard.

"Of course you could," I said, and I actually fought back tears. I had never been so proud, or thankful. You might say this was a peep at Atlantis.

Oddly enough, the idea of playing up to the audience was something I learned from Jack Benny. No, I didn't actually know Jack. But one night back in high school, Jack was on The *Tonight Show*. Johnny Carson asked him if there was any one thing to which he could attribute his success as a comedian.

"Well," Jack said, in his inimitable fashion, "I always play up to my audience."

It was like a gunshot. And I knew then what kind of actor I would like to be. I would develop other theories, but all have been colored by this simple approach. It remains the banner for everything I've tried to do.

***

In San Diego, I met a girl named Agnes. A brilliant girl, and very sweet. I liked her very much. I wasn't ready for a relationship, but we did become lovers, and were together most of the time. Agnes had a dog named Pomplemousse, which means grapefruit in French. Agnes had a terrific sense of humor.

She also had a terrific dog. And so when Pompei became pregnant, I thought maybe I *was* ready for a relationship. . . . At least, with a puppy. The pups were born, and sure enough, there was the most beautiful little girl I'd ever seen. She had a silver muzzle, and black markings around her eyes, and I would name her Tintagel, after the castle in Cornwall, but would come to call her—because it rhymed with Pomplemousse—Tint, the Goose. And finally, just Goose.

We spent that winter together, Agnes and I, and the "kids" as we came to call them. Agnes taught me how to train Goose, and she was brilliant at it. Goose turned out so well primarily because of her. For the first year of Goose's life, I didn't spend a single day away from her. She became the light of my life, and for the first time in many years I actually felt happy.

Spring arrived, and time to cast another season for the Shakespeare Festival. I had a meeting with Craig Noel, the artistic director of the theater. I said I felt the time had come to join the union, and be given my Equity card, as it was called. I said I would not be interested in another season as an apprentice.

Craig listened with respect to this, and then declared that there was no place for me that season except as an apprentice.

I told him that I would be leaving.

I said good-bye to Agnes, packed the car, put my motorcycle in Craig's garage, and planned to make the trip back to Florida, then once again to New York City.

The day I left, Craig handed me a card, and inside it was a hundred-dollar bill. He really was a wonderful and generous man. And I will never forget his generosity and support.

Back in Florida, Agnes wrote me every day, and

once a week or so we'd speak on the phone. I told her my plan was to save a little money for my return to the City, and to start over again. Agnes asked where she fit in to all this, and I told her I was very fond of her, but couldn't promise anything; it would be better not to count on me.

As fate would have it, while I was still in Florida, Craig placed a call to me from San Diego. One of the actors was leaving the company—could I get out there right away to replace him? And yes, I would get my Equity card.

I didn't gloat, exactly, but it was a wonderful day to be me.

Agnes picked me up at the airport, and we spent that night together. I think we both knew then that what we'd had was ending. Otherwise, it was great to be back home and working.

I was living at "the Alamo," the house next door to Craig's, which they reserved for "special members" of the company. I was happy as a clam.

But one morning Agnes called. "Well, I didn't think I'd be alive this morning, but I'd like you to come over and get the things you left here. And to read the diary I asked you to."

I went right over, and when she greeted me her wrists were bandaged. She had tried to kill herself the night before. A friend had found her, so she didn't make it. I collected my things, took the diary, and left. I was afraid to hear why she had done this, but at the same time furious with her.

In the pages of the diary I found a world of laughter, of cartoon drawings, and of adventures. Stories of "the kids," and how they had turned to a life of crime and terrorized the nation. They were finally arrested and sentenced to live out their days in the Federal Penitentiary for Dogs.

I laughed out loud. Agnes was so talented, so funny, and had one of the greatest imaginations I had ever known. Finally I realized how much she had loved our life together, and that the diary was her only way of telling me. She wasn't very good with words.

I tried to tell her I was sorry, that I did love her in a way; and I knew that wasn't enough, but hoped it was.

We didn't speak much after that. A month later, Agnes tried again, this time with pills. Again it didn't work. And once again she called me. And yes, again I went to see her. But this time I was furious enough to tell her how I felt. That what she was doing was an insult to all the people I had known who had wanted life but had it taken from them. That she degraded the memory of my sister. And that if she wanted to die, to do it and to leave me out of it.

We never spoke again.

So Far...

Years later, a friend told me that she had finally made it. That time I cried for Agnes, and for the girl who'd never felt that she belonged.

I spent another year in San Diego, and another summer, and that was when I met Ellen, an actress from New York.

That fall I felt the time had come to leave California and face once more the specter of New York. We drove to Florida together, as was my custom. It had become like a bad habit, I suppose, or maybe I needed to return to Florida because it had always been my staging area, a place to collect my thoughts, and to gird my loins for combat with the island of Manhattan.

7

New York, New York

Ellen went ahead of me, back to her apartment in New York. I would leave a month or so later to join her there.

I'd stayed in Florida a little longer than I had planned. It was just after Thanksgiving when I finally got on the road. Goose and I, and a fellow named Carl. He had been a friend of the family's son, who hitched a ride as far as Washington, D.C. As I was packing the trunk to leave, Carl kept saying that if I didn't mind, he'd keep his boots up front with us. It seemed a little weird to me, but he kept asking, so I agreed.

Two hours up the road, I got my first look at cocaine. He reached into his boot and pulled out a bagful, as long as his boots were tall. Had it been a few years later, this might have been the happiest day of my life. As it was, however, I was rather upset that I'd been lied to, but I bit my tongue because his family were good friends.

Just outside our nation's capital, we hit a blizzard. My poor old Fiat sputtered from time to time, so I'd have to jump out of the car to dry off my distributor cap. Standing outside in the snow, it suddenly struck me as funny that while I was standing outside in a blizzard, Carl was inside the car, sitting in a blizzard of his own.

I finally dropped him off in Georgetown and continued on my way. I wouldn't have my next encounter with the drug for two more years.

I came through the Lincoln Tunnel, and as I caught my first glimpse of the city after three years, it took my breath away. I woke Goose and said, "Look, Goose, look! There's our new home."

And I imagined her response: "Where the hell am I going to go to the bathroom?"

There it stood, a manmade mountain I would have to climb to find the promised land.

Over the years I had developed a theory about Manhattan. Almost completely rock, probably the largest chunk of granite in the world, the island seems magnetically assigned to be a forge for extraordinary thinking, as if the creative vectors of the world converge there. A holy place set aside by God for the ideas and dreams of man. But also a cruel place, where only the most tenacious of these flourish.

With that in mind, I have revised history's account of Henry Hudson's "bargain." My version goes like this: Except for the occasional hunting party or to harvest the abundant sealife from its crystal waters, the island was of little interest to the Native Americans of the region. There was something about Manhattan that made them feel uneasy. They couldn't quite put their finger on it, but decided it was the kind of place that was fun to visit but they'd never want to live there.

When the white ones first sailed up the river, the Indians were alarmed not by their presence but by their dreadful fashion sense. Funny hats and shoes, and enormous things called buckles at their waists; these pale faces were a strange bunch indeed.

"Let's trot on down and see what these idiots want."

"Oh, great-feathered, underdressed people. We would like to buy this magnificent island from you."

"I think they want to buy the island from us . . . but we don't own it, do we? Can we do that?" The native people powwowed a moment, then asked, "How much?"

"Oh, roughly, twenty-four bucks or so."

"We'll take it," said the Indians, and they left convinced that they had struck a wonderful bargain. As far back as they could remember, the only tribe that had ever tried to settle Manhattan had suffered a kind of mass insanity, attempting to build a multiple-level teepee. It was almost a relief to have the forbidding island in foreign hands. Of course, the Europeans knew a lot about vertical expression, and for them this place was perfect. And so Manhattan became a great canvas for glorious erections of the western mind. A place for the highly competitive to thrive or to fade into obscurity. It does not tolerate the mediocre, but imagination, talent, and tenacity—these it will embrace.

I think the reason so many Americans dislike New York is that they sense it really isn't part of the United States. Its energy demands the greatest of commitments, as if it had been set aside for those who think they're special to come and prove it.

Whether this is true or not doesn't really matter. The important thing is, it was true for me.

I was full of trepidation and feared that I might fail again as I had failed so miserably before. But Ellen pointed out that things were different now: I

Me in 7th grade, 12 years old, 1967 (*Sally Grammer*)

My sister Karen, 10 years old, 1966 (*Sally Grammer*)

In St. Thomas with my father and Karen (back row), and my half-siblings (L-R) John, Billy, Stephen and Betty. (*Sally Grammer*)

In training for a life of hard knocks, 15 years old, 1970 (*Sally Grammer*)

High school, sweet sixteen, 1971 (*Sally Grammer*)

On the road from Phoenix to Sedona with Goose, 1977 (*Sally Grammer*)

"*F*ield of Dreams" charity baseball (*Jonathan J. Malhalab*)

*S*inging the National Anthem at a Los Angeles Raiders game

A taste for fast cars. With Parnelli Jones and Dan Gurney, Long Beach Grand Prix

With Tammi and NBC president, Don Ohlmeyer, 1994

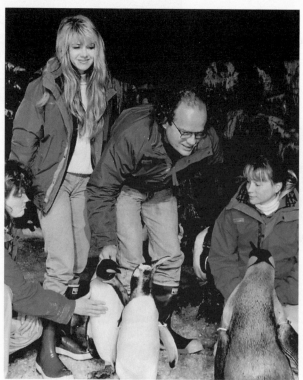

With Tammi at Sea World, 1995

*F*rasier and Niles
(*Photofest*)

*T*he cast of "Frasier." Left to right: David Hyde Pierce, Peri Gilpin, me, Jane Leeves, John Mahoney, and Moose. (*Courtesy of Paramount*)

"Hello, Seattle. I'm listening." (*Photofest*)

*E*x-wife Lilith shows up on "Frasier"! (*Photofest*)

As Dr. Frasier Crane
(*Andrew Eccles/EDGE*)

"Oh, Eddie, stop staring at me."
(*Photofest*)

Carving the Thanksgiving turkey, 1992 (*Sally Grammer*)

My daughter Kandace Greer Grammer

With my daughter Spencer, and fiancée, Tammi Baliszewski, 1995 (*Michele Laurita*)

With Leigh-Anne,
1992 (*Craig Schwartz
Photography*)

y mother,
Sally Grammer,
with Champ,
the racing dog,
1994

"Counseling" Sam on "Cheers" (*Photofest*)

Diane and Frasier in
a typical moment
on "Cheers"
(*Photofest*)

*T*he cast of "Cheers." Clockwise from left to right: Ted Danson, Kirstie Alley, Woody Harrelson, George Wendt, Rhea Perlman, John Ratzenberger, me, 1993 (*Photofest*)

Playing Sir Edward Mortimer in *Mary Stuart* at the Guthrie Theater in Minneapolis, 1980

Playing Richard II at the Mark Taper Forum, Los Angeles, 1992 (*Jay Thompson*)

James Earl Jones and Christopher Plummer in *Othello,* New York, 1982 (*Martha Swope © Time, Inc.*)

As Aubrey Bagot in George Bernard Shaw's *Too True to Be Good*. San Diego Old Globe Theatre, 1976

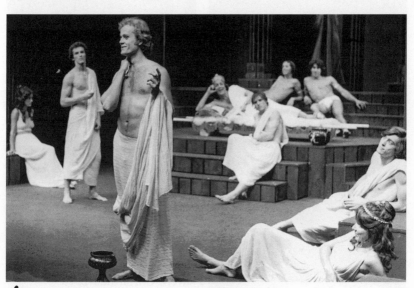

As Paris in Shakespeare's *Troilus and Cressida*. San Diego Old Globe Theatre, 1976

*S*till smiling, 1974
(*Sally Grammer*)

*D*ancing with Karen, Christmas
1973, Ft. Lauderdale, FL
(*Sally Grammer*)

*K*aren, Christmas 1973
(*Sally Grammer*)

was not the broken boy who'd left there in the past. She was right. I was a man now, and an actor. In San Diego I had played a variety of roles in a variety of plays, and had improved my skills. I was no longer just an acting student but a professional.

I came with ammunition. And came resolved, this time, to give no quarter and expect none.

I didn't move in right away with Ellen. She had an encumbrance to be dealt with, and room-mates to persuade to take me in. Finally the stage was set, and as I walked toward her apartment building to begin our life together, a funny thing happened. It was like a strange adventure in a Carlos Casteneda novel. I've always believed that the universe conspires to inform our choices, and if we listen carefully, we will not go astray. While standing on the corner of Fifty-seventh Street and Sixth Avenue, a fire engine roared by, sirens blaring, then another. And another. Ten in all. I thought they must be off to fight the largest blaze in history.

Goose began to howl along with the cacophony. And in that moment it occurred to me that moving in with Ellen was not the best idea. Perhaps this was a warning. But I guess I wasn't listening that day, and I proceeded on my way.

Life with Ellen and her roommates wasn't bad at first. We all got along pretty well, and things were good between Ellen and me. Her roommate Harry used his pull at the Magic Pan and helped get me a job there as a busboy. Not my cup of tea, but at least it made ends meet.

A few weeks later, I received a call from a casting director I had met (a story I will spare here, for the sake of telling this one). She had two days of work for me as an "under five," a part that has five lines or less, on the soap "One Life to Live." The pay would be $1,000. I gladly accepted.

I told the restaurant manager I had an acting job for the next two days and couldn't come to work.

"Sorry," he said, "you're on the schedule."

"I know, but I can't be here."

"Well then, you'll have to fill your shifts."

He gave me the numbers of three or four of my esteemed colleagues. I had no luck, and called to ask him if there was some way we could work this out.

"No," he said, "rules are rules. You'll have to be here."

Needless to say, I was not.

I enjoyed my first days on the set and discovered a newfound respect for daytime drama. I had no idea how hard they worked. I was impressed.

The night I finished, I called the manager and

asked if things had gone all right at the restaurant in my absence.

"No," he said, "I had to cover for you myself. Just come in tomorrow, and by the way, you're on report."

I walked through silent glances of reproach and accusation when I arrived at work.

"I'd like to see you in my office," the manager said.

I sat across the desk from him in silence.

Finally he said, "We have a problem."

"Oh, really? Would we have a problem if I had simply called in sick?"

"No," he said.

"Well, that's ridiculous," I said, and questioned the propriety of penalizing truthfulness and encouraging deceit. My honesty, I thought, should be rewarded, not "reported."

With that, he threw up his hands and told me, "Look, that's just the way it is. You're on report for the next two weeks, and I think that I should tell you, Kelsey—I'm not convinced that you are Magic Pan family material."

For a moment I sat paralyzed by the absurdity of what he'd said, then replied, "Well, let me clear this up for you. I *know* that I am not Magic Pan family material. I quit."

This did not go over well with Ellen. In fact, she seemed hysterical. I had trouble understanding why, but I had started having trouble understanding lots of things about her. It seemed that Ellen lived her life in a constant state of frenzy. For example, I would lie in bed each morning, literally in awe as she took garment after garment from her closet, until the floor was choked with clothing, and then protest, "I haven't got a thing to wear!"

Every morning she would wake me up at six a.m. "My agent isn't doing a goddamned thing for me. What should I do?"

"Honey, I don't know. It's six o'clock in the morning. Why don't you wait until ten when your agent will be in his office and then take this up with him? I would like to get some sleep."

This happened almost every day.

But Ellen was a brilliant actress, and perhaps it was our professional rather than personal compatibility that kept us together. In fact, the first time we were together back in San Diego, as we relaxed in the shadows of her room, I broached a rather sensitive subject. Her performance as Helen needed work. In a huff of dramatic indignation, she leaped from the bed and snarled, "How dare you!"

"Would you at least let me explain?" I asked.

She grabbed the text, handed it to me, and said, "Fine, explain."

And I did.

We studied through the night, poring over the language, and had a truly marvelous time. Ellen's tireless devotion to the work, and my ability to break down a text and find its thread, became a winning combination and bond between us. We'd spend hours in her apartment preparing for auditions—she the actress, I a director of sorts. Her trust in my opinion was so complete that she was fearless to try anything I might suggest. There were times she broke my heart when she would concentrate so fully that the truth would simply spill from her in a way that was breathtaking. Her talent was extraordinary.

As much as I admired her talent, Ellen's insecurity made her behave in ways that I found reprehensible. For instance, if a friend of hers was cast in a show, rather than be happy for the friend, Ellen would be furious. She'd rant and rave for days that she was a much better actress. She'd cry, "How could they cast that girl? She's terrible!"

Similarly, whenever anyone she knew became successful, whether male or female, it seemed to make Ellen miserable.

"Ellen," I said, "don't you get it? It's a good sign that people you know are getting work. At least it means that you're in the right room, and that you'll probably be working soon, too."

It fell on deaf ears. Ellen was locked in a fierce competition with everyone—it was her against the rest. Including me.

I got my first glimpse of this fairly early on. She had a big audition for a principle role on "One Life to Live," and she was very excited. She left the apartment and I agreed to meet her first at the audition, and then we'd go to lunch. I found her in the waiting room outside the casting director's office. She had not been in yet. A woman opened the door, a young actress walked out, and the woman called for the next. Ellen went into the office. The woman looked at me for a moment, and then closed the door.

Fifteen minutes later, Ellen emerged, and it was then the woman asked me, "Who are you? Are you an actor?"

"Yes, I am," I said. "But I'm not here for an audition, I'm with my girlfriend."

"Who's that?"

Ellen spoke up and said, "I'm his girlfriend."

"Oh, great. Yes, Ellen. And what's your name?" she asked.

"Kelsey."

"Well, Kelsey, you're very good-looking. Are you interested in doing soaps?"

"Sure."

"Come into my office for a minute."

So Far...

The woman was Mary Jo Slater, then casting director for "One Life to Live."

As I sat down she asked, "Do you have an agent?"

"No."

"Would you like one?"

"Sure."

So she made some calls, and the next day I had interviews with three of New York's biggest agents. By the way, it was Mary Jo who ruined my chances with the family of Magic Pan.

A fterward, I left for lunch with Ellen. As you can imagine, our luncheon conversation was strained at best. Almost nightmarish. Ellen grilled me on what had transpired, seeming to insinuate that what I'd done was unforgivable. Shamelessly opportunistic.

As I named the agents I would be meeting, with each one Ellen flinched with recognition.

"I can't believe this," she said. "I spent years beating at their doors. And then one day you show up at my audition and *bang*, you're in. How could you do this to me?"

I tried to explain that I had in fact done nothing, tried to remind her that she had invited me to join

121

her at her audition, and that her reaction was absurd.

She fell into a melancholy. Silent.

Had it not been for my early training with women of difficulty, I might have left her then and there. But this was not unusual behavior to my mind, not unreasonable—it was just the way of women. Something to be endured. For two more years we remained together, and that's the way things were until I left.

The agents were receptive when we met, and one of them was even enthusiastic, convinced that I had a future in commercials, and sent me out that winter on a number of auditions. Deep down, I had misgivings that a future in commercials would destroy my future as an actor. The easy money and security it promised would obscure my dreams and render me incapable, or perhaps too comfortable, to go on fighting for them.

One day I walked into the agency and announced that I was leaving them. I did not want to do commercials. I had nothing against them, but had something else in mind. I wanted to be an actor, and this, for now, was just a waste of time.

One of the agents, Scott, said he was flabbergasted. But he shook my hand and wished me luck.

So Far...

During that time, after the Pan debacle, I waited tables at O'Neal's, a restaurant on the corner of Fifty-seventh Street and Sixth Avenue. The money was pretty good; I was a damn good waiter, and proud to be one. When customers would ask what I did, I'd tell them, "I'm a waiter." It seemed ridiculous to me to talk of acting while serving burgers for a living.

On a high from having left my agent, it struck me that I could also never be an actor as long as I was a waiter. So resolved, I told the restaurant manager, "I quit." I didn't have a reason, or a job to go to, but the time had come to give up "waiting" and to proclaim myself an Actor.

Two days later, a call came from an old friend. He was directing *Hamlet* at the North Shore Music Festival in Massachusetts, and would I play Laertes? The universe had informed my choices.

"Yes, I'd love to play Laertes." And yes indeed, I was an Actor.

8

Along the Way

I spent a glorious spring in Massachusetts. My work was good—I even choreographed the fight scenes, which got rave reviews. And I made a friend or two. One was Lisa, as beautiful a girl as I had ever seen. But more important, intelligent and inquisitive. Her interest in the things I knew restored my sense of worth, a welcome change from the derision Ellen doled out on a daily basis. I even fell in love with her, I think. But it was not to be.

Another was Gregory, who played Horatio and would become a friend for life. We shared an equal passion for the work, but also tastes in art and literature, a thirst for the exceptional in life, and a fear of the mundane. I also fell in love with him, and knew that it would always be.

Hamlet closed, and I returned to Ellen. She had had a stroke of luck—she'd been cast as Viola, the lead in *Twelfth Night,* at the Shakespeare Festival in Stratford, Connecticut. So things were pretty good between us. She was working; I was unemployed. All was right with the world.

I was therefore free to coach her in the role, which turned out to be a blessing, since the director was a nincompoop. Ellen did a brilliant job in spite of him.

My own career was back on hold that summer, but I survived on the occasional "under five" that Mary Jo would send my way, and on unemployment. But the process of collecting unemployment benefits was so demeaning to me that I let it go. The work on soaps paid well enough to spare me the embarrassment of standing in line for my "unfit for work" insurance.

Instead, I took up running with a vengeance. Even though I wasn't working, running could provide me with a sense of accomplishment. Through running I established this philosophy: When in the worst of times, a daily promise kept can be salvation. A little promise to oneself each day, however small, can keep at bay the dread of insignificance as long as we fulfill it.

Every morning Goose and I would head to the bridle path in Central Park. There we'd run together, or rather, I would run while Goose raced hither and yon, terrorizing strangers, begging food, but always checking in with me to make sure I was all right and that I wasn't lost.

During these runs I would set goals for myself. "That man up there ahead of me—I'm going to lap him twice, or I'm not worth the feet God gave me." Parenthetically, the flatest feet in Christiandom. But nonetheless . . .

As I whistled by the octogenarian for the second time, I reveled in a glow of victory, assured once more that I was someone to be reckoned with. It was indeed a season of great triumph.

That fall I did a workshop production of Sam Shepard's *Icarus's Mother* with my friends Gail and Barry. Gail directed, Barry was a member of the cast. While in rehearsal, Barry complained that we, myself and the rest of the cast, were not doing enough to make him feel excluded—a necessary integer in his performance. At first his whining was something I ignored, but because he was my friend I contemplated how his problem could be solved.

And then it came to me: Barry's complaint became the genesis of a revelation about acting.

"Barry," I said, "it's not up to us to make you feel excluded; it's up to you to try to be included."

I had learned another lesson: The actor's obligation is solely to his character, not to the play. The play is the director's province. The actor's duty is to defend the rights and the desires of the character he plays.

It brought to mind a time in San Diego when I had played the Soldier in *Kennedy's Children* by Robert Patrick. Craig Noel, who was directing, questioned my reading of a certain line.

"Kels, wait a minute. Why would you say that line that way?"

I told him it was my belief that the Soldier, after months in Vietnam, had learned of reincarnation. And given that, there was no other way to read the line.

Craig responded, "Okay, makes sense. Let's move on." I didn't know it then, but what I had done was right. My instinct made me do by chance what Barry's quandary taught me I would have to do by choice.

A dreadful play, *Icarus's Mother* provided me this insight and, much to my chagrin, my first theatrical agent. I received a call from Jeffrey Lowenthal, who'd seen one of our performances and told me he thought I was terrific.

We met the next day, and Jeffrey told me he would like to be my agent—was I interested?

"Jeffrey," I said, "I have one question: Are you good?"

"Yes."

"This may sound strange," I said, "but I believe I'm going to be an actor of some importance, and I'd like to have one agent for the rest of my life. Are you that agent?"

"I believe I am," he said, and we shook hands.

"There's just one thing," I added, "never lie to me."

He accepted my terms, and both of us resolved that we would set the world on fire.

The next week, Jeffrey sent me to my first audition and I got the job, a production of *The Mousetrap* by Agatha Christie at the Studio Arena Theater in Buffalo, New York. Winter was approaching, and I'd heard some disconcerting things about the relationship between winter and the city of Buffalo. People froze to death there.

Nevertheless, I headed north with Goose, anticipating work and petrified that I would have to spend at least three paychecks to buy a coat warm enough to shelter me from the impending cold.

Although I enjoyed the play and the people I met, the thing that stands out most is what took place between the Goose and me. On the night of the first snow, we walked together until dawn—I in my super-duper mega-insulated parka, and she, for the first time, in her element. My Snow Dog. My Malamute. Dashing through the snow, beautiful, rejoicing in her heritage and blood.

Her blood was of the Yukon, and her heritage of frozen hills of winter. I watched her run and dance through falling snow, frolic in her being. From time to time she'd race toward me and stop, looking up at me as if to say, "Thank you, Daddy. Thank you so much. I never knew what I was meant to be, and now I do. Thanks, Dad." And with a wink she turned and ran into the night.

The time in Buffalo was not to Goose's benefit alone. I met a woman there named Barbara who showed me I was worthy of affection, and I believed her for a time. And in her arms I felt I too had found what I was meant to be. But once again it was not to be, because I lacked the courage to make it so. I returned to Ellen.

New Year's Eve, 1979, I walked alone the streets of New York City through the final hours of a trying year, and heard its dying breath proclaimed by cheers of celebration. It suddenly occurred to me that I was stepping into the first minutes of a promising new decade. Promising perhaps, but that was up to me.

I made a vow that night, beneath the midnight sky, that I would end the habit of losing. No longer would Manhattan be the backdrop for my failure. No longer would she trifle with me or my dreams.

From this day forward, I would be the master of my fate and not its victim. I determined I would visit every building, every street corner, every subway station, every fountain, monument, or park that made me feel invisible. I stood before each one of them and said, "Gone is my fear of you, gone your power to intimidate me, gone your power to defeat me."

Before these places that in the past had magnified my insignificance, I stood and made them mine. No longer enemies, but soldiers on my side.

The battle of New York was over.

9

Football Acting

I could not find employment the following summer. Ellen was on tour, so I decided to take the summer off, fly to San Diego, and drive my motorcycle back across the country. My friends said, "Kels, are you insane? You can't leave New York."

"Of course I can," I said. "Trust me. New York will still be here when I get back."

My acting friends' view was that if the powers-that-be can't see you, they can't hire you. So they were quite surprised when I returned six weeks later, got an audition for the Guthrie Theater in Minneapolis that same day, and got the job. The Guthrie was probably the most prestigious theater in the country outside of New York.

I called Ellen to tell her the good news.

There was silence. Then, "Sorry, I dropped the phone."

She must have flinched so hard it flew right out of her hand.

I had a week before I had to leave, and in that time I met a lovely girl. She was Peter's friend from Boston, Susan. Peter was an old buddy from O'Neal's who tended bar there. I popped in for a drink, and there she was.

I liked her right away, and Pete suggested that since he'd be working, Sue and I should spend the night together. Not *spend the night together*, but pass the time. It was a lovely time indeed.

We walked all over Manhattan. I pointed out some of my favorite buildings. She was enchanting company. I don't know why, but out of the blue I started telling her about W. H. Auden. I'd never read any of his poems, but I suddenly remembered the day he died. It was in 1973, my first year at Juilliard, and my literature teacher had spoken of his death as if it were a personal loss. She read us just a few of his lines, but I was impressed. I made a mental note that I would someday read this man.

So there I was, seven years later, telling Sue, "I think I need to read this guy."

Sue left New York and I never saw her again, but she sent me a gift in memory of our special time together—*The Collected Works of W. H. Auden.*

I was leaving for the Guthrie, so didn't read it right away, but shoved it in my bag to take along with me.

"Come on, Goose, let's go." We piled into the Fiat and headed off to Minneapolis. Goose and I loved to travel together, meet new people, and find new places. We loved adventure.

Two days later, I checked in to the Oak Grove hotel, housing provided by the theater. I had a fairly comfortable little efficiency: a murphy bed, a stove, and a partial view of the lake. I unpacked and came across the book. Well, now was as good a time as any, I thought. I sat at the kitchen table and prepared to meet Mr. Auden.

I like to read a book of poetry by shutting my eyes, letting the book fall open, and starting there. When I opened my eyes on this occasion, I looked down and saw this title: "Atlantis." I was amazed. I'd been looking for Atlantis all my life.

I began to read, and liked it. He was good. I learned later that the film *Ship of Fools* was based upon this poem. And then I turned the page. That's when I read the lines:

> Traveling and tormented,
> Dialectic and bizarre.
> Stagger onward rejoicing . . .

I couldn't believe it. Here, in this poem, were the very lines I'd written eleven years before, but by another's hand. Impossible, but there it was. I felt like I had found a long-lost brother, and I knew that W. H., or Wystan, as I've come to call him, would be a friend for life.

Strange that a girl I knew for only two days could have given me so wonderful a gift.

Thank you, Susan, thank you so much.

I read on into the night and was enthralled with this man's talent, thrilled by his words. And as I went to bed, I knew that this time when the play was over, I would not return to Ellen.

The next evening after my first rehearsal, I went to the little bar attached to the theater. An actor from New York named Richard Davidson came over and introduced himself. No one else had. I thought: Nice guy. "Let's have a drink."

We did.

The following morning we went for a run together. I liked him. Later that day, a member of the cast approached me. He'd seen us together and felt obliged to inform me, "Richard Davidson is an asshole. If I were you, I wouldn't hang out with him."

"Well, I'm not you, am I?" I replied.

Richard and I became the best of friends, and Minneapolis was a beautiful place to spend an autumn.

Life was very good indeed.

So Far...

B ack in New York, I told Ellen I was moving out. She and I were just too different in our approach to life. We stayed in touch for the next year or two, but mostly on a professional basis. That part of our relationship had always been good.

I moved in with Richard, and we found that we lived well together. We would read aloud to one another, barbecue, sunbathe on the roof, and in the evenings we'd hit our local, play the bowling game, and more often than not, get a little drunk and make fools of ourselves trying to pick up some girls. I was having a fabulous time.

And I had a job. For the first time I was actually being paid to act in New York City. The production was *Macbeth* at the Vivien Beaumont Theater in (and I still light up to think of it) Lincoln Center. Lincoln Center, the birthplace of so many of my dreams. And now the place where I was picking up my pay.

I n the spring of 1981 I heard that Stratford would be doing *Othello* starring James Earl Jones, and I was certain I should play the role of Cassio. In fact, I knew I would.

I auditioned for the part and didn't get it.

Peter Coe was the director. He had become famous for his production of *Oliver*. Very British, and very, very full of himself.

When I finished my monologue for him, he looked up and asked, dripping with condescension, "Why is your English so good?"

"It's my native language." What an asshole.

So I didn't get the part, but I was thrown: Whenever I "knew" I'd get a role, I did.

Rehearsals began and I turned my attention elsewhere. I shot an NYU student film and got my first taste of single-camera work, as it is called. A month had passed when my agent called. "Kels," said Jeffrey, "the actor playing Cassio just broke his leg. They want you there immediately."

I *knew* I'd get that role.

Recently I was asked, "Who was your favorite actor to work with, and who was your least favorite?"

After careful consideration I replied, "This may seem odd, but Christopher Plummer was both."

Chris was playing Iago in *Othello*, and I was jubilant that I'd be working with him. He was a kind of legend to me, hero, Baron von Trapp! As a boy I'd seen *The Sound of Music* at least a hundred times. I loved it, and I loved this man.

Boy, what a letdown.

I already knew what to expect from Peter Coe; imagine my surprise to find out he and Chris were cut from the same cloth. The rehearsal process was incredible.

At one point Peter interrupted. "Kelsey," he said, "I cannot understand a word you're saying."

"Are you telling me, Peter, that you literally don't understand a word I'm saying?"

"Yes, Kelsey. That is what I'm saying."

"Has this been a problem in the past?"

"No," he said.

"But it is a problem now."

"Yes."

"Peter," I said, "would you come down here please? I have something I would like to say, and I want to be sure that you will un-der-stand it."

He came down to the stage, and I knelt to look him in the eye. "Peter, the way I see it, you have two choices. One is to go on with rehearsal; the other is to fire me." I wasn't afraid to be fired, and it was important that he know it. Otherwise, his abuse would continue.

He considered his choices for a moment, and then said, "Let's continue with rehearsal."

My first indication that Chris would be a problem was soon to follow.

During rehearsal Chris and I were working through the "Reputation scene," Cassio's most famous, in which he rails against himself for brawling and soiling his good name. As we explored the scene, I made my way upstage, slumped against a wall, then slid down and sat upon a stool.

Chris looked out toward Peter, toward the darkness of the theater from which he was surely watching. "Uh, Peter. I'm so sorry," he said, "but Kelsey really can't sit there."

"Why not, Chris?"

"It's not . . . right."

I volunteered, "It made sense to me; the movement seemed organic."

There was a brief silence.

"Kelsey?" said Peter, "Chris is right. Don't sit there. In fact, why don't you cross the stage and deliver that speech from the other side?"

The next morning, I watched Chris and James rehearse the very famous "Temptation scene." As if to punctuate a poignant moment, Chris made his way upstage, slumped against the wall, then slid down and sat upon the stool. My stool.

I had my first glimpse into how insidious an evil I was facing.

We started previews and Chris tore up the stage, as the saying goes. He also tore up actors. Even James Earl Jones fell victim to his tyranny on stage. Watching Chris's performance, one might have thought the play was called *Iago*, not *Othello*. His domination was complete and ruthless, and Peter Coe his henchman.

Still in previews, the famous brawl in which I killed and maimed a dozen men didn't go so smoothly. I ended up a few feet farther stage left than usual. Chris was blocked to pull me from the fight all the way across the stage, and that way end the fracas.

On this particular night, however, he pulled so hard I rolled over my left ankle and broke my foot. I heard it snap, and I thought: My God, I broke my foot. How the hell did that happen?

It turned out to be a hairline fracture and I could still perform the play, but limping and in great pain for several weeks.

Finally we set out on the road. *Othello* was to tour the nation for the first six months and then move to Broadway for a limited run. As difficult as Chris was being, James Earl Jones was towering. I liked this man so much. He had a magnificence in the role, and an integrity that never faltered in spite of all Chris's machinations. I would stand on stage with James, and in my eyes he was entirely beautiful. Beautiful as a man and as an actor.

For those six months I felt at sea. I was an awful Cassio. Chris totally defeated me on stage. Try as I might, I could not find the means to be respected by him. In city after city I suffered this humiliation and was helpless to do anything about it. I felt desolate, and for the first time thought of quitting acting. Abandoning my dreams.

Opening night on Broadway, I entered the world-famous Sardi's for the party. Richard Davidson was with me. He had a date, and mine was a friend, Janine, whom I'd met in Minneapolis. Applause greeted me as we sat down at our table.

Richard turned to me and said, "Kels, it's your night. Enjoy it."

He was right, of course. But I couldn't enjoy it; I was lost in doubt and confusion about my choices and my future as an actor.

Later that night a feeling of despair came over me. I'd finally done what I had said I'd do so many years before: "One day, I'll be opening on Broadway." My family and friends would smirk, and I'd say, "Mark my words."

So there I was at last, and most of them were not. Karen was gone, Gordon and my father. Gam had died in the spring of '77, and Ray just after that. It was a hollow victory. My mom couldn't make it, but I was certain she was proud. Janine said, "Kels, I'm sure they're all proud." Maybe they were, I thought, but I was not.

I was constantly depressed, and felt like I was sinking deeper and deeper into an abyss of dissolution. Just when I had reached the lowest point, it happened.

It was a Wednesday matinee, and exactly as it had months and months before, the fight scene ended a bit too far stage left. And as before, Chris pulled me across the stage, but this time with greater vehemence. Again I rolled over my left ankle. I did not break my foot this time, but suddenly understood why I had.

In a flood of recognition, it dawned on me that when the fight ended too far stage left, Chris had to pull me that much harder so he could land precisely in the spot where his best light was. For this man's ego, I had broken my foot.

I was filled with rage, and all the pain and agony I had endured for almost a year, all the doubt and degredation, despair, and loss of faith—my God, I had almost quit acting because of this monstrosity—welled up in me and took him by the throat. I lifted him up and said quite audibly, "Fuck you."

With that, I grabbed him by the crotch and threw him off the stage.

I stood as if alive again. I had defended my talent and reclaimed my dream.

Chris stormed across the stage, seething, but it didn't frighten me. I was free. He had the power to fire me but not to harm me. Not any longer.

After that we played the Reputation scene together as we had never played it before. Chris listened to me, was respectful of my presence on the stage, and it was great to work with him.

The first act ended and I left the stage, convinced that I'd be leaving the show. But not a word was said.

From that day on, the work was wonderful with Chris. We even had fun, and I became quite fond of him. One time Chris was obviously disturbed about something when we were in the middle of a scene. I gripped his arm to get his attention and through my teeth said, "What the hell is wrong now?"

"The bells," he said, "the fucking bells. They're too loud. Listen to that. Why do I have to shout over that?"

And I thought, This is great. This guy almost destroyed me, and now we're talking seriously about production values.

This was my first and last experience with a

method I have come to call "Football Acting."
Its theory in a phrase: If you want to get another actor's attention, you've got to beat him up a
little.

10

My First Marriage—But Clearly Not My Last

I met Doreen at the thousandth performance party of *Evita*. She knew who I was—she'd seen me in *Othello* a night or two before. She was a dark-haired girl with beautiful big eyes, and she walked right up to me and said, "I saw you do Cassio. I thought you were great."

Doreen was a dancer in the Broadway musical *42nd Street*. I'd always had a thing for dancers, and I guess you could say I took a shine to her. The year was 1982, and I was in a different frame of mind than I had ever been. After months on the road, and a string of frivolous relationships, I was interested in something more significant. I had started thinking I would like to have a child, and longed to settle down. I dreamed of finding a woman with whom I could have a faithful relationship and raise a family.

I shared all that with Doreen, and she told me she would like the same.

We decided we should see each other with this in mind. Discover if we might be right together and qualified to give that gift to one another. I was very serious about this commitment and realized there were many things I'd have to know about her before we could proceed. There were questions that had to be asked, and answered.

My reasoning was sound and responsible, but I made one critical mistake. Rather than simply ask a question, I'd also include the answer I was hoping to hear. For instance, after I met her mother I had some concerns:

"I have to know that you and your mother have gone through a certain growing period, that she has released you and that you have released her too. Have you released her?"

"Yes, I have released her," Doreen answered.

Great, I thought, we can move on to the next question.

I suppose I should have let her answer without any prompting from me. But I did not. I wanted so badly to find stability, a relationship I could count on and a refuge from my loneliness.

Three months after we had met, we married.

We had planned to wait until the fall, but I had been offered a part in Santa Fe, New Mexico. I told Doreen I'd like to take the job, but I wanted to make sure she was all right with that.

"Fine," she said. "You can go as long as we get married first."

I accepted with one condition: If we should conceive, she had to promise me she'd have the baby.

She did, and we hastily made arrangements to be wed.

When I told Richard we were getting married, he was a little taken aback. He said, "You realize what this means, don't you? It means fidelity, and that you'll be responsible for another person. You may have to turn down jobs and sacrifice the luxury of going wherever your career might take you."

I told him I was aware of all that, but tired of the old life. I wanted this marriage.

With that he gave me his blessing.

I called Spencer in Florida and asked him to be my best man. My mother and he took the same flight to New York a few days before the wedding, and on May 30, 1982, I married Doreen Alderman at Jan Hus Presbyterian Church in Manhattan. It was a glorious day, certainly the finest day of our short-lived marriage.

Our friends gathered for the blessed event. After the ceremony all of us walked to the local where

I'd arranged to hold the reception. I fashioned a wedding cake of sorts from three wheels of brie, and enjoyed the moment when I announced that the time had come for the bride and groom to cut the cheese.

My friends had all chipped in to surprise us with a real wedding cake, which they promptly presented.

It was truly a wonderful day, filled with love and hope and happiness.

We spent the night in the Plaza Hotel, and in the morning I left for Santa Fe.

---

*I*n Santa Fe I played The Rover in an obscure Restoration play called *Wild Oats*. A. J. Antoon, a rather prestigious director, adapted the play and staged it in the American West, circa 1870. The Rover was the actor-manager of a traveling theater troupe. Half gunslinger, half thespian, he was a blast to play, and the show was very well received.

That same season the Santa Fe Festival Theater also produced a musical, *Amerika*, based on Franz Kafka's novel of the same title. I had agreed to play some minor roles. The composer was Shlomo Gronich, a famous Israeli recording artist. I liked him very much. He was extraordinarily gifted, and I dubbed him the Paul Simon of Tel Aviv. Shlomo was, in fact, the first conscientious objector in Israeli history. Rather than fight, he fulfilled his military obligation by giving concerts for the troops. So I admired him as well for his idealism and his willingness to stand up for his beliefs. We became great friends.

Outside Santa Fe I had discovered some diving pools in the mountains just above Los Alamos. It was a beautiful place: seven pools of pristine water descending one upon the other into a forest pond, edged by a crescent of sand, that fed a stream which cascaded down toward Santa Fe.

On my day off each week Goose and I would go there, make the three-mile hike along the stream, and revel in the magic of the place. A place of great serenity and power.

One week I invited Shlomo and his wife to join us. We spent an irreplaceable day. An afternoon of swimming and laughter, of breathing in the air of fondness and bathing in the glow of newfound friendship. Pausing on our way back down the mountain, we sat together on the enormous trunk of a fallen pine—Shlomo and I. His wife continued on with Goose, sensing perhaps an intimacy that should be respected. After a long silence, Shlomo turned to me and said, "Kelsey, I am missing my brother now. I miss him all the time. He was killed two years ago in the Golan Heights . . . I miss him so."

"I understand," I told him. "My sister, Karen, was murdered seven years ago, and not a day goes by that I don't think of her. But look around us. We're sitting with a family . . . in the midst of life's lesson. This fallen tree is the great-great grand-father of those that stand before us, and at their feet their children, saplings newly born to carry on the cycle of life. How beautiful it is to sit among them here, the generations of this family, and how beautiful life's passage."

To the reader these words may seem contrived, but I assure you they are genuine. Moments of great realization are often moments of eloquence.

We cried together for a time and held each other, then made our way along the stream toward Santa Fe. There never had been such a day.

In the fall of 1982 Goose and I flew home to Doreen. Instead of returning to the loving wife I'd left, I found a different woman. Doreen had changed. There was something terribly wrong. She wouldn't let me touch her. She wouldn't even talk to me. But she did tell me she was confused and didn't understand it herself.

I assured her that I understood, that things would be all right; it might take a little time, but I loved her and she was worth the wait.

But I didn't understand.

The truth was, I felt more alone than I could say—discarded and abandoned, and betrayed. I remember one night pleading through my tears, "Tell me, please, Doreen, why can't I touch you? What is wrong?"

Again she said, "I don't know, I just don't know. I couldn't take it when you were away, and now it feels like you're a stranger. I don't trust you anymore."

I broke down completely, sobbing uncontrollably. "Why, why, why, Doreen! Why can't I touch you? I've never felt so lonely in my life. I love you. I married you. Please. Please. Why?!"

On that night we finally made love. I'd been home for two months.

The walls were down, and now I prayed we could begin our marriage. I had resisted living in her old apartment, thinking we should start our lives together in a place entirely new to us both. As it turned out, that wasn't feasible and I relented. We took up housekeeping.

I was rehearsing *Plenty* at the Public Theater, and Doreen was plenty pleased that I was working, or so I thought. The hours were long, and as a rule we'd break around nine o'clock at night. The subway ride would get me home by ten.

Doreen would greet me with a frown and a look of disappointment. Once again she wouldn't speak to me. After a week of this behavior, I confronted her: why such coldness, why so angry?

"You should be home by six. A husband should be home by six o'clock for dinner and spend the evening with his wife." That was what she said.

I was nonplussed by the absurdity of this. I realized I was in way over my head; I was dealing with a mind beyond my comprehension. I summoned all my skills of reason and ventured this syllogism: "I am rehearsing a play. Rehearsal ends at nine o'clock. Therefore, I cannot be home to dine at six." My logic, though infallible, was unacceptable.

I think that was the night I penned these words:

> *I am tonight the mystery guest*
> *At a dinner thrown*
> *By my own*
> *Decisions.*

I finally gave in to the idea that our marriage had been a mistake—gave in to the greatest disappointment of my life. Our love was broken, and I was powerless to fix it. Nevertheless, I staggered on-

(*Michele Laurita*)

'd given my word, and my
nt to me than myself.

ained an odyssey through
of the irrational. Greeted
resentment, I was helpless
d only with my slim rapier
as outmatched by her ma-
and rage.

time to time, and it must
those that we conceived a
o labor on October 8, 1983.
I was in Virginia filming the
The producers put me on a
as I was flying home I smiled
ht be born on that day. Octo-
hday.

later, Doreen gave birth to
mmer, our little girl. She
ds, eleven ounces, and it was
n October 9 instead. She was
d I could almost hold her in
d. I was humbled by the mira-
and by the feeling that I'd had
th her creation. She was not
person. Unique and singular.
, my responsibility, my charge.
ensure her safe passage into

161

adulthood. On her second day of life I wrote these words; the original still hangs above her bed:

To my daughter Spencer:

I pray now only
That I will not corrupt your instincts
With my personal decisions;
That I will encourage you
To explore the choices you have made
And ease the pain you'll feel
In disappointment;
That I can,
Before you reach adulthood,
Hold back the frustration and fear
That inevitably come
In the search
Toward individuality.

...rds

...to the 1994 Emmy Awards: ...Tonda Baliszewski, Nancy ...e, Tammi, Jamie Miod, Donald ...n Bennett (*Donald Miod*)

11

The Face
of Love

I had to return to Virginia to complete the work there. As I arrived on the set, Jaclyn Smith, who was playing George's love interest, dashed toward me, and from across the parking lot she shouted, "What did you have?"

"A girl!" I cried.

"What did you name her?"

"Spencer!"

It was like she'd been hit on the head by an anvil. Her jaw dropped and she ran up to me, confiding, "That's incredible, I don't believe it. If I had had a little girl, I was going to name her Spencer."

This was truly serendipitous; it became my ace in the hole. Doreen, and Doreen's family, had great concern about the name. They allowed it on the birth certificate only for the time being. Their reservations were so strong that I had to be agreeable to changing the name should they come up with a better one. I called Doreen that night and recounted the story, being sure to stress that Jaclyn liked the name. *Jaclyn Smith.*

Well, it did the trick. Suddenly Doreen and her mother and everybody else thought Spencer was the best possible name for a girl. After all, Jaclyn Smith liked it!

I knew TV was powerful, but this was ridiculous. Nevertheless, it had worked to my advantage, and choirs of angels should sing the name of Jaclyn Smith forevermore. And Spencer.

I called Doreen from the airport to tell her I was on my way home, and that was when she dropped the bomb.

"Don't bother," she said, "I've had all the locks changed."

"Why?" I asked.

"During the delivery I started to think there was some hope for us, but now I know better."

I contained my rage. "I've got to go now," I said, "but I'll call when I get into the city and we can work things out."

I did, and asked if I could come over and talk. She refused. And when I asked where she expected me to spend the night, "Stay with Richard," she said. "Hell, sleep with him for all I care—you're probably just a couple of fags anyway."

The conversation ended. I knew it was useless to try to argue with Doreen. As you may recall, her rules of engagement were somewhat different from my own. I preferred to fight with honor; Doreen was ruthless in her attack and so vicious, it was almost beautiful. Standing in defeat, I would sometimes feel a perverse sense of privilege to witness such unvarnished selfishness and unapologetic rage. It was my second self again, the one who stood outside the circumstances, that could appreciate and record such inexcusable behavior. The actor who could marvel at the beast Doreen had become, a beast of mythological proportions.

I spent the night at Richard's, and I realize there was some basis for Doreen's resentment of him. As our marriage had deteriorated, I had spent a lot of time with Richard. He was my only link with sanity and became a kind of haven for me.

The next morning I went to the apartment. Doreen was civil and we spoke. She let me visit with Spencer, and we made arrangements: I would give her half the rent each month and pay for all the food and diapers Spencer would require, and I could see her as often as I wished.

Shortly thereafter, Doreen left Spencer with me and flew to the Bahamas with her girlfriend and two men I didn't know. Spencer was just six days old.

At first I felt overwhelmed, but it was an empowering experience. The most essential need for an infant is love, followed closely by food, and then fresh diapers. I realized I could supply all three with very little effort. Rather than a hardship, I discovered that caring for my little girl was a joy.

Doreen returned a few weeks later, and I remember feeling that I didn't want to share my daughter with her anymore. I was having too much fun. But I respected Doreen's rights and saw less of Spencer for a while—but just a little less. I still had her for days and sometimes weeks in a row.

I got a job in Buffalo that winter at the same theater where I'd worked before. I asked Doreen if I could take Spence (I called her Spence sometimes, or Spencer-butt, or Spenceroni) with me, and she agreed. I could keep her with me for three weeks, then fly her home to spend some time with her mother. If I wanted to, I could fly back again and return with her to Buffalo once more.

So Far...

In Buffalo, we made quite the little family: Spencer, Goose, and me. Goose's reaction to Spencer had been favorable. The day I introduced them, I looked at Goose and said, "Goose, this is my daughter, Spencer. And Spencer, this is my other daughter, Goose." I lowered Spencer toward the ground so Goose could sniff her, and whispered, "Goose, if you ever hurt her, I will have to kill you."

After a while Goose presented Spencer an approving lick of the tongue, and would have bathed the child in kisses if I hadn't stopped her.

Goose assumed a new identity: Aunt Goose, the Guardian Dog.

Our time in Buffalo was indescribable. Spencer charmed the pants off the entire theater. She became everyone's child. She would sleep in her bassinet in the dressing room, and when I was on stage the costume girls watched over her.

Goose was no slouch either. People would literally stop dead in their tracks and say, "My God, what a beautiful dog." She came to be known around the theater as "The Face."

When we left, the entire cast and crew presented a birthday card to Spencer. Everyone had signed it, and my instructions were that I should give it to her on her twelfth birthday. It seemed so far away, but incredibly, that birthday is this year.

No matter how bad things seem to be in my life,

I can look back and I see how blessed I've been. Blessed by so much love.

———

When I returned to New York we stayed with my friend Gregory. That was when I started watching television. Every night when Gregory came home from work he'd find us there, Spencer napping, I glued to the screen, and Goose curled up beside me. He let this go for a few days, and then it hit him: "My God," he said, "I know what you're up to. You're going to get a TV job next, aren't you."

"Yes," I said, "I think I am."

12

"Cheers"—Where Everybody Learned My Name

By the summer of 1984 Doreen and I had arrived at a truce of sorts, and when I got the role on "Cheers," the prospect of a life in California appealed to her. We decided to move there together and try to make our marriage work. I flew out ahead to look for a place to live and to begin work on the show.

On the day of my first rehearsal I drove my rented T-Bird to the studio. As I pulled up, the gates of Paramount loomed before me and I could hardly contain my excitement. The guard stepped up to the car and said, "Can I help you?"

"I'm Kelsey Grammer, I'm here to work on 'Cheers.'"

He looked down at his clipboard and said, "Oh,

yes, Mr. Grammer. Welcome." Then he told me where I could park and how to find Stage 25.

It's hard to describe the elation I felt as I drove onto the lot. I was entering the world of Hollywood, a world of glamour and prestige, of movie stars and power lunches, of fame and fortune. I walked past buildings that were drenched with history, and it exhilarated me that I was now to be a part of it.

I joined the cast of "Cheers," and the writers and producers, for my first read-through. Everyone greeted me with warmth and congratulations— they couldn't have been nicer. We sat down to read, gathered around that same enormous table that had so impressed me at my audition.

After the reading, which went very well (if I must say so myself), Nick Colossanto, who played Coach, approached me.

"You're really good, kid. You've got talent."

"Thanks," I said.

"No, I mean *really* good. Don't let 'em get you."

"Sorry?"

He looked me in the eye and told me, "I was born with one set of fingerprints. Don't ever forget that. One set of fingerprints. That's all you get."

I wasn't quite sure what to make of that, but it certainly stayed with me.

The night we shot my debut episode, it went off

without a hitch. I was funny; people really laughed. But my future with the show was still uncertain. The terms of my contract included a clause stating that after the first episode the producers would inform me if I'd be staying with the show. I waited for a few nerve-wracking days, and then the call came: I was in.

The thinking behind Frasier's arrival on "Cheers" was this: The character would be a writing device, a means to break up Sam and Diane. The producers had allowed the show to focus primarily on that relationship and felt that they had painted themselves into a corner. Frasier would provide them a way out, a way to rejuvenate the writing and keep the show alive. Seven episodes should do the trick.

But actors have a way of changing producers' minds. Actors are much more than writing devices.

The writers on "Cheers" were undoubtedly the best in television, but no matter how brilliant a script may be, a good actor always brings surprises to the language and different colors than the writers have imagined.

Somewhere around the filming of my fourth show, Les Charles, one of the creators and producers of "Cheers," told me it was too bad they hadn't known me better before they planned the season. The character of Frasier was much more interesting than they'd anticipated, and it was a shame I'd have to go.

That encouraged me; obviously the wheels were turning. Perhaps I would remain.

Though I was clearly responsible for the success of Frasier, I credit Shelley Long for his longevity. The rumors about her are numerous and often vicious, but grossly exaggerated. I have nothing against Shelley personally; I am even in her debt. But there was a problem. Shelley didn't want Frasier in the show.

Shelley was convinced that Diane and Sam should be together, that it was a terrible mistake to break them up. The writers were wrong about Frasier, and she took every opportunity to make that clear. She publicly campaigned against him, and it was difficult for me to ignore the obvious consequences should she succeed.

I remember the first time I attended the Golden Globe awards. The Golden Globe is given by the members of the Hollywood Foreign Press Association for outstanding performances in television and film. It's a very big night in Hollywood—all the stars turn out, and I was excited to be among them.

Shelley won for best performance by an actress in a comedy series. During her acceptance speech she spoke of how difficult the year had been for her and also for Diane. The show was terrible, and it broke her heart to get up each day and go to work. There was no longer any joy in it for her.

And the reason was Frasier.

I turned to the others at my table—some were from "Cheers," some from Paramount—and said, "Now, how can I ignore that?"

Yes, Shelley could be difficult. Not just for me, but for the rest of the cast as well. Nick's thinking was, "At least she's not a bitch." I took his meaning to be that at least she didn't plan these episodes, at least she didn't sit at home at night and calculate how to ruin everybody else's day. She wasn't evil, she was only capable of seeing things from one perspective—her own. And even though she was unpleasant, she was not a bitch.

I agreed with Nick, but explained that it was very hard for me to take it any other way than personally. Shelley's efforts to get me off the show were relentless. I learned that after read-throughs she would insist the writers take out every laugh I had. It became a kind of joke.

One night Glen Charles came up to me and said, "You know, Kels, you're amazing. All the writers have started taking bets on you. They try to write a line they're sure you can't make funny, but then you always do. I've won a lot of money."

That was when I realized Shelley was my angel; she had made it so much fun for everyone to keep me on the show. Every objection she made became a guarantee that I would never leave. Frasier would be around for years.

Things had worked out fine with Shelley—not, however, with Doreen. We separated in December of that year, and I found a little apartment on Venice Beach. When I told John Ratzenberger that my wife and I were breaking up, John, bless his heart, gave me some furniture and helped me move. That night Goose and I walked along the beach. There was a certain bounce in her step. It reminded me of how unhappy I had been, and so had she. Goose had spent the better part of a year cowering under the furniture, trying to hide from all the misery— she had witnessed so much sadness that it took its toll on her as well.

She jumped and wagged her tail and kissed me: "Welcome back, it's so good to see you again. Where have you been?"

Just as things were looking up, I got some devastating news. Jeffrey Lowenthal was dying of AIDS. Jeffrey, who had been my friend and agent for so many years. I remembered how I'd tried to warn him. Jeffrey had made no bones about his sexuality. He wasn't militantly gay, but he was

proud to be, and we would openly discuss his esca-
pades. "Just be careful," I would say. "Promise me
you're being careful."

With an evasive shrug he'd say, "Of course I
am."

I was heartbroken, but I was also incredibly
angry with him.

"What am I going to do?" he wailed over the
phone one night.

"Well, Jeffrey," I said, "you're going to live or
you're going to die. I don't know what else to tell
you. I'm sad for you, and frightened, but I can't
change what's happened. I love you, but I don't
know how to help you."

Jeffrey died a few months later.

It left me in a conflict of emotions: Had I been
right? Had I been wrong? Could I have helped;
could I have made a difference? I'll never know. I
am just left with it.

The years ahead would be filled with conflict,
also times of trial and triumph. Shelley Long
left "Cheers" at the end of the fifth season, and I
was now "the doctor in residence." People always
asked if "Cheers" was as much fun as it looked. Of
course it was, it was a blast. John and George and

Ted and, after Nick died, Woody; Rhea, and finally, Kirstie, were all people I loved and admired.

Those were wonderful times. The show was a hit, the work rewarding, and the money wasn't bad either. Of course it was fun, and we were like a family. But what family doesn't have its ups and downs?

I had plenty of them.

These were the days of my highly publicized cocaine addiction. The combination of divorce and alimony payments, and the mixed blessings of celebrity, sometimes overwhelmed me. I found escape in cocaine.

I had done a lot of blow back in New York. Hell, everybody did. And I'd be lying if I said I didn't enjoy it. I loved it. It meant I didn't have to sleep. Even as a child I'd hated going to sleep—life was so wonderful, so filled with exciting discoveries to be made, I didn't want to miss a second of it. Cocaine was the solution, and it was everywhere then—quite the thing to do. But the added pressures of my life in California, and my considerably larger salary, pushed it to the point where it became a problem. I'd stay up for days, and my work suffered. I was firmly in its grasp.

Everyone at "Cheers" was well aware of what was going on. It caused tension within the cast, but they did not abandon me. I remember with gratitude the day they met with me and, as a family, told me I should get some help. I did. And I guess you could say it saved my life.

Things got back on track. There were legal issues to address—a drunk-driving conviction, and another for possession of cocaine—and there was also the humiliation of the press to be endured. But I got through it.

Trials and triumphs, they come hand in hand. People often ask how I survived it all—they speak of hitting bottom and how hard it must have been. But they have no idea. Karen's death had been my bottom; everything else was a piece of cake. It's not really my intent to trivialize it, but a line of Auden's comes to mind: *Ordinary human unhappiness is life in its natural color; nothing to cavil of.*

And though those days may not have been so ordinary, they were most decidedly nothing to cavil of. So many many trials there were; but looking back: how great the triumph.

13

Another Day, Another Dolor

erlette Lamme was a woman of significance in my life. We spent seven years together, seven troubled years—my "years
of trial," as I now call them. She was a
support throughout them, but also she was one of
the trials.

I'll never forget the way we met. It was the summer of 1985. "Cheers" had ended for the season,
and I was playing Lucio in Shakespeare's *Measure
for Measure* at the Mark Taper Forum in Los
Angeles. We were well into the run, and the show
was under control.

It may surprise you to learn this, but as you
watch the actors on a stage perform from the safety
of the audience, they are also watching you. We
can see you out there, and since we can, we look.

We look, and as you watch, we check you out. It had always been a fantasy of mine to send a note at intermission to some stunning stranger I had spotted.

One night my buddy Carl and I made our exit after the opening scene. "Hey, did you see those two blondes?" he said.

"Fourth row, house left," I responded. "You bet your ass I saw them."

Apparently Carl shared my fantasy, and so he hatched a scheme. During intermission we composed a titillating note inviting them to join us for a drink after the show. We asked the house manager to deliver it to them, taking great pains to be sure he knew which girls we meant.

"Fourth row, house left. Yeah," he said, "I know the ones you mean."

It worked.

Cerlette and her friend met us at the Hungry Tiger restaurant around the corner from the theater. At first they didn't recognize us, probably because Carl and I, in our excitement, forgot to mention we had been wearing wigs on stage.

We sat down beside them.

"Hi. . . . We weren't sure you'd show," said Carl, very hot, very self-assured. "Buy you a drink?"

The girls exchanged a look of utter confusion.

Something had gone wrong, I thought. Maybe

we had the wrong girls. I turned to Cerlette and I asked, "So, did you two see the show tonight?"

"Yes," she said, "did you?"

"No," I answered, "I was in it."

She said, "Oh, really? We're here to meet a couple of the guys you work with. One of them played Lucio."

And then it dawned on me. The wigs.

"Oh, well. That would be me," I said.

"Really," she said, "I never would have known."

"I realize that," I muttered.

We ordered drinks. She told me they had loved the note, and that was why they'd come. I was in fact quite proud of the note, because I had written it. Its tone was very civil but peppered with the slightest hint of sexual innuendo. It was a brilliant note.

We went back to her apartment, but we did not have sex. I liked this girl. We kissed good night and I promised I would call her in the morning. I kept my promise and invited her to spend the day with me at Venice Beach. She came right over, and then we did have sex.

Cerlette was bouncy, pleasant, and romantic—Cerlette was fun: upright, as well as in bed. We fell in love.

She kept her own apartment, but she basically moved in with me. Although she wasn't the neediest woman I'd ever been with, she was needy enough. She fit perfectly into my pattern. I was not aware it was a pattern at the time, but years of therapy have shown me that it was. My understanding of love was that it meant being needed. I had no other frame of reference. The women of my childhood had given me a blueprint—need was love. The two were interchangeable. I was incapable of thinking any other way. As long as I was needed, it meant that I was loved.

It was a formula that backfired, because it was doomed to self-destruct. Being needed canceled out the possibility of ever being good enough. It also meant that eventually I would grow so tired of the constant disapproval that entailed—I would finally resent it so much I would leave, find another girl, and start all over again.

About a month into my relationship with Cerlette, she pretty much quit working and one night tearfully explained to me she couldn't pay her rent anymore. I didn't think it was time for us to live together yet (technically), so I volunteered to pay it for her. I was hooked. And so it began again.

It didn't take Cerlette very long to go from gratitude to resentment—two sides of the same coin—and fly into a rage if I bought the wrong kind of milk. She was bitter; I was worthless. All was right with the world.

So Far...

One day as I returned home from work, Cerlette ran out to meet me. "Please, please, promise me you won't be mad."

"What's happened?" I asked, "I won't be mad, just tell me." She was obviously distraught.

"Well, I took Goose to work with me today and she ran away. I can't find her."

Cerlette had been helping some friends of hers spruce up a home they'd bought. It wasn't in the best of neighborhoods, and she felt safer when she took Goose with her. Apparently they took a break, lit up a joint, and didn't keep an eye on Goose. A half hour later they got back to work, and that's when they noticed she was missing. The house was so far away from home, there was no way Goose could ever find her way back. I never saw her again.

The only thing I felt at the time was how much Cerlette needed my forgiveness, so I forgave her and I vowed to myself that no matter how bad things might get between us I would never throw this back at her.

But I felt then as I do now. There was really nothing quite so unforgivable. Cerlette had taken my greatest companion, the dog I cherished more than myself, and lost her. It was careless and selfish, and showed a total disregard of me. Cerlette had promised to take care of my dog. She didn't. I know she was miserable about it, but there was absolutely no excuse for what she did.

I miss Goose in a different way perhaps, but just as deeply as I miss my sister.

Shortly thereafter we moved to Van Nuys. We rented a house set on a fairly large piece of property—ideal for animals—so we adopted a variety of pets: five dogs, seven cats, a turtle, rabbits, guinea pigs, parrots, and ducks. I was working and, to her credit, Cerlette did a pretty good job of running the house and taking care of the chores. But like the lyrics of an old, familiar song, things between us weren't going so well. Every day there was some kind of crisis, some calamity that was either my fault or something I would have to attend to. It got to the point where I dreaded going home. Leaving work I'd think, I must be insane. I'm leaving the relatively stress-free environment of the workplace for the embroiled atmosphere of my anything but home-sweet-home.

I began to spend less time there. I'd stay out for nights in a row, or pass out on my boat instead. Cerlette accused me of cheating on her, which I had not. But once accused, I thought I might as well.

So Far...

Richard Davidson was in L.A. now, and the night he bailed me out of the Van Nuys jail, he asked, "Kels, what happened?"

"Richard," I said, "I stopped thinking."

It was true. I had stopped thinking. And this was how it happened.

It was one of the bad nights with Cerlette. Accusations were flying, tempers were high, and at the climax of her diatribe Cerlette concluded, "That's it, I'm out of here!"

She'd left her car at a friend's house. She wanted me to take her there, but I refused. I'd had a bit to drink that night, perhaps more than a bit—enough to know I shouldn't drive; so I told her, "I'll call you a cab."

"Oh, no, you won't," she said. "You'll take me there yourself."

"I've had too much to drink, Cerlette," I said. "I can't. I'll call you a cab."

"I won't take a cab; you'll drive me yourself."

"Oh, no, I won't."

"Oh, yes, you will."

"Oh, no, I won't."

"Oh, yes, you will."

I finally relented. "Oh, yes, I will."

We got in the car, and not two miles down the road we were pulled over by the cops. Two police-women came up to the car. They thought I was driving a little fast. "Have you been drinking?" they asked. I admitted that I had, but felt that I was all right to drive.

"Would you step out of the car, please?"

I did, and they administered an FST, Field Sobriety Test. I was actually doing pretty well when Cerlette began to wail from the car, "Oh, my God! I'm so sorry, honey, I'm so sorry. This is all my fault!"

One of the cops turned to me and said, "What's her problem?"

With that I knew my goose was cooked. They cuffed me, nestled me in their car, and drove me off to jail. I did the breathalyzer test and blew a .12, just above the legal limit at the time. I was booked for drunken driving, and one of the policewomen confided in me, "You know, I didn't really think you were drunk. But that girlfriend of yours—"

"I know, I know," I interrupted, "it's not your fault. It isn't even really hers. I just stopped thinking."

I was sentenced to fourteen days of CalTrans— basically highway cleanup—and was required to attend a class for DUI conviction. I did some of the workdays but blew off the class. Not the brightest thing I've ever done, but I suppose cocaine had magnified my problem with Authority to include the Law as well.

About a year later I was pulled over again, this

time for expired tags. I had just returned from Mexico, where I'd shot a two-hour TV pilot called "Lame Duck" with Bill Katt. I got the itch to drive my Triumph, threw on a jacket I hadn't worn in months, and took off for a spin. Cutting to the chase, they pulled me over, searched me, and in the pocket of my jacket found a quarter gram of coke. I had no idea it was there, but it was Providence, I guess. They hauled me off to jail and also toward recovery.

The trials I spoke of earlier were not just metaphorical; there were some Trials as well. For the possession charge I received ninety days' house arrest and three hundred hours of community service. Ironically, the DUI conviction, because I hadn't gone to class, landed me a stiffer penalty. I had to take the class, do twenty additional days of roadwork, and spend thirty days in county jail.

In the Los Angeles County Jail, I was given my own cell away from the general population in a maximum-security lockup. Before he took me there, the watch commander sat me down and said, "Look, we're putting you in 1100 with a couple of murderers, but we think it's better that way. The guys in general population would talk your ear off—you'd never get a moment's peace. Is that all right with you?"

"Sure."

1100 was a hall of seven cells and a shower with lockup doors at each end. In it was a cell that I'd call home for the next thirty days or so. Except for one hour each morning and evening, when we were given "hall time" to shower and watch TV and get the others coffee or hot water if they needed it, the inmates spent their time alone in their individual cells. We got three meals a day, and the routine of life in prison was, frankly, not so bad. I even made a friend, in Harvey. He'd been in jail for two years on a murder charge, and after two mistrials he was preparing to go to court for the third time. This shocked me because I was always under the impression that one mistrial, and that was it.

Harvey told me, "No, they get three chances. Three chances to nail you."

We became friends, and the deputies even relaxed the rules a little. Harvey and I were allowed a couple of hours in the hall together each night, when we'd play cards and watch television and talk. I liked him very much. Incidentally, Harvey was acquitted a year later.

Because of overcrowding I was released after only eleven of my thirty days. They were the best eleven days I'd had in years. Life was simple there, not full of turmoil as it was at home. No problems to take care of, no demands to meet, no frantic nights of accusation to bear. It was peaceful there. I was fed and warm, and I found solitude— something I hadn't had for a long, long time. In jail I had everything I needed—everything but freedom.

I learned a great deal in that time, but most important, I gained this knowledge: I was nothing if not free.

14

The Marriage
from Hell

The final years of "Cheers" were marvelous. Great fun. My troubles behind me, I felt my work had never been better. I was finally firing on all cylinders again. In fact, I was doing so well that in 1989, three years before "Cheers" ended, the folks at Paramount approached me about doing a show of my own. The deal was made to begin the show the minute "Cheers" shut down, though we didn't have a clue what it would be.

I decided it was time to buy a house, and it was Cerlette who found it. Thirty miles outside of Hollywood, it is set on five acres of land, in the middle of the Santa Monica mountains. A Mediterranean-style house with a pool and lots of fruit trees. Cerlette was so excited when she saw it. "Oh, honey," she said, "it's the perfect place for us."

It was incredibly hard for me to tell her of my decision. She'd stood by me through all the troubled times, so it pained me when I said, "Cerlette, I'm sorry. We are moving, but we won't be moving in together."

She seemed hurt, but she took it rather well. I guess she realized how bad things had become. I explained this didn't mean we wouldn't end up together someday. We'd still see each other, but for now I had to define a life on my own terms.

We found her an apartment, and I moved into the house that has become my home.

That first year on my own, I enjoyed my newfound independence. I saw a few women, but only casually; Cerlette actually remained the woman in my life. And things were pretty good. She was getting better, she seemed to have regained her self-respect and didn't need me quite as much. Perhaps we might, I thought, end up together after all.

But then I met Leigh-Anne, and the Pattern put my life on automatic pilot. Leigh-Anne was the essence of need itself, and once again I was a goner.

We did not meet in a strip joint, as is the popular version, but rather in a bar (a distinction I'd like to stress) in Calabassas. I was with some friends that night—they spotted her, liked her looks and started hitting on her. They pointed me out to her, which always embarrasses the hell out of me, and she blew them off and walked away. I was impressed. A little while later I saw her out on the patio. The truth is, I thought she was pretty cute myself, so I approached her and said, "I'd like to apologize for my friends. They're nice guys as a rule, but sometimes they act like assholes."

She said she really hadn't minded, she knew what they were doing. She did know who I was, but so what—I was no big deal. She had always hated Frasier.

It was love at first put-down. She was right—I was no big deal, and I thought how great it was that she had no regard for my celebrity. It occurred to me that this was a girl who might be interested in me for who I was, not what I did. She played me like a violin.

We ended up at my place that evening and played pool together until dawn, sharing our stories. Leigh-Anne was a stripper, and by the way she played pool you could tell she loved her work. She loved to tease a man, and feel his eyes upon her ass when she bent over. My God, she sure was sexy.

We started dating and I fell madly in love. She was everything I'd ever dreamed of—strong, sexy, independent, outspoken and unafraid of anyone or anything. Best of all, she didn't need me. She had no need at all.

They say great actors have great insight. If that is so, then I'm a fucking genius. A monument to perspicacity. There was no proof, no behavior to inform me, not a clue to tip me off—but I spotted it. Leigh-Anne had need beyond my wildest dreams. I knew it. I could see it buried deep within her, and I undertook its excavation.

All I had to do was take away her independence. The chief requirement for independence is having one's own money, so I insisted that she quit her job. It worked. She quit dancing, and a small corner of her need was unearthed. This may sound incredibly manipulative, but I was so deeply rooted in my pattern that I was completely unaware of it. Only through therapy have I learned to recognize and understand it.

For obvious reasons I have a great fear of abandonment. Everyone I've ever loved has left me. My father, Gordon, Karen, and even Goose. The pain of losing them was so unbearable, I had to find a way of making sure I'd never feel such pain again. Subconsciously I worked out this formula: If I can make them need me, they can never leave.

I realize now that to make a woman need me meant I had to destroy her. It's a terrible thing to destroy the one you love because, once successful, it destroys the love as well. It was a pattern of despair and loneliness, but I was trapped.

Not every woman in the world is susceptible to this kind of unhealthy seduction, but these I disregarded. I ruthlessly sought out my willing victims and started down the devastating path again.

———————

Leigh-Anne was locked in a pattern of her own. The means were different than mine, but the end was virtually the same—to destroy or, rather, to ensure that she would never be abandoned. Her method, however, was simpler and far more brutal. Ironically, to be sure I'd never leave her, she knew I'd have to need her. She had to convince me that I was nothing—unattractive, untalented, undeserving of love, and incapable of being loved by anyone but her. The way she achieved this was to break me down with verbal and physical abuse.

"You fucking pig." "You stink." "What a wimp." "Dickless." "You're disgusting." "What a piece of shit." "Your acting sucks." "You suck." "Fag." "Asshole." "Prick." "Bastard." "Fat pig." "You're so fucking stupid." "You're so fucking ugly." "I hate your guts." "You make me sick."

These were the verbal tools, but she had more.

She'd spit in my face. Slap me. Punch me. Kick

me. Break glasses over my head. Break windows. Tear up pictures of my loved ones. Threaten to kill me, kill herself. Cut my balls off. Chop me up. Put a bullet in my head.

These physical tools were not more devastating than her words, but more demeaning, more humiliating, because they had to be explained. They left evidence that could be seen in public. But then, public displays didn't matter to Leigh-Anne at all. She had no boundaries and felt no shame in her behavior no matter who was there to witness it.

It was hell. It was a nightmare. But I was paralyzed, trapped in a terrifying syndrome I couldn't stop.

How could this have happened? How could I have let it happen? Those are the questions everybody asks. Those are the questions I asked myself. Once again, therapy taught me why and how I'd let this happen, and also, through understanding, how to forgive myself.

It's called the battered-wife syndrome, but the name is misleading and because of my experience, I find it personally insulting. Battered spouse would be more accurate, and much more acceptable to me. It is a syndrome because in every case there are so many similarities.

The most common of these is the victim's inability to leave. Most victims share low self-esteem and fear of abandonment. The impact of abuse, the fact that it has even occurred, is so traumatic and hard to apprehend that it renders them incapable of ever leaving, or even thinking of it as an option. This is the most common reaction, but also the hardest to understand, and the most difficult to overcome.

Rather, as a rule battered spouses, because they themselves believe deep down that they deserve it, try to fix things. Promise that they'll be better, do anything to make the abuser happy.

Within the syndrome there is also a common cycle. It has three parts: first, the "honeymoon," a short-term period of bliss immediately following an episode; next, a time of calm, a temporary lull; until finally, the abuse explodes again.

Self-loathing is the cause of the abuse and also the acceptance of it. The cycle cannot be stopped until the victim leaves, or dies. Or the perpetrator goes to jail.

I now know why I married Leigh-Anne right after the first beating—just as soon as my black eye was gone. And why I stayed with her. I believed that she was right about me, that I was all the things she said. So I could not defend myself. Two things gave me the courage to leave her after only nine months. One was therapy; the other was my certain knowledge that if things continued it would ruin my career. Although I couldn't fight for myself, Christopher Plummer had taught me how to fight for my career. And that I would allow no one to take from me.

What would otherwise have been dramatic and scandalous events in my life became incidental during Hurricane Leigh-Anne. Not a national but most definitely a personal disaster.

On February 15, 1992, Barrie Buckner gave birth to our daughter, Kandace Greer Grammer. Naturally, her birth caused quite a fuss in the tabloids, but that was nothing compared to the blizzard that hit when I told Leigh-Anne.

Barrie and I had been friends for years. Cerlette had introduced us, but she was never Barrie's best friend, as has been reported. She was in fact one of my best friends. When they began, Cerlette's accusations of infidelity focused on Barrie. After two years of dealing with the same amount of flak I'd get had it actually happened, finally it did. What the hell? I thought. If I'm going to get blamed for it anyway, it might as well be true.

Barrie and I would from time to time spend an evening together, and she became another refuge in my life. With her there was no torment, no expectation—only kindness and affection with no strings attached. But that all changed when Barrie got pregnant.

The timing was unfortunate; I had just moved in to my new house to begin a less encumbered existence. This was not the best of news, and even though we once discussed how beautiful a child of ours might be, a life with Barrie was the furthest thing from my mind. The baby was a problem; Barrie wanted it, I had reservations.

In retrospect, I am delighted. Barrie chose to have our little girl, and even though I've lost her friendship, I've gained another miracle in my life: Greer, my daughter. An ineffable joy.

The ending of "Cheers" seems almost like a coda, a punctuation, to the brief but dense— perhaps the densest—two years of my life.

The night "Cheers" closed was one of the greatest events in television history. The years of its run had been a party, so it was fitting that it end with the biggest and most marvelous party of them all. An entire city was invited, an entire nation—and everybody came.

The evening air was charged with excitement. Thousands of fans gathered outside Boston's fabled Bull & Finch, the bar where "Cheers" had been born. I was sad and joyful at the same time. "Cheers" was ending, and my future was uncertain, but I reveled in a mixture of nostalgia and anticipation. I think we all did. It was a night filled with a contradiction of feelings, a contradiction that was indescribably intoxicating.

That final night of "Cheers" was so extraordinary, an occasion so exceptional, that even Leigh-Anne's considerable gifts were powerless to spoil it.

I remember Ted and I standing together talking on the third floor of the Bull & Finch. In mid-sentence, with a mischievous grin, Ted stopped and said, "Come on, Kels, let's go to the window." We walked to the casement together, stuck our heads out, and the crowd erupted with cheers and applause. We stepped back in, and Ted turned to me and said, "Isn't that great? Let's do it again." We did, and the crowd erupted again, and Ted said what can be said of all those years: "Wasn't that fun?"

Jimmy Burrows, creator and director of "Cheers," and my friend, sent a card. There was just one line. *It was the best of times . . . it was the best of times.*

15

Truth, Justice, and the American Way

The genesis of "Frasier," the show, began in 1990. We weren't sure when exactly "Cheers" would definitely be ending—that season or the next—so I put my mind to laying the groundwork for my own series with Paramount. I met with a number of producers—"show runners," as they're called. Rudy Hornish, a longtime friend and now director of development for my company, Grammnet, Inc., met with Dan Fauci, a vice-president of development for television at Paramount, and me for lunch. I'd asked Rudy to come along because, having just joined the company, I wanted to encourage him to feel included, and also encourage the powers at Paramount to get to know him. Dan mentioned the writing team of Angel, Casey, and Lee (a.k.a. Grubb Street). I knew them well. They had been writers and then producers on "Cheers" years before and then created "Wings." They were good, and I agreed it was a good idea to have a talk with them. Rudy made arrangements to meet with them the following week.

We all sat down together and I said, "Guys, I've got a deal with Paramount to do my own show as soon as 'Cheers' is over. I was wondering if you'd like to do it with me."

They exchanged looks for a moment, and Peter Casey spoke for the three of them when he said, "Yeah, Kels, we'd like that."

And so it began.

We still weren't sure what the show would be yet, but we had the first pieces of the puzzle in place. That was a year and a half before "Cheers" ended. As the time approached to present the network with a concept, I had decided Frasier should retire into history along with the show. The boys of Grubb Street agreed, and came up with this idea: I would play a bedridden mogul who had been crippled in a motorcycle accident. A man so driven and wealthy that being in bed didn't stop him from virtually running the country as he'd done before. They wrote a script, and afterward John Pike, the president of Paramount TV, gave me a call and invited me to dinner. Leigh-Anne and I joined John and his wife at a famous little Italian joint in Brentwood, and after a lovely meal John finally said these words: "Kels, I think a comedy should be funny."

I nodded. "Uh-huh."

"I just don't think a guy in a bed is funny."

That pretty much said it all.

The next week, John and I met in his office.

"Why not stick with Frasier?" he said. "The character's established, it's got a built-in audience, and I'd like to hit a home run with this show, wouldn't you?"

It was a very convincing argument.

"What do you think about a show with Lilith?" he asked.

"I don't think so, John," I said without hesitation. I had already considered the idea. In my opinion, that relationship had been pretty much played out on "Cheers." Bebe Neuwirth was wonderful as Lilith, but I was certain that if the show was to be centered around an old character, everything else about it should be new.

So this was the rough concept we presented to the boys—David, Peter, and David—to be filled in by them. They sharpened their pencils and went to work.

A few weeks later we had our next meeting. Frasier would be divorced, leave Boston, give up his psychiatric practice for a talk radio show in Seattle, his old hometown. There his father, Martin, a retired policeman who had been partially disabled in a shooting, would move in with him. There would also be a health-care worker, Daphne, a brother, Niles, and a radio producer, Roz, to round out the cast.

"Sounds pretty good," I said. "But just two things: Frasier doesn't have a brother, and his father's dead."

"Huh? We hadn't really thought of that," they said. And then, "So we take a license."

I thought for a moment, then said, "What the hell, let's do it."

David, Peter, and David started writing and having preliminary meetings with actors.

David Hyde Pierce was settled on for the role of Niles without a second thought. Months before, our casting director, Jeffrey Greenberg, brought in David's picture and said, "If you ever need a brother for Kelsey, this is the guy."

He was dead-on. In fact, David's picture could easily be mistaken for a younger version of me.

Daphne was a different story. One morning I got a call. "We need you to come in right away and read with an actress," said Jeffrey.

"Right away—are you kidding?" I asked. "I'm on vacation."

"Well, she has something else going on, and this is the only time she can make it."

"See if we can work out another time," I said, "and have somebody call me."

It was David Lee. "We've worked out another time," he said, "but while I have you, let me give you a rundown on the character. Daphne is a British housekeeper and physical therapist."

A red flag went up in my mind. "David, um, it makes me a little nervous. The British thing. It reminds me of the old show 'Nanny and the Professor.' I'm just afraid the idea of a British woman and an American man could become a little cutesy and predictable. It's been done before, and I personally never cared for it."

There was silence on the other end of the phone. Finally David said, "God, Kelsey, these are the only scenes we have that even work at all so far. But if you're really that concerned about it maybe we should talk."

The day of Jane Leeves's audition, I walked into the office and there she was. Beautiful, gorgeous, wonderful Jane. I introduced myself and went in ahead of her to speak with the boys.

"Well, she sure looks good," I said, "but I'm still not sure. I'll tell you what. Let's bring her in, read through the scenes, and we'll just see."

She came in and read, we thanked her, and she

left. I turned to the producers. "Okay," I said, "you got me. She's great. She was brilliant." And she most certainly is.

John Mahoney, who plays my father, had done an episode of "Cheers" in its final year, and I thought then, as I do now, that John was a wonderful actor. After working with him, I discovered that he's an equally wonderful man. We all agreed that we would love to have him play the father. I asked Jeffrey Greenberg for his number, and I called him that night in Chicago.

"John, I just want to put in my two cents worth," I said. "I'd love to work with you, and I think we could have a lot of fun together. Read the script and see what you think."

After he read it, John agreed to do the show.

The character of Roz was hard to get a handle on at first, so it was hard to cast someone to play her. We took a shot on a very talented actress to play her in the pilot, but it just didn't work. So we recast the role with Peri Gilpin. We all knew Peri as a gifted actress, and trusted that in her hands Roz Doyle, through the writers' exploration and Peri's skills, would eventually come to life. Today, Roz is very much alive and doing splendidly at KACL, 780 AM.

As for David, of course, finding Niles shot out of him like poop through a goose. Working with him is effortless. He is exquisite as Niles, a lovely man and an amazing actor.

It feels like I'm forgetting someone. Now, let me see . . . who could it be? Oh, yes, Moose. The Dog. Or Eddie, Martin's beloved sidekick and the bane of Frasier's existence. It's widely rumored that I hate the dog, and it's kind of fun to perpetuate that myth. The truth is, I have nothing against Moose. The only difficulty I have is when people start believing he's an actor. Acting to me is a craft, not a reflex. It takes years to master, and though it does have its rewards, the reward I seek is not a hot dog. Moose does tricks; I memorize lines, say words, even walk around and stuff. But I don't need a trainer standing off-camera, gesticulating wildly and waving around a piece of meat, to know where I'm supposed to look.

I will give him this, though. Moose, like any good actor, doesn't lie.

Which brings me to a little story. It was back in Buffalo, during my first winter there. The theater arranged privileges for the actors at the Jewish Y, so every night before the show I would go there to take some steam. One evening three of us were sitting in our towels and struck up a conversation. It got around to our individual careers—one was an insurance salesman, the other a real estate agent, and I of course was an actor.

"Wow, an actor," said the insurance salesman. "That's pretty tough."

"Yeah," I said, "but it's a good life. I love my work."

It went on like that for a while until finally he said, "You know, we're not so different—in fact, we have a lot in common. The truth is, I act every day."

Suddenly I was seized by a great revelation, and my actor's indignation welled up from deep within me. I looked him in the eye and told him, "No, you don't. The truth is, you *lie* every day." I guess that kind of pissed him off because he left immediately, mumbling, "Jeez, don't get so bent out of shape."

The guy in real estate followed, adding, "Yeah, what an asshole."

Let me explain. Actors don't lie, because to be effective as an actor, you have to tell the truth. Truth is the only thing the audience can recognize, the only thing that helps them accept the fantasy of what they're watching. For a play or a film or a television show to be believable, it has to be authentic. Authenticity is truth. That's what I meant.

Subtle perhaps, but in my experience I've never known a good actor who could get away with a lie.

But I digress. Now that I've taken care of Moose, let's get on with the show. We shot the pilot in the spring of 1993, two months after "Cheers" had ended. It was fantastic. The show went like clockwork; it felt like we'd been doing it for years. And when we finished, the studio audience gave us a standing ovation. Now, that I'd never seen before. Not at a pilot filming, not from a bunch of industry people who usually sit on their hands looking like an old oil painting. It was thrilling, and we were all convinced we had a hit.

Just one thing remained: the American public. America's a tough audience. No matter how good you think something is, America, bless its heart, might not agree. Fortunately for the cast and the crew of "Frasier," its producers and creators, my children, my mother, my fiancée, my dogs, my ex-wives, my attorneys, my business manager, my agents, my birds, my fish (I could go on), and me . . . America loved the show. "Frasier" was a hit. Whew!

After our first season "Frasier" won four Emmys: Best Director, Best Show, Best Writing, and even one for me—Best Actor in a Comedy Series. To everyone who had a hand in shaping Frasier—thank you. I always knew I liked that guy.

McGraw-Hill
Mathematics

Transition Handbook

Bridge the Gaps!

What Do I Need to Know?

Skill Builder

Challenge

6

 McGraw-Hill
School Division

New York   Farmington

McGraw-Hill School Division 🐝

A Division of The McGraw·Hill Companies

Copyright © McGraw-Hill School Division,
a Division of the Educational and Professional Publishing Group of The McGraw-Hill Companies, Inc.
All rights reserved.

McGraw-Hill School Division
Two Penn Plaza
New York, New York 10121-2298

Printed in the United States of America

ISBN 0-02-100166-9 / 6

2 3 4 5 6 7 8 9 024 05 04 03 02 01

GRADE 6
Contents

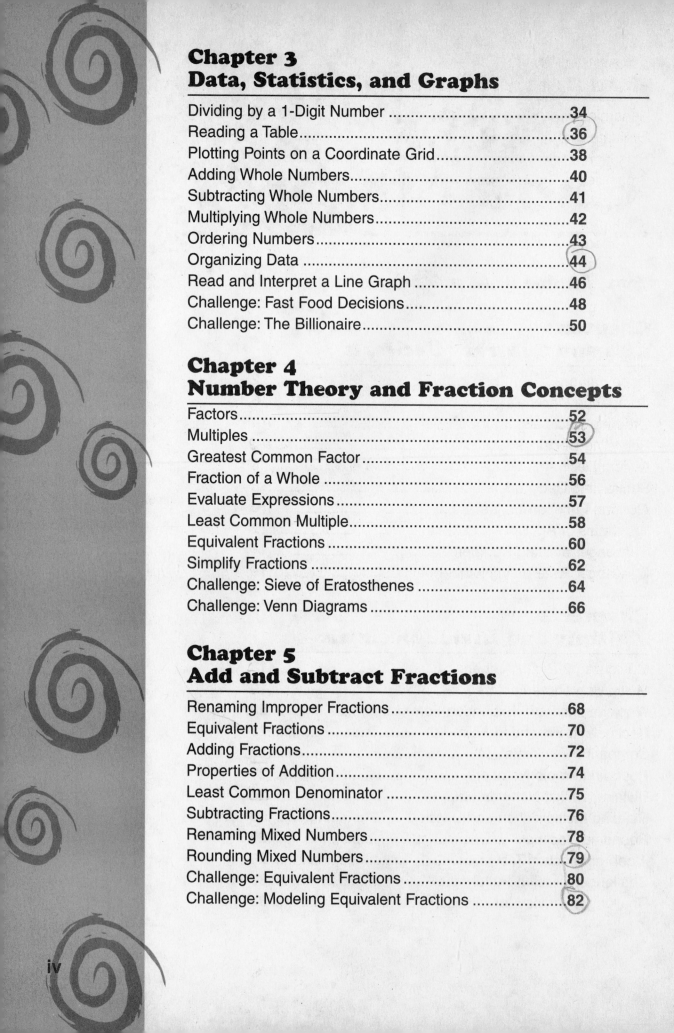

Chapter 3
Data, Statistics, and Graphs

Chapter 4
Number Theory and Fraction Concepts

Chapter 5
Add and Subtract Fractions

Chapter 6
Multiply and Divide Fractions

Chapter 7
Measurement

Chapter 8
Algebra: Functions and Equations

Chapter 9
Integers and Rational Numbers

Chapter 10
Geometry

Chapter 11
Perimeter, Area, and Volume

Chapter 12
Ratio and Proportion

Chapter 13
Percents

Chapter 14
Probability

Your Handbook

Welcome to *McGraw-Hill Mathematics Transition Handbook: Bridge the Gaps!* We hope you find this handbook enjoyable as well as useful in improving your math skills.

Your teacher will assign *Skill Builder* lessons from the handbook based on the work you do on pages given to you called *What Do I Need To Know?*

Each *Skill Builder* begins with a section called *Learn*, in which a student asks *What Can I Do?* to learn a specific math skill. Stepped-out models and one or more strategies are presented that will help you strengthen that skill.

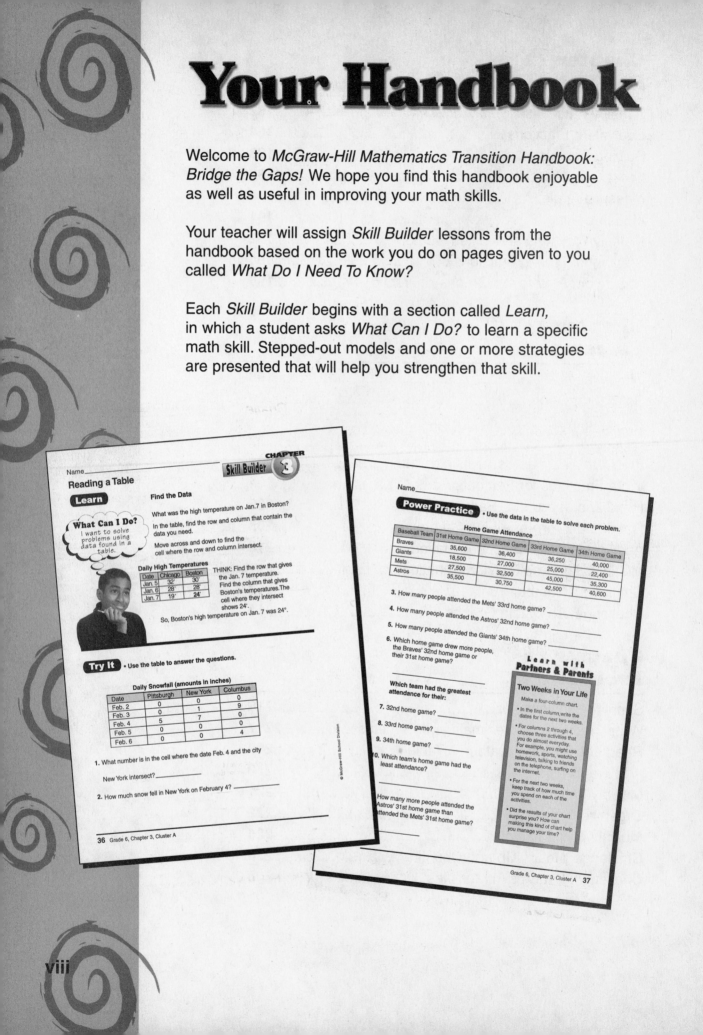

Name_____

Reading a Table

Skill Builder CHAPTER 3

Learn

What Can I Do?
I want to solve problems using data found in a table.

Find the Data

What was the high temperature on Jan. 7 in Boston?

In the table, find the row and column that contain the data you need.

Move across and down to find the cell where the row and column intersect.

Daily High Temperatures

Date	Chicago	Boston
Jan. 5	32°	30°
Jan. 6	28°	28°
Jan. 7	19°	24°

THINK: Find the row that gives the Jan. 7 temperature. Find the column that gives Boston's temperatures. The cell where they intersect shows 24°.

So, Boston's high temperature on Jan. 7 was 24°.

Try It • Use the table to answer the questions.

Daily Snowfall (amounts in inches)

Date	Pittsburgh	New York	Columbus
Feb. 2	0	0	0
Feb. 3	0	1	9
Feb. 4	5	7	0
Feb. 5	0	0	0
Feb. 6	0	0	4

1. What number is in the cell where the date Feb. 4 and the city New York intersect? _____

2. How much snow fell in New York on February 4? _____

36 Grade 6, Chapter 3, Cluster A

Name_____

Power Practice • Use the data in the table to solve each problem.

Home Game Attendance

Baseball Team	31st Home Game	32nd Home Game	33rd Home Game	34th Home Game
Braves	35,600	36,400	36,250	40,000
Giants	18,500	27,000	25,000	22,400
Mets	27,500	32,500	45,000	35,300
Astros	35,500	30,750	42,500	40,600

3. How many people attended the Mets' 33rd home game? _____

4. How many people attended the Astros' 32nd home game? _____

5. How many people attended the Giants' 34th home game? _____

6. Which home game drew more people, the Braves' 32nd home game or their 31st home game? _____

Which team had the greatest attendance for their:

7. 32nd home game? _____

8. 33rd home game? _____

9. 34th home game? _____

10. Which team's home game had the least attendance? _____

How many more people attended the Astros' 31st home game than attended the Mets' 31st home game? _____

Learn with Partners & Parents

Two Weeks in Your Life

Make a four-column chart.

• In the first column, write the dates for the next two weeks.

• For columns 2 through 4, choose three activities that you do almost everyday. For example, you might use homework, sports, watching television, talking to friends on the telephone, surfing on the internet.

• For the next two weeks, keep track of how much time you spend on each of the activities.

• Did the results of your chart surprise you? How can making this kind of chart help you manage your time?

Grade 6, Chapter 3, Cluster A **37**

viii

At a Glance . . .

The *Try It* section gives you a chance to try the strategy or strategies. Often the *Try It* exercises will give some hints to help you get started.

The *Power Practice* section gives you lots of opportunities to practice the lesson skill. This will help you succeed in solving the problems that come up within the corresponding chapter of your textbook.

At least once per chapter, you will see *Learn with Partners & Parents*, an activity that you can use at home with your parents, other family members, and friends, or at school with a partner.

Your teacher may assign a *Challenge* activity. Each *Challenge* provides a special math experience, such as a puzzle, code, or riddle.

We wish you success and enjoyment in your math experiences throughout the year!

Learn

What Can I Do?
I want to write how many tenths or hundredths.

Use a Decimal Model
How many tenths and hundredths are in 0.24?

Think: 1 shaded column = 1 tenth or 10 hundredths
2 shaded columns = 2 tenths or 20 hundredths
4 shaded boxes = 4 hundredths
0.24 = 2 tenths 4 hundredths or 24 hundredths

Try It
• Use the model. Write how many tenths and hundredths.

1. 0.35 = __3__ tenths __5__ hundredths

0.35 = __35__ hundredths

Power Practice
• Write how many tenths and hundredths.

2. 0.08 = __0__ tenths __8__ hundredths

0.08 = __8__ hundredths

3. 0.12 = __1__ tenth __2__ hundredths

0.12 = __12__ hundredths

Write the decimal.

4. 4 tenths 4 hundredths = __0.44__

5. 0 tenths 5 hundredths = __.05__

Comparing Decimals

Learn

What Can I Do?
I want to compare decimals.

[number line from 0.20 to 0.50 with arrows pointing to 0.37 and 0.40]

0.20   0.30   0.37 0.40   0.50

Use a Number Line

Think: 0.4 is farther right on the number line. Therefore, 0.4 > 0.37

Use Place Value

Think: Look at the digits in the tenths place. 4 > 3, so 0.4 > 0.37.

Try It • Compare. Write >, <, or =. Use the number line.

0.20   0.30   0.40   0.50   0.60   0.70

1. 0.51 ___<___ 0.62   **2.** 0.63 ___>___ 0.6   **3.** 0.34 ___>___ 0.2

Power Practice • Compare. Write >, <, or =.

4. 0.7 ___<___ 0.9   **5.** 0.05 ___>___ 0.03   **6.** 0.15 ___>___ 0.13   **7.** 0.6 ___>___ 0.23

8. 0.5 ___=___ 0.50   **9.** 0.04 ___<___ 0.4   **10.** 0.72 ___<___ 0.74   **11.** 0.44 ___>___ 0.4

12. 0.20 ___>___ 0.02   **13.** 0.03 ___<___ 0.10   **14.** 0.92 ___>___ 0.29   **15.** 0.59 ___>___ 0.57

16. 0.1 ___>___ 0.09   **17.** 0.06 ___<___ 0.60   **18.** 0.7 ___=___ 0.70   **19.** 0.55 ___>___ 0.51

Ordering Decimals

Learn

What Can I Do?
I want to write decimals in order.

Use These Steps.

Write the numbers in a column. Line up the decimal points. Compare each digit in a column, starting with the column at the left. Find digits that are not equal.

3.06	3.06
3.6	3.**6**
2.8	2.8

Think:
2 < 3
2.8 is the least.

Think:
0 < 6
3.06 < 3.6

The order from least to greatest is:
2.8, 3.06, 3.6

Try It • **Find the greatest decimal in each set.**

1. 3.2, 3.7, 4.5 ___4.5___

2. 0.14, 0.32, 0.19 ___0.32___

3. 5.6, 5.45, 5.47 ___5.6___

4. 1.2, 1.6, 1.53, 1.41 ___1.6___

5. 0.42, 0.5, 0.53, 0.48 ___0.53___

6. 0.7, 1.4, 0.99, 1.26 ___1.4___

Power Practice • **Order from least to greatest.**

7. 0.33, 0.71, 0.17, 0.2 ___0.17, 0.2, 0.33, 0.71___

8. 2.1, 0.67, 1.9, 2.06 ___0.67, 1.9, 2.06, 2.1___

9. 1.65, 3.04, 2.67, 3.1 ___1.65, 2.67, 3.04, 3.1___

10. 0.2, 0.11, 0.04, 0.17 ___0.04, 0.11, 0.17, 0.2___

11. 3.3, 3.16, 3.2, 3.02, 3.19 ___3.02, 3.16, 3.19, 3.2, 3.3___

Rounding Decimals

Learn

What Can I Do?
I want to round decimals to the nearest whole number.

Use a Number Line

The decimal 3.4 is between 3 and 4. It is closer to 3.

3.0   3.4   4.0

So, 3.4 rounds to 3.

The decimal 5.7 is between 5 and 6. It is closer to 6.

5.0   6.0

So, 5.7 rounds to 6.

Use the Tenths Digit

Look at the digit in the tenths place.

If it is less than 5, round down.

If it is 5 or greater. Round up.

Round 3.**4** down to 3.
Round 5.**7** up to 6.

Try It

• Use the number line or tenths digit. Round to the nearest whole number.

1. 7.7 __8__

7.0   8.0

2. 5.2 __5__

5.0   6.0

3. 0.3 __0__

0.0   1.0

4. 6.6 __7__

6.0   7.0

Power Practice

• Round each decimal to the nearest whole number.

5. 7.3 __7__

6. 9.2 __9__

7. 1.8 __2__

8. 6.5 __7__

9. 4.5 __5__

10. 7.6 __8__

11. 0.4 __0__

12. 0.6 __1__

13. 2.17 __2__

14. 2.71 __3__

15. 5.83 __6__

16. 5.38 __5__

17. 2.26 __2__

18. 6.53 __7__

19. 6.45 __6__

20. 9.91 __10__

21. 22.65 __23__

22. 17.67 __18__

23. 35.19 __35__

24. 11.18 __11__

Adding Decimals

Learn

What Can I Do?
I want to add decimals.

Use These Steps

Add: 3.4 + 6.21 + 0.83 = ?

Write the numbers in a column. Line up the decimal points. Add.

$$
\begin{array}{r}
1 \\
3.40 \\
6.21 \\
+\ 0.83 \\
\hline
10\ 44
\end{array}
$$

Think:
Write zeros as placeholders, if necessary.
3.4 = 3.40

Place the decimal point in the sum.

$$
\begin{array}{r}
1 \\
3.40 \\
6.21 \\
+\ 0.83 \\
\hline
10.44
\end{array}
$$

3.4 + 6.21 + 0.83 = 10.44

Try It • Complete each addition.

1.
$$
\begin{array}{r}
1\ \ \\
3.2 \\
0.6 \\
+\ 2.9 \\
\hline
6.7
\end{array}
$$

2.
$$
\begin{array}{r}
1\ \ \\
5.6 \\
8.3 \\
+\ 0.5 \\
\hline
14.4
\end{array}
$$

3.
$$
\begin{array}{r}
2\ 1\ \\
18.2 \\
9.4 \\
+\ 23.5 \\
\hline
51.1
\end{array}
$$

4.
$$
\begin{array}{r}
1\ 1\ \ \\
7.03 \\
2.66 \\
+\ 5.57 \\
\hline
15.26
\end{array}
$$

5.
$$
\begin{array}{r}
2\ \ \\
4.5 \\
1.8 \\
+\ 3.7 \\
\hline
10.0
\end{array}
$$

6.
$$
\begin{array}{r}
1\ \ \\
6.2 \\
9.4 \\
+\ 1.6 \\
\hline
17.2
\end{array}
$$

7.
$$
\begin{array}{r}
1\ \ \\
25.3 \\
9.7 \\
+\ 10 \\
\hline
45.0
\end{array}
$$

8.
$$
\begin{array}{r}
1\ 1\ \ \\
4.3 \\
6.58 \\
+\ 2.93 \\
\hline
13.81
\end{array}
$$

Name_____

Power Practice • Find each sum.

9.
   0.8
   0.3
+ 0.7
_____
1.8

10.
   5.1
   0.6
+ 3.9
_____
9.6

11.
  24.1
  16.6
+ 39.9
_____
80.6

12.
  6.6
  7.7
+ 8.8
_____
23.1

13.
  3.52
  0.27
+ 7.08
_____
10.87

14.
  0.12
  0.85
+ 3.91
_____
4.88

15.
  50.34
  70.45
+ 30.36
_____
151.15

16.
  82.69
  71.19
+ 80.85
_____
234.63

17.
  1.2
  5.71
+ 3.8
_____
10.71

18.
  5.49
  0.70
+ 5.86
_____
12.05

19.
  0.7
  62.14
+ 9.7
_____
72.54

20.
  44.83
  7.51
+ 0.8
_____
53.14

21.
  15.1
  7.5
  26.09
+ 7.44
_____
56.13

22.
  0.56
  80.67
  9.3
+ 9.8
_____
100.33

23.
  22.22
  2.8
  8.1
+ 37.25
_____
70.37

24.
  31
  5.48
  24.08
+ 99.88
_____
160.44

25. 7.4 + 3.5 + 80.2 = ___91___

26. 0.37 + 0.73 + 0.37 + 0.73 = ___4___

27. 6.23 + 7.1 + 0.72 + 62.3 = ___67___

28. 0.38 + 45.2 + 7.9 + 14.8 = ___72___

29. 51.2 + 5.21 + 0.89 + 8.9 = ___89___

30. 67.3 + 8.44 + 25 + 17.97 = ___92___

31. 6.48 + 19 + 56.29 + 20.56 = ___122___

32. 57 + 36.51 + 0.76 + 6.2 = ___545___

© McGraw-Hill School Division

Subtracting Decimals

Learn

What Can I Do?
I want to subtract decimals.

Subtract: 17 − 5.91 = ?

Write the numbers in a column.
Line up the decimal points. Subtract.

```
    9
  6 10 10
 1̸7̸.0̸0̸
 − 5.91
  11 09
```

Think: Write zeros as placeholders if necessary.
17 = 17.00

Place the decimal point in the difference.

```
    9
  6 10 10
 1̸7̸.0̸0̸
 − 5.91
  11.09
```

So, 17 − 5.91 = 11.09

Try It • Complete each subtraction.

1.
```
  4 13
  5̸.3̸
 − 0.6
    7
```

2.
```
  8 12
  9̸.2̸
 − 7.3
    9
```

3.
```
  4 16
  5̸6̸.5
 − 37.4
     1
```

4.
```
  8 10
  9̸.0̸9
 − 5.64
     5
```

5.
```
  8 10
  9̸.0̸
 − 8.3
    7
```

6.
```
  0 16
  51.6̸
 − 30.8
     8
```

7.
```
  8 10
  9̸0̸.3
 − 8.3
     0
```

8.
```
  6 10
  0.7̸0̸
 − 0.41
     9
```

Name_____

Power Practice • Find each difference.

9. 6.2
   − 0.8

10. 5.17
   − 4.67

11. 30.1
   − 26.5

12. 56.02
   − 40.53

13. 5.03
   − 3.80

14. 70.07
   − 43.75

15. 51.6
   − 38.09

16. 60.78
   − 58.79

17. 27
   −8.4

18. 13.5 − 6.7 = _____

19. 56.09 − 8.8 = _____

20. 81 − 5.35 = _____

21. 42.5 − 37.85 = _____

22. 12.04 − 9.9 = _____

23. 50.13 − 38.2 = _____

24. 60.03 − 7.64 = _____

25. 81.17 − 70.6 = _____

Learn with Partners & Parents

The Moving Decimal Points

Use these decimals:
   0.1234   0.4321

• Subtract the decimals.

• Change the position of the decimal point in one number and subtract again.

• Make as many different subtraction problems as you can by moving the decimal points around.

• What is the largest difference? the smallest difference?

Algebra: Function Tables

Learn

Rule: Add _____

Input	6	24	45	53	?
Output	9	27	48	?	86

What Can I Do?
I want to complete a function table.

Look for a Relationship

Look at the first column of numbers. What number is added to 6 to give an output of 9?

Think: 6 + ___ = 9
Since 6 + 3 = 9, the rule is "Add 3."

Check your rule.
Look at the next columns.
24 + 3 = 27
45 + 3 = 48

Look at the fourth column. To find the output for the input 53, use your rule. Since 53 + 3 = **56**, the output is **56**.

Look at the last column. To find the input for the output 86, use your rule. Since **83** + 3 = 86, the input is **83**.

Try It • Complete each table.

1. Rule: Subtract _____

Input	15	30	41	59	
Output	8	23	34		95

Find the rule: 15 – ___ = 8

Check your rule: 30 – ___ = 23

Use your rule: 59 – ___ = ___

and ___ – ___ = 95

Power Practice • Complete each table.

2. Rule: Add _____

Input	10	15	25	35	
Output	30	35	45		75

3. Rule: Add _____

Input	19	28	50	65	
Output	40	49	71		90

4. Rule: Subtract _____

Input	12	19	25	40	
Output	6	13	19		74

5. Rule: Subtract _____

Input	31	44	55	70	
Output	19	32	43		79

6. Rule: Add _____

Input	153	190		535	700
Output	255	292	401		

7. Rule: Subtract _____

Input	360	440	505		963
Output	270		415	875	

8. Rule: Subtract _____

Input	1.4	3.0		6.27	7.91
Output	1.1		4.28		

9. Rule: Add _____

Input	2.15	9.1	6.04		
Output	4.23			7.23	8.07

Properties of Addition

Learn

What Can I Do?
I want to add three numbers mentally.

Use Addition Properties

Use the **Commutative Property** to change the order of the addends.

$8 + (44 + 2) = 8 + (2 + 44)$

Use the **Associative Property** to regroup the addends.

$8 + (2 + 44) = (8 + 2) + 44$

Add.

$8 + 2 = 10$
$10 + 44 = 54$

So, $8 + (44 + 2) = 54$

Try It   • Add. Identify the property used.

1. $(7 + 35) + 5 = 7 + (35 + 5)$ ←Step 1

   $= 7 +$ _____

   $=$ _____

Property Used in Step 1:

_____

2. $(3 + 16) + 57 = (16 + 3) + 57$ ←Step 1

   $= 16 + (3 + 57)$ ←Step 2

   $= 16 +$ _____

   $=$ _____

Property Used in Step 1:

_____

Property Used in Step 2:

_____

Name_____

Power Practice • **Add using the properties of addition.**

3. $45 + 6 + 5 = 45 +$ _____ $+ 6$

$=$ _____ $+ 6$

$=$ _____

4. $79 + 34 + 21 = 34 +$ _____ $+ 21$

$= 34 +$ _____

$=$ _____

5. $27 + 9 + 13 + 1 = 27 + 13 +$ _____ $+ 1$

$= 40 +$ _____

$=$ _____

6. $15 + 8 + 35 + 22 = 15 +$ ____ $+ 8 + 22$

$=$ _____ $+ 30$

$=$ _____

7. $55 + (63 + 7) + 45 = (63 +$ _____ $) + 55 + 45$

$= ($ _____ $) + 100$

$=$ _____

8. $29 + 68 + (32 + 11) = 29 + (11 +$ _____ $) + 68$

$= (29 + 11) +$ _____ $+ 68$

$= 40 +$ _____

$=$ _____

9. $348 + 12 + 22 + 50 + 3 = 348 + 12 + 22 +$ _____ $+ 50$

$= 348 + 12 +$ _____ $+ 50$

$= 360 +$ _____

$=$ _____

10. $717 + (92 + 4) + (78 + 5) = 717 + (78 +$ _____ $) + (92 + 4)$

$= 717 + ($ _____ $) + ($ _____ $)$

$=$ _____ $+$ _____

$=$ _____

Building Numbers

Use each of the digits 0, 1, 2, 3, 4, 5, 6, 7, 8, and 9 once and only once to make the number described in each problem. Each number should have three decimal places. Do not use 0 in either the millions or the thousandths place.

? , ? ? ? , ? ? ? . ? ? ?
__ __ __ __ __ __ __ __ __ __

1. What is the greatest number you can make?

987,654,210

2. What is the least number you can make?

012,345,678

3. When rounded to the nearest tenth, what is the greatest number that rounds to 5 tenths?

9876,432,510

4. When rounded to the nearest tenth, what is the least number that rounds to 5 tenths?

0,123,567,498

5. What decimal gives the least odd whole number when rounded?

0,123,4567,89

6. What decimal gives the greatest odd whole number when rounded?

1,234,567,89

© McGraw-Hill School Division

7. What decimal gives the greatest even whole number when rounded?

_____

8. What decimal gives the least even whole number when rounded?

_____

9. What is the greatest number less than 5 million?

_____

10. What is the least number greater than 8 million?

_____

11. What is the number closest to 2 million 6 hundred thousand?

_____

12. What is a number with a 3 in the millions place in which the sum of the first four digits equals the sum of the last four digits?

_____

13. Write another number with 3 in the millions place. The sum of the first four digits should equal the sum of the last four digits, but the three digits in the decimal places should be different from those you wrote for problem 12.

_____

Patterns in Numbers

Write the number that continues the pattern. Then write the rule.

1. 3.1, 4.3, 5.5, _____

Rule:_____

2. 0.4, 1.1, 1.8, _____

Rule:_____

3. 0.1, 1.2, 2.3, _____

Rule:_____

4. 12.5, 11.9, 11.3, _____

Rule:_____

5. 15, 13.8, 12.6, _____

Rule:_____

6. 0.55, 0.7, 0.85, _____

Rule:_____

7. 8.7, 8.57, 8.44, _____

Rule:_____

8. 0.4, 3.6, 6.8, _____

Rule:_____

Name_____

Write three decimal patterns of your own. Write a rule for each.

9. _____

   Rule:_____

10. _____

   Rule:_____

11. _____

   Rule:_____

In each of the following number patterns, a decimal number has been added to or subtracted from the first number and each succeeding number in the sequence. One pattern has an alternating sequence. For each sequence,

   a. identify the operation or operations being performed.

   b. identify the number.

12. 111.11, 122.22, 133.33, 144.44

   a._____   b._____

13. 456, 443.86, 431.72, 419.58

   a._____   b._____

14. 359, 379.01, 399.02, 419.03

   a._____   b._____

15. 444, 454.5, 452.25, 462.75

   a._____   b._____

Multiplying 2-Digit Numbers

Learn

What Can I Do?
I want to multiply a 2-digit number by a 1-digit number.

Think of a Multiplication Fact
$4 \times 90 = ?$ Think: $4 \times 9 = 36$
So, $4 \times 90 = 360$

Multiply each digit. Begin with the ones digit.

$\begin{array}{r} 1 \\ 14 \\ \times 3 \\ \hline 2 \end{array}$ Think: 3×4 ones $= 12$ ones
 12 ones $= \mathbf{1}$ ten $\mathbf{2}$ ones

Multiply the tens digit. Then add on the renamed tens.

$\begin{array}{r} 1 \\ 14 \\ \times 3 \\ \hline 42 \end{array}$ Think: 3×1 ten $= 3$ tens
 3 tens $+ 1$ ten $=$
 **4** tens

So, $14 \times 3 = 42$.

Try It • Complete each multiplication.

1. $3 \times 40 = 120$
2. $6 \times 90 = 540$
3. $9 \times 70 = 630$

4. $\begin{array}{r} 52 \\ \times 4 \\ \hline 208 \end{array}$
5. $\begin{array}{r} 1 \\ 13 \\ \times 5 \\ \hline 65 \end{array}$
6. $\begin{array}{r} 46 \\ \times 3 \\ \hline 138 \end{array}$
7. $\begin{array}{r} 3 \\ 74 \\ \times 9 \\ \hline 666 \end{array}$
8. $\begin{array}{r} 3 \\ 39 \\ \times 6 \\ \hline 214 \end{array}$

Power Practice • Multiply.

9. $5 \times 80 = 400$
10. $2 \times 60 = 120$
11. $4 \times 20 = 80$
12. $8 \times 30 = 240$
13. $6 \times 40 = 240$
14. $7 \times 50 = 350$

15. $\begin{array}{r} 13 \\ \times 3 \\ \hline 39 \end{array}$
16. $\begin{array}{r} 21 \\ \times 4 \\ \hline 84 \end{array}$
17. $\begin{array}{r} 2 \\ 53 \\ \times 8 \\ \hline 424 \end{array}$
18. $\begin{array}{r} 16 \\ \times 3 \\ \hline 48 \end{array}$
19. $\begin{array}{r} 8 \\ 45 \\ \times 6 \\ \hline 270 \end{array}$

20. $\begin{array}{r} 73 \\ \times 4 \\ \hline 292 \end{array}$
21. $\begin{array}{r} 6 \\ 58 \\ \times 8 \\ \hline 464 \end{array}$
22. $\begin{array}{r} 2 \\ 94 \\ \times 5 \\ \hline 570 \end{array}$
23. $\begin{array}{r} 4 \\ 36 \\ \times 7 \\ \hline 252 \end{array}$
24. $\begin{array}{r} 8 \\ 29 \\ \times 9 \\ \hline 261 \end{array}$

Multiplying Three Factors

Learn

What Can I Do?
I want to find the product of three 1-digit numbers.

Use Multiplication Facts

Multiply the first two factors.

5 × 5 × 5

Think: 5 × 5 = 25

Multiply the product of the first two factors by the last factor.

$$\begin{array}{r} 25 \\ \times\ 5 \\ \hline 125 \end{array}$$

So, 5 × 5 × 5 = 125

Try It • Complete each multiplication.

1. 2 × 4 × 2 = ?

8 × 2

16

2 × 4 × 2 = _16_

2. 3 × 5 × 2 = ?

15 × 2

30

3 × 5 × 2 = _30_

3. 3 × 3 × 3 = ?

9 × 3

27

3 × 3 × 3 = _27_

Power Practice • Multiply.

4. 2 × 2 × 3 = _12_

5. 4 × 4 × 4 = _54_

6. 3 × 5 × 6 = _____

7. 5 × 7 × 0 = _6_

8. 6 × 1 × 2 = _12_

9. 7 × 7 × 7 = _____

10. 8 × 3 × 5 = _120_

11. 6 × 6 × 6 = _____

12. 9 × 2 × 7 = _____

13. 9 × 9 × 9 = _____

14. 8 × 6 × 7 = _____

15. 8 × 8 × 8 = _____

Whole Numbers in Expanded Form

Learn

What Can I Do?
I want to write a number in expanded form.

Use Place Value

Start at the greatest place. Use the place to find the place value of each non-zero digit. Express as a sum.

1,305
Think: 1 thousand = **1**,000

1,**3**05
Think: 3 hundreds = **3**00

1,30**5**
Think: 5 ones = **5**

1,305 = 1,000 + 300 + 5

Try It • Complete to show expanded form.

1. 563 = 500 + _____ + 3

2. 2,047 = 2,000 + _____ + 7

3. 2,407 = 2,000 + _____ + _____

4. 8,124 = 8,000 + 100 + _____ + 4

5. 9,103 = _____ + _____ + 3

Power Practice • Write in expanded form.

6. 89 = _____ + _____

7. 910 = _____ + _____

8. 6,045 = _____ + _____ + _____

9. 809 = _____ + _____

10. 5,003 = _____ + _____

11. 6,400 = _____ + _____

12. 3,435 = _____ + _____ + _____ + _____

13. 6,732 = _____ + _____ + _____ + _____

Decimals in Expanded Form

Learn

What Can I Do?
I want to write a decimal in expanded form.

Use Place Value

Start at the greatest place. Find the place value of each digit. Express as a sum.

0.**4**62
Think: 4 tenths = 0.**4**

0.4**6**2
Think: 6 hundredths = 0.0**6**

0.46**2**
Think: 2 thousandths = 0.00**2**

So, 0.462 = 0.4 + 0.06 + 0.002.

Try It • Complete to show expanded form.

1. 5.63 = 5 + _____ + 0.03

2. 0.47 = 0.4 + _____

3. 3.59 = 3 + 0.5 + _____

4. 1.72 = 1 + _____ + 0.02

5. 4.016 = _____ + 0.01 + _____

Power Practice • Write in expanded form.

6. 0.89 = _____ + _____

7. 0.525 = _____ + _____ + _____

8. 0.41 = _____ + _____

9. 3.031 = _____ + _____ + _____

10. 6.07 = _____ + _____

11. 3.406 = _____ + _____ + _____

12. 5.003 = _____ + _____

13. 12.09 = _____ + _____ + _____

14. 0.804 = _____ + _____

15. 4.074 = _____ + _____ + _____

Comparing Decimals

Learn

What Can I Do?
I want to compare decimals.

Compare Whole Number Parts

Which decimal is closest to 20?

0.2135, 2.135, 21.35, 213.5

Align the decimals.

0.2135

2.135

21.35

213.5

20.0

Think: 21.35 and 20 each have two places to the left of the decimal point.

So, 21.35 is closest to 20.

Try It • Compare whole number parts. Which decimal is closest?

1.   1.093
10.93
109.3

<u>109.3</u> is closest to 100.

2.   4.617
46.17
461.7

<u>4.617</u> is closest to 5.

3.   2.945
29.45
294.5

<u>29.45</u> is closest to 30.

Power Practice • Find the decimal that is closest to the number shown.

4. 70 <u>68.45</u>   6.845   68.45   684.5

5. 500 <u>513.6</u>   5.136   51.36   513.6

6. 90 <u>87.91</u>   8.791   87.91   879.1

7. 8 <u>7.634</u>   7.634   76.34   763.4

8. 700 <u>690.5</u>   6.905   69.05   690.5

Rounding Whole Numbers

Learn

What Can I Do?
I want to round to the nearest hundred.

Use the Tens Digit

If the tens digit is less than 5, round down to the lesser hundred.

hundreds	tens	ones
4	2	9

Think: 2 < 5,
   Round 429 down to 400.

If the tens digit is 5 or greater, round up.

hundreds	tens	ones
2	7	2

Think: 7 > 5,
   Round 272 up to 300.

Try It • Use the tens digit. Round to the nearest hundred.

1. 7<u>0</u>2 _700_   2. 2<u>5</u>3 _300_   3. 3<u>1</u>9 _300_   4. 8<u>7</u>7 _900_

Power Practice • Round each number to the nearest hundred.

5. 244 _200_   6. 391 _400_   7. 150 _200_   8. 717 _700_

9. 440 _200_   10. 628 _600_   11. 563 _600_   12. 365 _400_

13. 982 _1000_   14. 525 _500_   15. 439 _400_   16. 662 _700_

17. 2,462 _2,500_   18. 3,053 _3100_   19. 1,174 _1200_   20. 5,628 _5600_

21. 6,389 _6400_   22. 7,145 _7000_   23. 2,090 _2100_   24. 9,961 _1000_

Name_____

Dividing 2-Digit Numbers

Skill Builder **CHAPTER 2**

Learn

Use Place Value

$$\begin{array}{r} ? \\ 3\overline{)46} \end{array}$$

Divide the tens.

$$\begin{array}{r} 1 \\ 3\overline{)46} \\ -3 \\ \hline 1 \end{array}$$

Think: 4 tens ÷ 3 = 1 ten
1 ten is left over.

What Can I Do?

I want to divide a 2-digit number.

Rename the ten as 10 ones.
Then divide the ones.

$$\begin{array}{r} 15 \\ 3\overline{)46} \\ -3 \\ \hline 16 \\ -15 \\ \hline 1 \end{array}$$

Think: 16 ones ÷ 3 = 5 ones
1 one is left over.

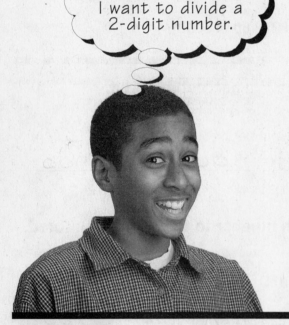

Try It • Complete each division.

1.
$$\begin{array}{r} 1 \\ 4\overline{)75} \\ -4 \\ \hline 35 \end{array}$$

2.
$$\begin{array}{r} 2 \\ 3\overline{)87} \\ -6 \\ \hline 27 \end{array}$$

3.
$$\begin{array}{r} 1 \\ 5\overline{)68} \\ -5 \\ \hline 1 \end{array}$$

4.
$$\begin{array}{r} 2\overline{)90} \\ -8 \end{array}$$

© McGraw-Hill School Division

Name_____

Power Practice • Divide. Write each quotient and remainder.

5. $3\overline{)75}$ — 25

6. $6\overline{)93}$ — 15 r 3

7. $5\overline{)80}$ — 16

8. $7\overline{)92}$ — 13 r 1

9. $2\overline{)50}$ — 25

10. $3\overline{)70}$ — 26 r 2

11. $6\overline{)71}$ — 11 r 5

12. $4\overline{)55}$ — 13 r 3

13. $4\overline{)85}$ — 21 r 1

14. $6\overline{)74}$ — 12 r 2

15. $5\overline{)59}$ — 11 r 4

16. $8\overline{)90}$ — 11 r 2

17. $2\overline{)39}$ — 19 r 1

18. $3\overline{)56}$ — 18 r 2

19. $5\overline{)64}$ — 12 r 2

20. $6\overline{)88}$ — 14 r 4

21. $5\overline{)97}$ — 19 r 2

22. $8\overline{)83}$ — 13 r 6

23. $2\overline{)68}$ — 34

24. $3\overline{)80}$ — 26 r 2

Learn with Partners & Parents

Telephone Division

- Use the first 3 digits of your telephone number to write three different division problems:

  $\square\square \div \square$

  (Remember, you can't divide by zero.)

- Find each quotient and remainder.

- Discard the remainders and add the three quotients. The player with the highest total gets 1 point.

- For the next round, use the middle three digits of your phone number. For the final round, use the last three digits.

Relating Multiplication and Division

Skill Builder

Learn

What Can I Do?
I want to use related multiplication and division sentences.

Multiplication and division are inverse operations. You can use a multiplication sentence to divide.

$3 \times 13 = 39, 39 \div 3 = ?$

Multiplication sentence
Factor × factor = product
$3 \times 13 = 39$

Related division sentences
Product ÷ factor = factor
$39 \div 3 = 13$
$39 \div 13 = 3$

You can use a division sentence to multiply.
$58 \div 2 = 29, 2 \times 29 = ?$

Division sentence
Dividend ÷ divisor = quotient
$58 \div 2 = 29$

Related multiplication sentences
Quotient × divisor = dividend
$29 \times 2 = 58$
Divisor × quotient = dividend
$2 \times 29 = 58$

Try It • Complete.

1. $4 \times 14 = 56$

factor ___ × factor ___ = product ___

product ___ ÷ factor ____ = factor ____

2. $75 \div 5 = 15$

dividend ___ ÷ divisor ___ = quotient ___

divisor ___ × quotient ___ = dividend ___

Power Practice • Complete using related factors.

3. $3 \times 29 = 87$, so $87 \div 3 =$ _____

4. $8 \times 26 = 208$, so $208 \div$ _____ $= 26$

5. $56 \div 2 = 28$, so $2 \times 28 =$ _____

6. $90 \div 5 = 18$, so $18 \times$ _____ $= 90$

7. _____ $\div 6 = 23$, so $6 \times 23 = 138$

8. $5 \times$ _____ $= 240$, so $240 \div 5 = 48$

9. $192 \div$ _____ $= 32$, so $32 \times 6 = 192$

10. $9 \times 33 =$ _____, so $297 \div 9 = 33$

Rounding Decimals

 Learn

Use the Hundredths Digit

If the hundredths digit is less than 5, round down.

What Can I Do?
I want to round to the nearest tenth.

ones		tenths	hundredths
6	.	3	2

Think: 2 < 5,

Round 6.32 down to 6.3.

If the hundredths digit is 5 or greater, round up.

ones		tenths	hundredths
2	.	0	9

Think: 9 > 5,

Round 2.09 up to 2.1.

Try It • **Use the hundredths digit. Round to the nearest tenth.**

1. 7.5<u>3</u> _7.5_   2. 9.1<u>5</u> _9.2_   3. 6.4<u>4</u> _6.4_   4. 8.0<u>8</u> _8.1_

Power Practice • **Round each decimal to the nearest tenth.**

5. 0.49 _.5_   6. 3.13 _3.1_   7. 6.53 _6.5_   8. 9.59 _9.6_

9. 7.45 _7.5_   10. 9.34 _9.3_   11. 0.75 _.8_   12. 2.17 _2.2_

13. 4.02 _4.0_ 14. 8.96 _9_   15. 0.51 _.5_   16. 1.76 _1.8_

17. 3.452 _3.5_ 18. 9.105 _9.1_ 19. 5.432 _5.4_ 20. 7.678 _7.7_

Algebra: Function Tables

Learn

Rule: Multiply by ?					
Input	11	15	25	30	?
Output	22	30	50	?	84

What Can I Do?

I want to complete a function table.

Look for a Relationship

Look at the first column of numbers.
What number is 11 multiplied by to give an output of 22?

Think: ___ × 11 = 22
Since 2 × 11 = 22, the rule is "Multiply by 2."

Check your rule.
Look at the next columns.
2 × 15 = 30   2 × 25 = 50

Look at the fourth column.
To find the output for the input 30, use your rule.
Since 2 × 30 = **60**, the output is **60**.

Look at the last column.
To find the input for the output 84, use your rule.
Since 2 × **42** = 84, the input is **42**.

Try It • Complete the table.

1.

Rule: Divide by _____				
Input	24	36	45	69	
Output	8	12	15		32

Find the rule: 24 ÷ ___ = 8

Check your rule: 36 ÷ ___ = 12

45 ÷ ___ = 15

Use your rule: 69 ÷ ___ = ___

and   ___ ÷ ___ = 32

Power Practice • Complete each table.

2.

Rule: Multiply by _____				
Input	7	13	22	35	
Output	28	52	88		96

3.

Rule: Multiply by _____				
Input	6	12	14	18	
Output	30	60	70		95

4.

Rule: Divide by _____				
Input	120	100	88	66	
Output	60	50	44		27

5.

Rule: Divide by _____				
Input	200	120	96	88	
Output	50	30	24		16

6.

Rule: Multiply by _____				
Input	13	20		42	56
Output	91	140	210		

7.

Rule: Divide by _____				
Input	186	126			72
Output	31	21	19	14	

8.

Rule: Multiply by _____				
Input	0.4	0.7	1.3		2.6
Output	1.6	2.8		6.0	

9.

Rule: Multiply by _____				
Input	2.1	3.3	3.7		
Output	10.5	16.5		21.5	50.5

Division Patterns
You can find patterns in these division problems.

1. Find each quotient.

$80 \div 40 =$ _____

$80 \div 20 =$ _____

$80 \div 10 =$ _____

$80 \div 5 =$ _____

$80 \div 2.5 =$ _____

$80 \div 1.25 =$ _____

2. What pattern do you see in the dividends, divisors, and quotients?

_____

_____

3. Find each quotient.

$60,000 \div 12,000 =$ _____

$6,000 \div 1,200 =$ _____

$600 \div 120 =$ _____

$60 \div 12 =$ _____

$6 \div 1.2 =$ _____

4. What pattern do you see in the dividends, divisors, and quotients?

_____

_____

5. Use what you know about the patterns above to find each quotient.

$72 \div 36 =$ _____

$72 \div 18 =$ _____

$72 \div 9 =$ _____

$72 \div 4.5 =$ _____

$72 \div 2.25 =$ _____

6. When did you stop calculating and start using what you know about patterns? Why?

_____

_____

7. Use what you know about the patterns above to find each quotient.

$400 \div 200 =$ _____

$40 \div 20 =$ _____

$4 \div 2 =$ _____

$0.4 \div 0.2 =$ _____

$0.04 \div 0.02 =$ _____

8. When did you stop calculating and start using what you know about patterns? Why?

_____

_____

Lattice Multiplication

About 400 years ago in England, a simple method for finding a product was developed. It is called the lattice method. Here is how to use this method to multiply 6,184 by 235.

1. First draw a 3-by-4 lattice with diagonals in each cell.

2. Next, write the factors on the top and right side.

3. Multiply the 4 by each number on the side. Fill in the products as shown. If the product has only a ones digit, write a 0 in the tens place above the diagonal.

4. Now it's your turn. Multiply the 8, the 1, and the 6 in the same way. Fill in the products.

© McGraw-Hill School Division

5. Find the final product by adding the numbers along each diagonal. Regroup to the next diagonal when needed. Work from the bottom right to the top left. Fill in the sums. Read the answer from the top left.

Carry this 2

$8 + 1 + 4 + 4 + 5 = 22$

Write this 2

$6,184 \times 235 = \underline{\hspace{1cm}}, 240$

6. Use the lattice method to find the product of $83 \times 3,982$.

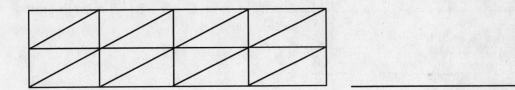

_____

7. Use the lattice method to find the product of $2,008 \times 365$

_____

Dividing by a 1-Digit Number

Learn

Use Place Value

You can think of 2,968 as:

2 thousands + 9 hundreds + 6 tens + 8 ones

What Can I Do?

I want to divide by a 1-digit number.

$$\begin{array}{r} 7 \\ 4\overline{)2,968} \\ -\ 28 \\ \hline 1 \end{array}$$

Think: You cannot divide 2 thousands by 4.
Divide 29 *hundreds* by 4.
$\qquad 4 \times 7 = 28 \qquad 29 - 28 = 1$

$$\begin{array}{r} 74 \\ 4\overline{)2,968} \\ 28\ \downarrow \\ \hline 16 \\ -\ 16 \\ \hline 0 \end{array}$$

Think: Bring down 6 tens.
Divide 16 *tens* by 4.
$\qquad 4 \times 4 = 16 \qquad 16 - 16 = 0$

$$\begin{array}{r} 742 \\ 4\overline{)2,968} \\ -\ 28\ \big| \\ \hline 16\ \big| \\ -\ 16\ \downarrow \\ \hline 08 \\ -\ 08 \end{array}$$

Think: Bring down 8 ones.
Divide 8 *ones* by 4.
$\qquad 4 \times 2 = 8 \quad 8 - 8 = 0$ No Remainder

Try It • Complete the division.

1.
$$\begin{array}{r} 89 \\ 4\overline{)357} \\ -\ 32 \\ \hline 37 \\ -\ \\ \hline \end{array}$$

2.
$$\begin{array}{r} 30 \\ 3\overline{)929} \\ -\ 9 \\ \hline 029 \\ -\ 27 \\ \hline 2 \end{array}$$

3.
$$\begin{array}{r} 1,4 \\ 5\overline{)7,145} \\ -\ 5 \\ \hline 21 \\ -20 \\ \hline \\ -\ \\ \hline \end{array}$$

4.
$$\begin{array}{r} 63 \\ 9\overline{)5,758} \\ -\ 54 \\ \hline 35 \\ -27 \\ \hline \\ \end{array}$$

Name_____

Power Practice • Divide. Write the quotient and remainder.

5. $3\overline{)197}$ **6.** $7\overline{)931}$ **7.** $6\overline{)804}$

8. $5\overline{)296}$ **9.** $2\overline{)4,767}$ **10.** $3\overline{)7,135}$

11. $4\overline{)6,071}$ **12.** $6\overline{)8,439}$ **13.** $5\overline{)3,195}$

14. $8\overline{)4,327}$ **15.** $9\overline{)6,444}$ **16.** $5\overline{)5,020}$

17. $7\overline{)8,405}$ **18.** $9\overline{)7,309}$ **19.** $4\overline{)3,256}$

20. $6\overline{)4,000}$ **21.** $3\overline{)5,281}$ **22.** $8\overline{)6,745}$

23. $7\overline{)2,947}$ **24.** $5\overline{)8,195}$ **25.** $9\overline{)4,725}$

Reading a Table

Learn

Find the Data

What Can I Do?
I want to solve problems using data found in a table.

What was the high temperature on Jan.7 in Boston?

In the table, find the row and column that contain the data you need.

Move across and down to find the cell where the row and column intersect.

Daily High Temperatures

Date	Chicago	Boston
Jan. 5	32°	30°
Jan. 6	28°	28°
Jan. 7	19°	**24°**

THINK: Find the row that gives the Jan. 7 temperature. Find the column that gives Boston's temperatures. The cell where they intersect shows 24°.

So, Boston's high temperature on Jan. 7 was 24°.

Try It
• **Use the table to answer the questions.**

Daily Snowfall (amounts in inches)

Date	Pittsburgh	New York	Columbus
Feb. 2	0	0	0
Feb. 3	0	1	9
Feb. 4	5	7	0
Feb. 5	0	0	0
Feb. 6	0	0	4

1. What number is in the cell where the date Feb. 4 and the city New York intersect? _____7_____

2. How much snow fell in New York on February 4? ____7 inches____

Name_____

Power Practice • Use the data in the table to solve each problem.

Home Game Attendance

Baseball Team	31st Home Game	32nd Home Game	33rd Home Game	34th Home Game
Braves	35,600	36,400	36,250	40,000
Giants	18,500	27,000	25,000	22,400
Mets	27,500	32,500	45,000	35,300
Astros	35,500	30,750	42,500	40,600

3. How many people attended the Mets' 33rd home game? ___4500___

4. How many people attended the Astros' 32nd home game? ___30 750___

5. How many people attended the Giants' 34th home game? ___2240___

6. Which home game drew more people, the Braves' 32nd home game or their 31st home game?

___32cd home game___

Which team had the greatest attendance for their:

7. 32nd home game? ___Braves___

8. 33rd home game? ___Metz___

9. 34th home game? ___Astros___

10. Which team's home game had the least attendance?

___The giants___

11. How many more people attended the Astros' 31st home game than attended the Mets' 31st home game?

 ___6000___

Learn with Partners & Parents

Two Weeks in Your Life

Make a four-column chart.

• In the first column, write the dates for the next two weeks.

• For columns 2 through 4, choose three activities that you do almost everyday. For example, you might use homework, sports, watching television, talking to friends on the telephone, surfing on the internet.

• For the next two weeks, keep track of how much time you spend on each of the activities.

• Did the results of your chart surprise you? How can making this kind of chart help you manage your time?

Plotting Points on a Coordinate Grid

Learn

What Can I Do?

I want to plot a point for an ordered pair.

Use a Coordinate Grid

An ordered pair names a point on a grid.

To plot a point, start at the origin (0, 0). The first number in the pair tells you how far to move *across* the x-axis. The second number tells you how far to move *up* the y-axis.

Point *A* is at (2, 4)
Point *B* is at (4, 2).

Try It • Use the ordered pair to complete the sentence. Then plot each point on the grid.

Point *F* (3,1)

1. To plot point *F*,

move _____ units across the x-axis,

and _____ unit up the y-axis.

Point *G* (1, 5)

2. To plot point *G*,

move 1 unit _____ the x-axis,

and 5 units _____ the y-axis.

Power Practice • Plot each point.

3. Point *L* (6, 2)   **4.** Point *M* (10, 2)   **5.** Point *N* (0, 9)

6. Point *O* (5, 12)   **7.** Point *P* (3, 15)   **8.** Point *Q* (9, 0)

9. Point *R* (1, 7)   **10.** Point *S* (3, 10)   **11.** Point *T* (5, 5)

12. Point *V* (8, 7)   **13.** Point *X* (9, 9)   **14.** Point *Z* (13, 5)

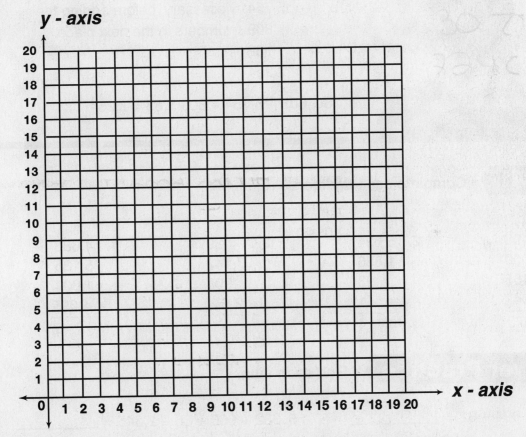

Answer these questions after plotting all the points named above.

15. What point lies on the *x*-axis? _____

16. What point lies on the *y*-axis? _____

17. Which point is the farthest across the grid? _____

18. Which point is the highest up the grid? _____

Adding Whole Numbers

Learn

What Can I Do?

I want to add three or more addends.

Add. 608 + 5,754 + 809 + 83 = ?

Use These Steps

Write the numbers in a column. Line up the digits that are in the same place. Add, beginning with the ones column.

```
  2 1 2
    608    Remember to regroup when
  5,754    necessary, before adding the
    809    numbers in the next place.
+    83
  7,254
```

So, 608 + 5,754 + 809 + 83 = 7,254

Try It • Complete each addition.

1.	2.	3.	4.
¹² 408 60 155 + 2,047 —— 70	¹ 5,634 1,866 93 + 551 —— 4	² 39 7,143 908 + 2,641 —— 1	¹ 4,683 5,135 1,004 + 4,095 —— 7

Power Practice • Find each sum.

5. 95 + 804 + 82 = _____

6. 382 + 660 + 85 + 2,345 = _____

7. 3,523 + 747 + 109 + 96 = _____

8. 515 + 4,629 + 2,432 + 87 = _____

9. 6,988 + 1,954 + 803 + 5,512 + 444 = _____

10. 77 + 3,190 + 6,840 + 903 + 5,662 = _____

11. 205 + 584 + 2,387 + 68 + 7,346 = _____

12. 3,095 + 3,905 + 359 + 395 + 5,955 = _____

Subtracting Whole Numbers

Learn

What Can I Do?

I want to subtract whole numbers.

Subtract. 6,402 – 876 = ?

Use These Steps

Write the numbers in a column. Line up the digits that are in the same place. Subtract, beginning with the ones column.

```
    9 13
  5 10 3 12
  6,042    Remember to regroup when
 – 876     necessary, before subtracting.
  5,166
```

So, 6,042 – 876 = 5,166

Try It • Complete the subtraction.

1.
```
   3 10
  4Ø8
 – 64
    4
```

2.
```
   3 15
  64̸5̸
 – 429
    6
```

3.
```
      10
   1 Ø11
  2,1̸1̸9
 – 987
     32
```

4.
```
        12 9
   3 2 1Ø 12
  4,3Ø2̸
 –3,945
      7
```

Power Practice • Find each difference.

5. 950 – 78 = _____

6. 414 – 386 = _____

7. 732 – 581 = _____

8. 3,149 – 875 = _____

9. 8,047 – 5,897 = _____

10. 6,324 – 5,849 = _____

11. 7,002 – 583 = _____

12. 4,513 – 686 = _____

13. 2,301 – 1,743 = _____

14. 9,432 – 87 = _____

15. 6,315 – 5,908 = _____

16. 8,920 – 7,945 = _____

Name_____

Multiplying Whole Numbers

Learn

What Can I Do?
I want to find a product.

1-Digit Multiplier

$3 \times 438 = ?$
Multiply each place in the other factor by the multiplier. Begin with the ones place.

```
  1 2
  438
×   3
1,314
```

Remember to regroup when necessary, before multiplying the numbers in the next place.

So, $3 \times 438 = 1,314.$

2-Digit Multiplier

$42 \times 36 = ?$
Multiply each place in the other factor by the ones digit of the multiplier

```
   1
   36
×  42
   72
```

Remember to regroup when necessary.

Multiply each place in the other factor by the tens digit of the multiplier. Then add both products

```
   2
   /
   36
×  42
   72
+1,440
 1,512
```

Think:
144 tens = 1,440.
Remember the 0 in the ones place.
So, $42 \times 36 = 1,512.$

Try It • Complete the multiplication.

1.
```
  2
  352
×   4
   08
```

2.
```
  5
  719
×   6
   14
```

3.
```
 1
 /
  85
× 24
 340
  00
```

4.
```
  2
  59
× 63
 177
____
```

Power Practice • Find each product.

5. $4 \times 87 =$ _____

6. $6 \times 75 =$ _____

7. $8 \times 46 =$ _____

8. $9 \times 163 =$ _____

9. $8 \times 628 =$ _____

10. $4 \times 505 =$ _____

11. $13 \times 58 =$ _____

12. $95 \times 47 =$ _____

13. $28 \times 82 =$ _____

14. $52 \times 31 =$ _____

15. $14 \times 68 =$ _____

16. $37 \times 77 =$ _____

Ordering Numbers

Learn

Line Up the Numbers

Line up the ones digit. Look for numbers that have the least or greatest number of places.

 45   Think: 45 has the least number of places.
387   45 is the least.
370
405
308

What Can I Do?
I want to order a set of numbers.

Compare the digits starting in the greatest place to determine the order.

Compare hundreds.

387
370
405   Think: 4 > 3, so 405 is the greatest.
378

Compare tens.

387   Think: 8 > 7 and 7 > 0
370   387 > 370 > 308
308

So the order from greatest to least is 405, 387, 370, 308, 45.

Try It • Find the greatest number in each set.

1. 56	2. 502	3. 763	4. 612
962	488	317	643
587	76	752	599
_____	_____	_____	_____

Power Practice • Order from greatest to least.

5. 904, 940, 87, 807, 780 _____

6. 467, 409, 555, 515, 551, 49 _____

7. 293, 195, 307, 78, 254, 183 _____

Organizing Data

Learn

What Can I Do?
I want to organize data to make it easy to interpret.

Make a Frequency Table

List the categories of your data in the left column.

In the second column, make a tally mark (/) next to the category each time it occurs. Cluster the tally marks by five (ℋℋ) to make counting the total easier.

In the third column, write the total number.

Hours Students Watch TV Daily		
Hours	Tally	Number
less than 1	//	2
1	ℋℋ /	6
2	ℋℋ ///	8
3	ℋℋ ℋℋ /	11
4	//	2
4 or more	/	1

Try It • Use the collected data to complete the frequency table.

1. Hours Spent Doing Homework
Responses: 4 h, 3 h, 1 h, 2 h, 2 h, 2 h, 1 h, 3 h, 4 h, 4 h, 3 h, 3 h, 1 h, 5 h, 2 h, 2 h, 3 h, 2 h, 2 h, 3 h, 4 h

Hours Spent Doing Homework		
Hours	Tally	Number
less than 1		0
1	///	3
2	ℋℋ //	7
3	ℋℋ /	6
4	/·//	3
4 or more	/	1

Power Practice • Make a frequency table for the collected data.

2. Math Test Scores: 75, 80, 80, 90, 85,
70, 65, 95, 100, 80, 85, 90, 65, 50, 65,
85, 90, 65, 85, 90, 95, 75, 65, 70, 90,
90, 90, 80, 70, 75, 85, 90, 80

Math Test Scores		

3. Favorite Shirt Color

Boys: Blue, White, Red, Black, White,
Blue, Blue, Blue, Brown, White,
Blue, Blue, Red, White, Brown,
Black, Blue, Black, White, Red

Girls: Brown, Red, Red, Blue, Red, White,
Black, Red, Black, Black, Red, Blue,
White, Red, Black, Brown, Black,
Red, White, Blue, White, Red, Red

Favorite Shirt Color			
Boys' Choices		Girls' Choices	

4. Time It Takes to Make Breakfast:
10 min, 10 min, 15 min, 20 min,
5 min, 10 min, 15 min, 10 min,
15 min, 5 min, 15 min, 10 min,
10 min, 15 min, 5 min, 20 min,
10 min, 5 min, 10 min, 15 min,
10 min, 10 min, 5 min

Time It Takes to Make Breakfast		

Read and Interpret a Line Graph

Learn

What Can I Do?

I want to read data from a line graph.

Seeing Trends

A line graph helps you to see changes that happen over time.

A **flat** line means **no change**. A line that **rises** means an **increase**. A line that **falls** means a **decrease**.

The level of water in the Mill Town reservoir:

• stayed the same from July to September.

• increased from September to October and from October to November.

• decreased from November to December.

Water in Mill Town's Reservoir

Depth of Water (ft)

Months of the Year

Try It • **Use the graph to complete each statement. Write *increased* or *decreased*.**

1. The number of people who attended the carnival _____ from week 1 to week 2.

2. The number of people who attended the carnival _____ from week 2 to week 3.

3. The number of people who attended the carnival _____ from week 4 to week 5.

Bayside Carnival Attendance

Number of People

week 1   week 2   week 3   week 4   week 5

Power Practice • **Use the line graph to answer questions 4-8.**

4. In which year did Auto City sell the least number of cars? _____

5. In which two years were Auto City's car sales the same?

_____

6. In which year did Auto City's sales decrease? _____

7. In which years did Auto City's sales increase? _____

8. In which year did Auto City's sales increase the most ? _____

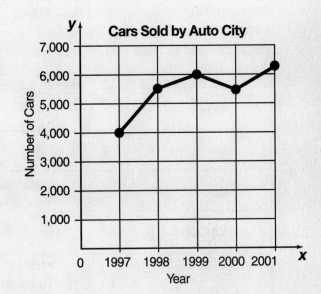

Use the line graph to answer questions 9 -12

9. Between which hours did the temperature steadily increase ?

_____

10. Between which two hours did the temperature decrease the most?

_____

11. Between which two hours did the temperature increase the most?

_____

12. Between which two hours did the temperature not change?

_____

Fast Food Decisions

You own a fast-food restaurant.
You need to make some decisions
about menu items, hours of operation,
and worker staffing. Use the data in
these graphs to help you make these decisions.

Customer Food Preferences

KEY = 10 customers

Food Sales by Time of Day

Food Preparation Time

1. What will be your hours of operation? _____

2. How will you decide which hours to be open?

_____

_____

3. During which hours will you need the largest crew of workers?

_____

_____

4. Explain why you chose those times.

_____

_____

5. If food preparation time were your only concern, which foods would you have on your menu? Explain.

_____

_____

6. If customer preference were your only concern, which foods would you have on your menu? Explain.

_____

_____

7. Which foods would you decide to have on your menu, taking into consideration both preparation time and customer preferences? Explain.

_____

_____

_____

Name_____

The Billionaire

You have been given one billion dollars by an eccentric billionaire who made only two rules:

- You may not spend any of it until you have counted every single dollar.

- You may only count for 8 hours a day.

There are three facts you must know:

- You can count one dollar every second.

- There are 60 seconds in a minute.

- There are 60 minutes in an hour.

1. How many dollars can you count in an 8-hour day?

_____

2. At this rate, how many dollars can you count in a year?

_____

3. How many years would it take to count one billion dollars?

_____

4. How old will you be when you are through counting?

_____

5. How many dollar bills you can count in 10 years? Record your number.

_____

Name_____

6. Calculate the number of bills you could count in 50 years, 60 years, 70 years, 80 years, and 90 years. Record the products for each calculation.

50 years_____

60 years_____

70 years_____

80 years_____

90 years_____

7. A trillion dollars ($1,000,000,000,000) is one thousand times as much as a billion. How long would it take to count a trillion dollars at the same rate?

_____

8. A quadrillion dollars ($1,000,000,000,000,000) is one million times as much as a billion. How long would it take to count this many dollars at the same rate?

_____

9. How will you spend the billion dollars? Use the space below to plan your billion dollar budget. Share your ideas with your classmates.

_____

_____

_____

_____

_____

Factors

Learn

What Can I Do?
I want to list all the factors of a number.

Find Factor Pairs

All numbers have at least two factors, the number 1 and the number itself.

$3 = 1 \times 3$
The factors of 3 are 1 and 3.

Some numbers have more than two factors. Look for all factor pairs whose product is equal to that number.

$18 = 1 \times 18$
$18 = 2 \times 9$
$18 = 3 \times 6$

The factors for 18 are 1, 2, 3, 6, 9 and 18.

Try It

. **Find the missing factors. Then list all the factors of each number.**

1. $20 = 1 \times$ _____

$20 = 2 \times$ _____

$20 = 4 \times$ _____

Factors of 20:

_____

2. $32 = 1 \times$ _____

$32 =$ _____ $\times 16$

$32 =$ _____ $\times 8$

Factors of 32:

_____

3. $45 = 1 \times$ _____

$45 =$ _____ $\times 15$

$45 = 5 \times$ _____

Factors of 45:

_____

Power Practice

• **List all the factors of each number.**

4. 27 _____

5. 19 _____

6. 71 _____

7. 35 _____

8. 68 _____

9. 55 _____

10. 47 _____

11. 33 _____

12. 53 _____

13. 48 _____

14. 88 _____

Name_____

Multiples

Learn

What Can I Do?
I want to list the first five non-zero multiples of a number.

What are the first five non-zero multiples of 6?

Multiply by Factors of 1–5

Find the product of 1 and 6, 2 and 6, 3 and 6, 4 and 6, and 5 and 6.

$1 \times 6 = 6$
$2 \times 6 = 12$
$3 \times 6 = 18$
$4 \times 6 = 24$
$5 \times 6 = 30$

Skip-Count by the Number

Skip-count by 6.

0 6 12 18 24 30

So, 6, 12, 18, 24, 30 are the first five multiples of 6.

Try It • Find the missing products. Then list the first five non-zero multiples of each number.

1.
4	4	4	4	4
×1	×2	×3	×4	×5
4	8	12	16	20

First 5 multiples of 4: _4, 8, 12, 16, 20_

2. 15, 30, 45, __60__ , __75__   First 5 multiples of 15: _15, 30, 45, 60, 75_

Power Practice • List the first 5 non-zero multiples of each number.

3. 3 _6, 9, 12, 15_   4. 5 _10, 15, 20, 25_   5. 8 _16, 24, 32, 40_

6. 10 _20, 30, 40, 50_   7. 40 _80, 125, 160, 200_   8. 22 _80, 90, 100, 60_

9. 25 _50, 75, 100, 123_   10. 18 _90, 45, 60, 70_   11. 16 _89, 10, 23, 45_

12. 60 _120, 180, 240, 300_   13. 24 _1, 23, 45, 67_   14. 32 _67, 89, 107, 37_

© McGraw-Hill School Division

Greatest Common Factor

Learn

What Can I Do?
I want to find the greatest common factor of a pair of numbers.

What is the greatest common factor (GCF) of 24 and 36?

Find Common Factors

Find the factors of each number.

24: 1, 2, 3, 4, 6, 8, 12, 24
36: 1, 2, 3, 4, 6, 9, 12, 18, 36

Look for the common factors.

24: **1**, **2**, **3**, **4**, **6**, 8, **12**, 24
36: **1**, **2**, **3**, **4**, **6**, 9, **12**, 18, 36

The common factors of 24 and 36 are 1, 2, 3, 4, 6, and 12.

Find the Greatest Common Factor

12 is the greatest of the common factors of 24 and 36.

Try It • List the factors and common factors of each number. Then find the greatest common factor.

1. 4 and 20

   factors of 4: 1, 2, 4

   factors of 20: _____

   common factors of 4 and 20: _____

   GCF of 4 and 20: _____

2. 25 and 40

   factors of 25: 1, 5, 25

   factors of 40: _____

   common factors of 25 and 40: _____

   GCF of 25 and 40: _____

3. 15 and 45

   factors of 15:

   _____

   factors of 45:

   _____

   common factors of 15 and 45: _____

   GCF of 15 and 45: _____

4. 28 and 32

   factors of 28:

   _____

   factors of 32:

   _____

   common factors of 28 and 32: _____

   GCF of 28 and 32: _____

Name_____

Power Practice • Find the greatest common factor.

5. 8 and 64 _____   **6.** 5 and 35 _____   **7.** 8 and 48 _____

8. 10 and 55 _____   **9.** 30 and 75 _____   **10.** 28 and 63 _____

11. 27 and 72 _____   **12.** 18 and 60 _____   **13.** 24 and 78 _____

14. 14 and 56 _____   **15.** 72 and 96 _____   **16.** 88 and 96 _____

17. 55 and 65 _____   **18.** 40 and 100 _____   **19.** 54 and 63 _____

Fraction of a Whole

 Learn

Find out if the region shows equal parts.

A fraction tells how many equal parts a region has been divided into.

 What Can I Do?
I want to find a fraction of a region.

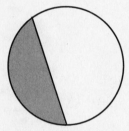

This circle has been divided into 2 *equal* parts. One of the 2 parts is shaded.

So, $\frac{1}{2}$ of the circle is shaded.

This circle has been divided into 2 *unequal* parts. Neither part is $\frac{1}{2}$ of the circle.

numerator → $\underline{1}$ ← part shaded
denominator → 2 ← total number of equal parts

Try It • **Is the rectangle divided into sixths? Write *yes* or *no*.**

1. _____

2. _____

3. _____

Power Practice • **Write the fraction for the shaded part.**

4. ___

5. ___

6. ___

Evaluate Expressions

Learn

What Can I Do?
I want to evaluate an expression.

Draw a Picture

How many boxes?

Think: Multiply, then add.

4 rows of 7 and 5 more

$4 \times 7 = 28$ and $28 + 5 = 33$

There are 33 boxes in all.

Try It • Complete to find the number of boxes in all.

1.

___ rows of ___ and ___ more

___ × ___ + ___ = ___

There are ___ in all.

Power Practice • Evaluate.

2. $5 \times 9 + 2$ _____

3. $6 \times 7 + 1$ _____

4. $8 \times 4 + 6$ _____

5. $3 \times 10 + 4$ _____

6. $9 \times 11 + 3$ _____

7. $5 \times 12 + 1$ _____

8. $10 \times 10 + 6$ _____

9. $11 \times 6 + 5$ _____

10. $12 \times 12 + 10$ _____

Least Common Multiples

What Can I Do?
I want to find the least common multiple of a pair of numbers.

What is the least common multiple (LCM) of 6 and 15?

Find Common Multiples
List non-zero multiples of each number.
6: 6, 12, 18, 24, 30, 36, 42, 48, 54, 60
15: 15, 30, 45, 60

Find common multiples.

6: 6, 12, 18, 24, **30**, 36, 42, 48, 54, **60**
15: 15, **30**, 45, **60**

30 is the least of the common multiples.

Try It · List non-zero multiples of each number. Then find the least common multiple.

1. 3 and 4

multiples of 3:
3, 6, 9, 12, 15, 18, 21, ____

multiples of 4:
4, 8, ____, 16, ____, ____

common multiples of 3 and 4:
_____

LCM of 3 and 4: _____

2. 5 and 10

multiples of 5:
5, 10, 15, 20, ____, ____, ____

multiples of 10:
10, ____, ____, ____

common multiples of 5 and 10:
_____

LCM of 5 and 10: _____

3. 6 and 12

multiples of 6:
____, ____, ____, ____

multiples of 12:
____, ____, ____, ____

common multiples of 6 and 12:
_____

LCM of 6 and 12: _____

4. 14 and 28

multiples of 14:
____, ____, ____, ____

multiples of 28:
____, ____, ____, ____

common multiples of 14 and 28:
_____

LCM of 14 and 28: _____

Name _____

Power Practice • **Find the least common multiple.**

5. 7 and 21 _____

6. 5 and 25 _____

7. 6 and 8 _____

8. 2 and 12 _____

9. 4 and 10 _____

10. 8 and 12 _____

11. 3 and 7 _____

12. 14 and 35 _____

13. 30 and 45 _____

14. 13 and 52 _____

15. 8 and 28 _____

16. 12 and 18 _____

17. 9 and 24 _____

18. 20 and 32 _____

19. 5 and 35 _____

Equivalent Fractions

Learn

Use Fraction Bars

$\frac{1}{2}$	$\frac{1}{2}$

$\frac{1}{6}$	$\frac{1}{6}$	$\frac{1}{6}$	$\frac{1}{6}$	$\frac{1}{6}$	$\frac{1}{6}$

$\frac{1}{8}$	$\frac{1}{8}$	$\frac{1}{8}$	$\frac{1}{8}$	$\frac{1}{8}$	$\frac{1}{8}$	$\frac{1}{8}$	$\frac{1}{8}$

$$\frac{1}{2} = \frac{3}{6} = \frac{4}{8}$$

Multiply the Numerator and Denominator

To find fractions equivalent to $\frac{1}{2}$, multiply the numerator and denominator by the same non-zero numbers.

$$\frac{1}{2} = \frac{1 \times 3}{2 \times 3} = \frac{3}{6}$$

$$\frac{1}{2} = \frac{1 \times 4}{2 \times 4} = \frac{4}{8}$$

Think: Multiplying by $\frac{3}{3}$ and $\frac{4}{4}$ is the same as multiplying by 1.

So, $\frac{3}{6}$ and $\frac{4}{8}$ are equivalent to $\frac{1}{2}$.

What Can I Do?
I want to find fractions equivalent to a given fraction.

Try It • Use the fraction bars to write an equivalent fraction.

1.

$\frac{1}{9}$	$\frac{1}{9}$	$\frac{1}{9}$	$\frac{1}{9}$	$\frac{1}{9}$	$\frac{1}{9}$	$\frac{1}{9}$	$\frac{1}{9}$	$\frac{1}{9}$

$\frac{1}{3}$	$\frac{1}{3}$	$\frac{1}{3}$

$$\frac{2}{3} = \frac{6}{} = \underline{}$$

2.

$\frac{1}{8}$	$\frac{1}{8}$	$\frac{1}{8}$	$\frac{1}{8}$	$\frac{1}{8}$	$\frac{1}{8}$	$\frac{1}{8}$	$\frac{1}{8}$

$\frac{1}{4}$	$\frac{1}{4}$	$\frac{1}{4}$	$\frac{1}{4}$

$$\frac{1}{4} = \frac{}{8} = \underline{}$$

3.

| $\frac{1}{12}$ | $\frac{1}{12}$ | $\frac{1}{12}$ | $\frac{1}{12}$ | $\frac{1}{12}$ | $\frac{1}{12}$ | $\frac{1}{12}$ | $\frac{1}{12}$ | $\frac{1}{12}$ | $\frac{1}{12}$ | $\frac{1}{12}$ | $\frac{1}{12}$ |

| $\frac{1}{4}$ | $\frac{1}{4}$ | $\frac{1}{4}$ | $\frac{1}{4}$ |

$$\frac{3}{4} = \frac{}{12} = \underline{}$$

4.

| $\frac{1}{6}$ | $\frac{1}{6}$ | $\frac{1}{6}$ | $\frac{1}{6}$ | $\frac{1}{6}$ | $\frac{1}{6}$ |

| $\frac{1}{3}$ | $\frac{1}{3}$ | $\frac{1}{3}$ |

$$\frac{2}{3} = \frac{4}{} = \underline{}$$

Power Practice • Complete. Then write the equivalent fraction.

5. $\frac{1}{2} = \frac{}{10} = \underline{}$

6. $\frac{2}{3} = \frac{}{15} = \underline{}$

7. $\frac{3}{4} = \frac{}{8} = \underline{}$

8. $\frac{1}{3} = \frac{}{9} = \underline{}$

9. $\frac{5}{6} = \frac{}{18} = \underline{}$

10. $\frac{7}{8} = \frac{}{24} = \underline{}$

11. $\frac{3}{7} = \frac{}{21} = \underline{}$

12. $\frac{5}{9} = \frac{}{27} = \underline{}$

13. $\frac{2}{3} = \frac{}{12} = \underline{}$

14. $\frac{2}{5} = \frac{}{20} = \underline{}$

15. $\frac{1}{4} = \frac{}{36} = \underline{}$

16. $\frac{5}{8} = \frac{}{32} = \underline{}$

17. $\frac{3}{4} = \frac{}{16} = \underline{}$

18. $\frac{5}{7} = \frac{}{14} = \underline{}$

19. $\frac{1}{8} = \frac{}{24} = \underline{}$

20. $\frac{1}{3} = \frac{}{15} = \underline{}$

21. $\frac{3}{5} = \frac{}{10} = \underline{}$

22. $\frac{1}{9} = \frac{}{90} = \underline{}$

Simplify Fractions

Learn

What Can I Do?
I want to write a fraction in simplest form.

Use Common Factors

A fraction is in **simplest form** when the numerator and denominator have no common factors other than 1.

To find the simplest form of $\frac{24}{30}$, begin by dividing the numerator and denominator by a common factor.

Common factors for 24 and 30 are 1, 2, 3, and 6.

$$\frac{24}{30} = \frac{24 \div 3}{30 \div 3} = \frac{8}{10}$$

Think: 8 and 10 still have 2 as a common factor. Divide by 2.

$$\frac{8}{10} = \frac{8 \div 2}{10 \div 2} = \frac{4}{5}$$

Use the GCF

To find the simplest form of a fraction in one step, divide by the GCF.

Think: The GCF of 24 and 30 is 6.

$$\frac{24}{30} = \frac{24 \div 6}{30 \div 6} = \frac{4}{5}$$

Try It • Complete. Write the fraction in simplest form.

1. $\frac{12}{15} = \frac{12 \div 3}{15 \div 3} = \frac{4}{\underline{\hphantom{0}}}$

2. $\frac{30}{40} = \frac{30 \div 10}{40 \div 10} = \frac{\underline{\hphantom{0}}}{4}$

3. $\frac{8}{14} = \frac{8 \div 2}{14 \div 2} = \underline{\hphantom{00}}$

4. $\frac{24}{36} = \frac{24 \div 12}{36 \div 12} = \underline{\hphantom{00}}$

5. $\frac{20}{25} = \frac{20 \div 5}{25 \div 5} = \underline{\hphantom{00}}$

6. $\frac{34}{42} = \frac{34 \div 2}{42 \div 2} = \underline{\hphantom{00}}$

7. $\frac{9}{27} = \frac{9 \div 9}{27 \div 9} = \underline{\hphantom{00}}$

8. $\frac{20}{80} = \frac{20 \div 20}{80 \div 20} = \underline{\hphantom{00}}$

Name_____

Power Practice • Write in simplest form.

9. $\frac{6}{27}$ = _____

10. $\frac{12}{48}$ = _____

11. $\frac{21}{30}$ = _____

12. $\frac{20}{45}$ = _____

13. $\frac{11}{55}$ = _____

14. $\frac{24}{48}$ = _____

15. $\frac{9}{63}$ = _____

16. $\frac{12}{60}$ = _____

17. $\frac{10}{74}$ = _____

18. $\frac{24}{56}$ = _____

19. $\frac{13}{39}$ = _____

20. $\frac{28}{46}$ = _____

21. $\frac{16}{80}$ = _____

22. $\frac{32}{84}$ = _____

23. $\frac{15}{70}$ = _____

24. $\frac{26}{52}$ = _____

25. $\frac{17}{68}$ = _____

26. $\frac{35}{55}$ = _____

27. $\frac{48}{80}$ = _____

28. $\frac{84}{96}$ = _____

Learn with Partners & Parents

Number Lines for Equivalent Fractions

- Create a number line showing the fractions from $\frac{0}{8}$ to $\frac{8}{8}$.

- Simplify as many of these fractions as you can. Write the simplest form fraction underneath the fraction.

- Repeat the activity for fractions between 0 and 1 with denominators of 12, 16, 24, and 32. Draw one number line for each different denominator.

Sieve of Eratosthenes

A prime number is a number that has only two factors, itself and 1.
Any number greater than 1 that has more than two factors is a composite
number. About 2,200 years ago, Eratosthenes, a Greek mathematician, devised a
"sieve" for finding prime numbers. You can make your own sieve.

1	2	3	4	5	6	7	8	9	10
11	12	13	14	15	16	17	18	19	20
21	22	23	24	25	26	27	28	29	30
31	32	33	34	35	36	37	38	39	40
41	42	43	44	45	46	47	48	49	50
51	52	53	54	55	56	57	58	59	60
61	62	63	64	65	66	67	68	69	70
71	72	73	74	75	76	77	78	79	80
81	82	83	84	85	86	87	88	89	90
91	92	93	94	95	96	97	98	99	100

You will cross out all composite numbers and circle all prime numbers.

1. Cross out 1 because 1 is **not** a prime number.

2. Is 2 a prime number? _____ Circle 2.

3. Could any multiples of 2 other than 2 be prime? _____

4. Cross out every multiple of 2 except 2 itself. List those numbers.

_____

_____

_____

_____

5. The next numeral that you have neither circled nor crossed out is 3. Is 3 a prime
number? _____ Circle 3.

6. Could any multiples of 3 other than 3 be prime? _____

7. Except for 3, cross out every multiple of 3 that you have not already crossed out. List those numbers.

_____

_____

8. The next numeral that you have neither crossed out nor circled is 5. Is 5 a prime

number?_____ Circle 5.

9. Cross out every multiple of 5 that you have not already crossed out. List those numbers.

_____

_____

10. Continue until you have either circled or crossed out every numeral. Write the prime numbers you found.

_____

_____

11. Are all the numbers that have been crossed out except 1 prime or composite?

_____

12. Are all odd numbers prime? Explain. _____

_____

13. Is the number 2 the only even prime number? Explain. _____

_____

14. How many prime numbers are there from 1 through 100? _____

Venn Diagrams

Special circle diagrams, called Venn diagrams, can be used to display factors.

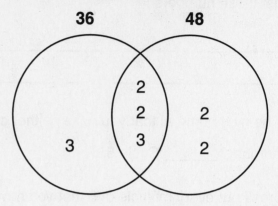

Prime Factors of 36 and 48

1. What does this Venn diagram show?

_____

2. What are the prime factors of 36?

_____

3. What are the prime factors of 48?

_____

4. What are the common prime factors of 36 and 48 ?

_____

To find the greatest common factor (GCF) of 36 and 48, multiply all the factors in the overlap of the circles.

5. What are the numbers in the overlap? _____

6. To find the GCF, multiply: $2 \times 2 \times 3 =$ _____

7. What is the greatest common factor of 36 and 48? _____

To find the least common multiple (LCM) of 36 and 48, multiply all the factors in each circle, using those in the overlap only once.

8. What are the factors in each circle that are not in the overlap?

_____

9. Least common multiple = ____ × ____ × ____ × ____ × ____ × ____ = ____

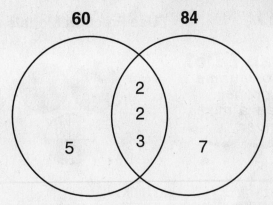

Prime Factors of 60 and 84

10. Write the prime factorization of each number.

60 = _____

84 = _____

11. What is the greatest common factor of 60 and 84? _____

12. What is the least common multiple of 60 and 84? _____

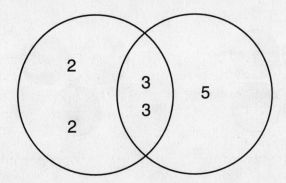

The Venn diagram shows the prime factors of two numbers.

13. What is the greatest common factor of the two numbers? _____

14. What is the least common multiple of the two numbers? _____

15. What are the two numbers? _____

Renaming Improper Fractions

Learn

What Can I Do?
I want to rename an improper fraction as a mixed number.

Use Fraction Models

Think:

$\frac{10}{4}$ are shaded. Two whole circles and $\frac{2}{4}$ of the last circle is shaded.

$$\frac{10}{4} = 2\frac{2}{4} = 2\frac{1}{2}$$

Use Division

Divide the numerator by the denominator.

$$\frac{10}{4} = 10 \div 4 \qquad 4 \overline{)10} \quad \begin{array}{r} 2\ R2 \\ -\ 8 \\ \hline 2 \end{array}$$

Think: Express the remainder as a fraction, where the remainder is the numerator and the divisor is the denominator.

$$10 \div 4 = 2\frac{2}{4} = 2\frac{1}{2}$$

So, $\frac{10}{4} = 2\frac{1}{2}$

Try It • Use the models to complete the sentences.
• Then rename the fraction as a mixed number.

1. $\frac{5}{3} = ?$

_____whole circle is shaded.

_____of the last circle is shaded.

$\frac{5}{3} =$ _____

2. $\frac{7}{2} = ?$

_____whole circles are shaded.

_____of the last circle is shaded.

$\frac{7}{2} =$ _____

3. $\frac{22}{8} = ?$

_____whole circles are shaded.

_____of the last circle is shaded.

$\frac{22}{8} =$ _____

Name_____

Complete the division. Then write the quotient as a whole or mixed number.

4. $\frac{7}{5} = ?$

$$\begin{array}{r} 1 \text{ R}\underline{} \\ 5\overline{)7} \\ -5 \\ \hline 2 \end{array}$$

$\frac{7}{5} = 1\frac{}{5}$

5. $\frac{19}{4} = ?$

$$\begin{array}{r} 4 \text{ R}\underline{} \\ 4\overline{)19} \\ -16 \\ \hline 3 \end{array}$$

$\frac{19}{4} = 4\frac{}{4}$

6. $\frac{16}{8} = ?$

$$\begin{array}{r} 2 \text{ R}\underline{} \\ 8\overline{)16} \\ -16 \\ \hline 0 \end{array}$$

$\frac{16}{8} = 2\frac{}{8}$

7. $\frac{33}{6} = ?$

$$\begin{array}{r} 5 \text{ R}\underline{} \\ 6\overline{)33} \\ -30 \\ \hline 3 \end{array}$$

$\frac{33}{6} = 5\frac{}{6} = 5\frac{}{2}$

8. $\frac{21}{8} = ?$

$$\begin{array}{r} 2 \text{ R}\underline{} \\ 8\overline{)21} \\ -16 \\ \hline 5 \end{array}$$

$\frac{21}{8} = 2\frac{}{8}$

9. $\frac{28}{7} = ?$

$$\begin{array}{r} 4 \text{ R}\underline{} \\ 7\overline{)28} \\ -28 \\ \hline 0 \end{array}$$

$\frac{28}{7} = 4\frac{}{7}$

10. $\frac{33}{9} = ?$

$$\begin{array}{r} 3 \text{ R}\underline{} \\ 9\overline{)33} \\ -27 \\ \hline 6 \end{array}$$

$\frac{33}{9} = 3\frac{}{9} = 3\frac{}{3}$

11. $\frac{50}{12} = ?$

$$\begin{array}{r} 4 \text{ R}\underline{} \\ 12\overline{)50} \\ -48 \\ \hline 2 \end{array}$$

$\frac{50}{12} = 4\frac{}{12} = 4\frac{}{6}$

Power Practice • **Write as a whole or mixed number in simplest form.**

12. $\frac{10}{3} = $ _____

13. $\frac{17}{4} = $ _____

14. $\frac{30}{8} = $ _____

15. $\frac{15}{5} = $ _____

16. $\frac{30}{7} = $ _____

17. $\frac{19}{3} = $ _____

18. $\frac{40}{8} = $ _____

19. $\frac{25}{6} = $ _____

20. $\frac{35}{2} = $ _____

21. $\frac{21}{6} = $ _____

22. $\frac{44}{9} = $ _____

23. $\frac{27}{12} = $ _____

24. $\frac{41}{6} = $ _____

25. $\frac{66}{9} = $ _____

26. $\frac{84}{7} = $ _____

27. $\frac{34}{6} = $ _____

28. $\frac{33}{3} = $ _____

29. $\frac{60}{8} = $ _____

30. $\frac{55}{4} = $ _____

31. $\frac{65}{5} = $ _____

32. $\frac{49}{7} = $ _____

33. $\frac{28}{6} = $ _____

34. $\frac{27}{16} = $ _____

35. $\frac{80}{12} = $ _____

Name_____

Learn Equivalent Fractions

What Can I Do?
I want to find equivalent fractions.

Multiplying the Numerator and Denominator

To find an equivalent fraction, multiply the numerator and denominator by the same non-zero number.

Think: Multiplying by $\frac{2}{2}$ is the same as multiplying by 1.

$$\frac{1}{2} = \frac{1 \times 2}{2 \times 2} = \frac{2}{4}$$

Divide the Numerator and Denominator

To find an equivalent fraction, divide the numerator and denominator by the same non-zero number.

Think: Dividing by $\frac{3}{3}$ is the same as dividing by 1.

$$\frac{3}{9} = \frac{3 \div 3}{9 \div 3} = \frac{1}{3}$$

Try It • Multiply to find an equivalent fraction. Then write the fraction.

1. $\frac{2}{5} = \frac{2 \times 4}{5 \times 4} = \frac{8}{}$ _____

2. $\frac{3}{7} = \frac{3 \times 2}{7 \times 2} = \frac{}{14}$ _____

3. $\frac{4}{9} = \frac{4 \times 5}{9 \times 5} = \frac{}{}$ _____

4. $\frac{5}{8} = \frac{5 \times 3}{8 \times 3} = \frac{}{}$ _____

• Divide to find an equivalent fraction. Then write the fraction.

5. $\frac{12}{8} = \frac{12 \div 4}{8 \div 4} = \frac{3}{}$ _____

6. $\frac{30}{10} = \frac{30 \div 5}{10 \div 5} = \frac{}{2}$ _____

7. $\frac{4}{14} = \frac{4 \div 2}{14 \div 2} = \frac{}{7}$ _____

8. $\frac{9}{24} = \frac{9 \div 3}{24 \div 3} = \frac{}{}$ _____

Name_____

9. $\frac{1}{3} = \frac{}{18}$ _____

10. $\frac{30}{24} = \frac{5}{}$ _____

11. $\frac{14}{20} = \frac{}{10}$ _____

12. $\frac{16}{40} = \frac{}{5}$ _____

13. $\frac{2}{5} = \frac{}{25}$ _____

14. $\frac{5}{9} = \frac{}{36}$ _____

15. $\frac{2}{9} = \frac{16}{}$ _____

16. $\frac{15}{35} = \frac{}{7}$ _____

• Circle the fraction(s) equivalent to the given fraction.

17. $\frac{3}{4}$ a. $\frac{9}{7}$ b. $\frac{9}{12}$ c. $\frac{2}{3}$

18. $\frac{10}{20}$ a. $\frac{1}{2}$ b. $\frac{15}{25}$ c. $\frac{20}{40}$

19. $\frac{8}{12}$ a. $\frac{3}{4}$ b. $\frac{18}{36}$ c. $\frac{2}{3}$

20. $\frac{7}{21}$ a. $\frac{3}{7}$ b. $\frac{1}{7}$ c. $\frac{14}{42}$

21. $\frac{8}{14}$ a. $\frac{5}{7}$ b. $\frac{4}{7}$ c. $\frac{16}{24}$

22. $\frac{4}{5}$ a. $\frac{28}{35}$ b. $\frac{14}{15}$ c. $\frac{16}{24}$

23. $\frac{12}{36}$ a. $\frac{1}{3}$ b. $\frac{3}{8}$ c. $\frac{6}{18}$

24. $\frac{6}{11}$ a. $\frac{60}{100}$ b. $\frac{12}{21}$ c. $\frac{12}{22}$

25. $\frac{16}{20}$ a. $\frac{4}{5}$ b. $\frac{8}{10}$ c. $\frac{3}{4}$

Learn Adding Fractions

Use These Steps

Add the numerators.
Use the common denominator.

$\frac{2}{3} + \frac{2}{3} = \frac{4}{3}$

| $\frac{1}{3}$ | $\frac{1}{3}$ | $\frac{1}{3}$ | $\frac{1}{3}$ |

What Can I Do?
I want to add fractions.

Write the sum in simplest form.

$\frac{4}{3} = 1\frac{1}{3}$

| $\frac{1}{3}$ | $\frac{1}{3}$ | $\frac{1}{3}$ | $\frac{1}{3}$ |

| 1 | $\frac{1}{3}$ |

So, $\frac{2}{3} + \frac{2}{3} = 1\frac{1}{3}$.

 Try It • Use the fraction bars to find each sum.

1. $\frac{2}{8}$ | $\frac{1}{8}$ | $\frac{1}{8}$ | | $\frac{1}{8}$ | $\frac{1}{8}$ | $\frac{1}{8}$ |

    $+\frac{3}{8}$
    _____

2. $\frac{3}{5}$ | $\frac{1}{5}$ | $\frac{1}{5}$ | $\frac{1}{5}$ | | $\frac{1}{5}$ | $\frac{1}{5}$ |

    $+\frac{2}{5}$
    _____ | 1 |

Power Practice

• Find each sum. Write the answer in simplest form.

3. $\dfrac{2}{5}$
$+\dfrac{2}{5}$
_____

4. $\dfrac{3}{8}$
$+\dfrac{3}{8}$
_____

5. $\dfrac{1}{10}$
$+\dfrac{7}{10}$
_____

6. $\dfrac{7}{9}$
$+\dfrac{5}{9}$
_____

7. $\dfrac{5}{12}$
$+\dfrac{5}{12}$
_____

8. $\dfrac{3}{5}$
$+\dfrac{1}{5}$
_____

9. $\dfrac{3}{4}$
$+\dfrac{3}{4}$
_____

10. $\dfrac{7}{10}$
$+\dfrac{9}{10}$
_____

11. $\dfrac{5}{6}$
$+\dfrac{5}{6}$
_____

12. $\dfrac{5}{12}$
$+\dfrac{7}{12}$
_____

13. $\dfrac{2}{5}$
$+\dfrac{3}{5}$
_____

14. $\dfrac{5}{9}$
$+\dfrac{8}{9}$
_____

15. $\dfrac{7}{8}$
$+\dfrac{3}{8}$
_____

16. $\dfrac{5}{12}$
$+\dfrac{1}{12}$
_____

17. $\dfrac{3}{10}$
$+\dfrac{7}{10}$
_____

18. $\dfrac{1}{9}$
$+\dfrac{5}{9}$
_____

19. $\dfrac{7}{8}$
$+\dfrac{5}{8}$
_____

20. $\dfrac{6}{11}$
$+\dfrac{5}{11}$
_____

21. $\dfrac{4}{5}$
$+\dfrac{3}{5}$
_____

22. $\dfrac{5}{16}$
$+\dfrac{13}{16}$
_____

23. $\dfrac{4}{9} + \dfrac{7}{9} =$ _____

24. $\dfrac{3}{8} + \dfrac{6}{8} =$ _____

25. $\dfrac{5}{10} + \dfrac{3}{10} =$ _____

Properties of Addition

Learn

What Can I Do?
I want to add three numbers using the properties of addition.

Use Addition Properties

Add: 125 + (9 + 125) = ?
Use the **Commutative Property**
to change the order of the addends.

125 + (9 + 125) = 125 + (125 + 9)

Use the **Associative Property**
to regroup the addends.

125 + (125 + 9) = (125 + 125) + 9

Think: Find the sum of 125 and 125.
Then add 9 to this sum.

125 + 125 = 250   250 + 9 = 259
So, 125 + (9 + 125) = 259

Try It • **Complete to find the sum. Then identify the property used.**

1. 750 + (68 + 50)

= 750 + (_____ + 68) ←step 1

= (750 + _____) + 68 ←step 2

= (_____) +68

= _____

Property Used in Step 1:

_____

Property Used in Step 2:

_____

2. 149 + (51 + 352)

= (149 + _____) + 352 ←step 1

= _____ + 352

= _____

Property Used in Step 1:

_____

Power Practice • **Add using the properties of addition.**

3. 574 + (57 + 6) = _____

4. (735 + 84) + 16 = _____

5. (613 + 85) + 67 = _____

6. 855 + (103 + 145) = _____

7. (373 + 96) + 124 = _____

8. (609 + 832) + 41 = _____

Name _____

Learn Least Common Denominator

What Can I Do?
I want to find LCD (least common denominator).

What is the least common denominator (LCD) of $\frac{1}{3}$, $\frac{3}{4}$, and $\frac{5}{6}$?

Find the LCM

The least common denominator is the LCM (least common multiple) of the denominators.
Think:

$\frac{1}{3}$ Multiples of 3: 3, 6, 9, **12**, 15

$\frac{3}{4}$ Multiples of 4: 4, 8, **12**, 16, 20

$\frac{5}{6}$ Multiples of 6: **12**, 18, 24, 30

The LCM is 12.
So, the LCD of $\frac{1}{3}$, $\frac{3}{4}$, and $\frac{5}{6}$ is 12.

Try It • Complete. Find the LCD.

1. $\frac{1}{2}$, $\frac{2}{5}$

Multiples of 2: 2, 4, 6, ____, ____

Multiples of 5: 5, ____, ____, ____

LCM of 2 and 5: ____

LCD of $\frac{1}{2}$ and $\frac{2}{5}$: ____

2. $\frac{1}{2}$, $\frac{2}{3}$, $\frac{7}{9}$

Multiples of 2: 2, 4, 6, 8, 10, __, __, __, __

Multiples of 3: __, __, __, __, __, __

Multiples of 9: __, __, __

LCM of 2, 3, and 9: ____

LCD of $\frac{1}{2}$, $\frac{2}{3}$, and $\frac{7}{9}$: ____

Power Practice • Find the least common denominator.

3. $\frac{1}{4}$, $\frac{3}{8}$ ____

4. $\frac{2}{3}$, $\frac{1}{5}$ ____

5. $\frac{1}{2}$, $\frac{3}{8}$ ____

6. $\frac{5}{6}$, $\frac{4}{9}$ ____

7. $\frac{1}{2}$, $\frac{7}{12}$ ____

8. $\frac{3}{4}$, $\frac{5}{6}$ ____

9. $\frac{4}{5}$, $\frac{5}{8}$ ____

10. $\frac{2}{3}$, $\frac{5}{7}$ ____

11. $\frac{1}{2}$, $\frac{2}{3}$, $\frac{5}{6}$ ____

12. $\frac{2}{3}$, $\frac{4}{5}$, $\frac{1}{6}$ ____

13. $\frac{1}{4}$, $\frac{5}{6}$, $\frac{5}{9}$ ____

14. $\frac{1}{3}$, $\frac{3}{4}$, $\frac{3}{5}$ ____

Subtracting Fractions

 Learn

$$\frac{4}{6} - \frac{1}{6} = ?$$

Use These Steps

Subtract the numerators.
Use the common denominator.

What Can I Do?

I want to subtract fractions.

$$\frac{4}{6} - \frac{1}{6} = \frac{3}{6}$$

$\frac{1}{6}$	$\frac{1}{6}$	$\frac{1}{6}$	$\frac{1}{6}$

Write the difference in simplest form.

$$\frac{3}{6} = \frac{1}{2}$$

$\frac{1}{6}$	$\frac{1}{6}$	$\frac{1}{6}$	$\frac{1}{6}$

$\frac{1}{2}$

So, $\frac{4}{6} - \frac{1}{6} = \frac{1}{2}$

Try It • Use the fraction bars to find each difference.

1. $\frac{6}{8}$

   $-\frac{3}{8}$

   ___

$\frac{1}{8}$	$\frac{1}{8}$	$\frac{1}{8}$	$\frac{1}{8}$	$\frac{1}{8}$	$\frac{1}{8}$

2. $\frac{10}{12}$

   $-\frac{7}{12}$

   $\frac{}{} = \frac{}{4}$

$\frac{1}{4}$

Name_____

Power Practice
Find each difference.
Write the answer in simplest form.

3. $\dfrac{4}{5}$ $-\dfrac{2}{5}$ _____

4. $\dfrac{7}{8}$ $-\dfrac{5}{8}$ _____

5. $\dfrac{9}{10}$ $-\dfrac{7}{10}$ _____

6. $\dfrac{11}{12}$ $-\dfrac{5}{12}$ _____

7. $\dfrac{13}{16}$ $-\dfrac{9}{16}$ _____

8. $\dfrac{3}{5}$ $-\dfrac{1}{5}$ _____

9. $\dfrac{7}{8}$ $-\dfrac{3}{8}$ _____

10. $\dfrac{7}{10}$ $-\dfrac{3}{10}$ _____

11. $\dfrac{5}{6}$ $-\dfrac{1}{6}$ _____

12. $\dfrac{8}{9}$ $-\dfrac{5}{9}$ _____

13. $\dfrac{3}{4}$ $-\dfrac{1}{4}$ _____

14. $\dfrac{7}{9}$ $-\dfrac{2}{9}$ _____

15. $\dfrac{11}{12}$ $-\dfrac{1}{12}$ _____

16. $\dfrac{7}{8}$ $-\dfrac{2}{8}$ _____

17. $\dfrac{4}{5} - \dfrac{1}{5} =$

18. $\dfrac{5}{8} - \dfrac{1}{8} =$

19. $\dfrac{8}{9} - \dfrac{1}{9} =$

20. $\dfrac{11}{16} - \dfrac{5}{16} =$

Learn with Partners & Parents

Make One Half

Write these fractions on cards or slips of paper.

$\dfrac{1}{12}, \dfrac{5}{12}, \dfrac{1}{10}, \dfrac{3}{10}, \dfrac{1}{9}, \dfrac{2}{9},$

$\dfrac{4}{9}, \dfrac{1}{8}, \dfrac{3}{8}, \dfrac{1}{6}, \dfrac{1}{5}, \dfrac{2}{5},$

$\dfrac{1}{4}, \dfrac{1}{3}.$

- Turn the cards over and mix them up. A player draws a card.

- Players give the fraction that, when added to the fraction on the card, will make one half.

- The player who gets the correct answer first gets 1 point.

- The first player with 7 points is the winner.

Name_____

Renaming Mixed Numbers

Learn

$2\frac{1}{4} = 1\frac{?}{4}$

Regroup 1 as a Fraction

2 wholes and 1 fourth

$2\frac{1}{4}$

To make more fourths, divide a whole into fourths.

Think: $1 = \frac{4}{4}$

1 whole and 5 fourths

$1\frac{5}{4}$

So, $2\frac{1}{4} = 1\frac{5}{4}$

What Can I Do?

I want to rename a mixed number.

Try It • Use the models to rename the mixed number.

1. $2\frac{5}{8} = 1\frac{}{8}$

Power Practice • Complete. Then write each whole or mixed number.

2. $5\frac{2}{3} = 4\frac{}{3}$ _____

3. $6\frac{5}{8} = 5\frac{}{8}$ _____

4. $2\frac{4}{9} = 1\frac{}{9}$ _____

5. $5 = 4\frac{}{8}$ _____

6. $7\frac{3}{5} = 6\frac{}{5}$ _____

7. $10\frac{2}{3} = 9\frac{}{3}$ _____

8. $12\frac{7}{8} = $ _____

9. $3\frac{7}{10} = $ _____

10. $5\frac{7}{12} = $ _____

11. $15\frac{6}{15} = $ _____

12. $8\frac{13}{16} = $ _____

13. $9\frac{11}{18} = $ _____

Rounding Mixed Numbers

Learn

What Can I Do?
I want to round a mixed number to the nearest whole number.

Use a Number Line

$4\frac{4}{5}$ is between 4 and 5.
It is closer to 5.

4   $\frac{1}{5}$ $\frac{2}{5}$ $\frac{3}{5}$ $\frac{4}{5}$ 5

So, $4\frac{4}{5}$ rounds up to 5.

$6\frac{3}{8}$ is between 6 and 7.
It is closer to 6.

6   $\frac{1}{8}$ $\frac{2}{8}$ $\frac{3}{8}$ $\frac{4}{8}$ $\frac{5}{8}$ $\frac{6}{8}$ $\frac{7}{8}$ 7

So, $6\frac{3}{8}$ rounds down to 6.

Use the Fraction Part

Compare the fraction to $\frac{1}{2}$.
If it is less than $\frac{1}{2}$, round down. If it is $\frac{1}{2}$ or greater, round up.

$1\frac{3}{4}$ Think: $\frac{1}{2} = \frac{2}{4}$

$\frac{3}{4} > \frac{2}{4}$

So, round $1\frac{3}{4}$ up to 2.

$3\frac{2}{5}$ Think: $\frac{2}{5} = \frac{4}{10}$ and $\frac{1}{2} = \frac{5}{10}$

$\frac{4}{10} < \frac{5}{10}$

So, round $3\frac{2}{5}$ down to 3.

Try It • Round to the nearest whole number.

1. $5\frac{5}{6}$ ___6___

5   $\frac{1}{6}$ $\frac{2}{6}$ $\frac{3}{6}$ $\frac{4}{6}$ $\frac{5}{6}$ 6

2. $4\frac{1}{3}$ ___4___

4   $\frac{1}{3}$ $\frac{2}{3}$ 5

3. $2\frac{3}{7}$ ___2___

2   $\frac{1}{7}$ $\frac{2}{7}$ $\frac{3}{7}$ $\frac{4}{7}$ $\frac{5}{7}$ $\frac{6}{7}$ 3

4. $1\frac{4}{8}$ ___2___

1   $\frac{1}{8}$ $\frac{2}{8}$ $\frac{3}{8}$ $\frac{4}{8}$ $\frac{5}{8}$ $\frac{6}{8}$ $\frac{7}{8}$ 2

Power Practice • Round to the nearest whole number.

5. $5\frac{2}{3}$ ___6___ **6.** $3\frac{1}{2}$ ___4___ **7.** $1\frac{4}{9}$ ___1___ **8.** $6\frac{7}{12}$ ___7___

9. $11\frac{2}{8}$ ___11___ **10.** $6\frac{5}{10}$ ___7___ **11.** $3\frac{4}{7}$ ___4___ **12.** $9\frac{7}{16}$ ___9___

13. $15\frac{11}{12}$ ___16___ **14.** $7\frac{11}{16}$ ___8___ **15.** $8\frac{21}{32}$ ___9___ **16.** $14\frac{5}{12}$ ___14___

Equivalent Fractions

A fraction has been assigned to each president's name. Compare the fractions. Find the fraction that is not equivalent to the others. The president's name next to this fraction is the correct answer to the question under the item.

$\dfrac{4}{8}$ Abraham Lincoln $\dfrac{5}{12}$ Theodore Roosevelt

$\dfrac{2}{4}$ Thomas Jefferson $\dfrac{8}{16}$ William Howard Taft

1. Which president, at the age of 42, was the youngest person ever elected president?

_____

2. Which fractions are equivalent? _____

3. Explain how you know they are equivalent?

_____

$\dfrac{3}{9}$ Franklin D. Roosevelt $\dfrac{9}{12}$ William McKinley

$\dfrac{3}{4}$ Woodrow Wilson $\dfrac{12}{16}$ Herbert Hoover

4. Which president was the only president to serve more than two terms in office?

_____

5. Which fraction is not equivalent to the others?

_____

6. Write two more fractions that are equivalent to that fraction.

_____

$\frac{10}{12}$ Calvin Coolidge

$\frac{12}{18}$ Grover Cleveland

$\frac{20}{24}$ Zachary Taylor

$\frac{5}{6}$ Franklin Pierce

7. Which president served from 1885–1889 and again from 1893–1897?

_____

8. Which fractions are equivalent? _____

9. Change the numerator of the non-equivalent fraction to make it equivalent to the other three. What is the new fraction?

_____

10. Describe the method you used to find out the non-equivalent fractions.

_____

_____

11. Write three fractions equivalent to $\frac{1}{2}$.

_____

_____

12. Describe the method you used to find the equivalent fractions.

_____

_____

13. Write three fractions equivalent to $\frac{3}{4}$.

_____

14. Describe the method you used to find the equivalent fractions.

_____

_____

CHALLENGE

CHAPTER 5

Modeling Equivalent Fractions

The fraction $\frac{3}{4}$ can be modeled in a variety of ways. Two ways are shown below.

 $= \frac{3}{4}$

 $= \frac{6}{8}$

In each of the following problems, the first square represents a fraction.

• Write a fraction with a denominator of 4 for the shaded part.

• Shade the second square to show a fraction that is equivalent to the first fraction. For problem 1, the denominator of the second fraction is given.

• Under the second square, write the equivalent fraction you have modeled.

1. Sixteenths

Fraction: _____ /16

Equivalent fraction

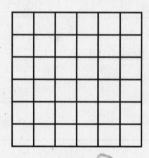

Fraction: _____ /36

2. Fourths

Fraction: _____ /4

Equivalent fraction

Fraction: ___36___

© McGraw-Hill School Division

Name_____

3. Fourths

Fraction: ___$\frac{2}{4}$___

Equivalent fraction

Fraction: ___$\frac{40}{100}$___

4. Fourths

Fraction: ___$\frac{3}{4}$___

Equivalent fraction

Fraction: ___$\frac{60}{100}$___

5. Fourths

Fraction: ___$\frac{1}{4}$___

Equivalent fraction

Fraction: ___$\frac{20}{100}$___

Renaming a Whole or Mixed Number

Learn

Use Fraction Models

$2\frac{5}{8}$ circles are shaded.

Two whole circles and $\frac{5}{8}$ of the third circle are shaded.

Think: $\frac{21}{8}$ are shaded.

What Can I Do?

I want to rename a mixed number as a fraction.

Use Multiplication and Addition

Multiply the whole number part by the denominator of the fraction. Then add on the numerator.

$2\frac{5}{8}$ $8 \times 2 = 16$

Think: There are 16 eighths in 2 wholes.

$16 + 5 = 21$

So, $2\frac{5}{8} = \frac{21}{8}$

Try It • Use the models to complete the sentences. Then rename the mixed number as a fraction.

1.

$1\frac{1}{6} = \frac{?}{6}$

_____ sixths are shaded in the first circle.

_____ sixth is shaded in the last circle.

$1\frac{1}{6} = \frac{}{6} + \frac{1}{6} = \frac{}{6}$

2.

$2\frac{3}{4} = \frac{?}{4}$

_____ fourths are shaded in the first two circles

_____ fourths are shaded in the last circle.

$2\frac{3}{4} = \frac{}{4} + \frac{3}{4} = \frac{}{4}$

Name_____

Complete the multiplication and addition to write the whole or mixed number as a fraction.

3. $3\dfrac{1}{5} = \dfrac{?}{5}$

denominator × whole number = product   product + numerator

$5 \times 3 =$ _____   _____ $+ 1 =$ _____

$3\dfrac{1}{5} = \dfrac{}{5}$

4. $5\dfrac{7}{12} = \dfrac{?}{12}$

denominator × whole number = product   product + numerator

_____ × _____ = _____   _____ + _____ = _____

$5\dfrac{7}{12} = \dfrac{}{12}$

Power Practice

• **Complete. Then write each whole or mixed number as a fraction.**

5. $5\dfrac{2}{3} = \dfrac{}{3}$ ___

6. $7\dfrac{1}{4} = \dfrac{}{4}$

7. $3\dfrac{7}{8} = \dfrac{}{8}$ ___

8. $4\dfrac{4}{5} = \dfrac{}{5}$ ___

9. $7 = \dfrac{}{2}$ ___

10. $6 = \dfrac{}{8}$ ___

11. $4\dfrac{5}{12} = \dfrac{}{12}$ ___

12. $9\dfrac{5}{6} = \dfrac{}{6}$ ___

13. $10\dfrac{2}{3} = \dfrac{}{3}$ ___

14. $8\dfrac{7}{16} = \dfrac{}{16}$ ___

15. $11\dfrac{8}{9} = \dfrac{}{9}$ ___

16. $14\dfrac{2}{3} = \dfrac{}{3}$ ___

17. $18 = \dfrac{}{4}$ ___

18. $5\dfrac{9}{32} = \dfrac{}{32}$ ___

19. $13\dfrac{6}{7} = \dfrac{}{7}$ ___

20. $7\dfrac{11}{15} = \dfrac{}{15}$ ___

21. $7 = \dfrac{}{9}$ ___

22. $5\dfrac{5}{8} = \dfrac{}{8}$ ___

Evaluate Expressions

Learn

What Can I Do?
I want to evaluate an expression.

Use a Picture

How many boxes are in 2 rows?

Think: There are 15 boxes in 3 rows.

number of boxes in 1 row: $15 \div 3$

number of boxes in 2 rows: $15 \div 3 \times 2$

Divide, then multiply.

$15 \div 3 = 5$ $5 \times 2 = 10$

There are 10 boxes in 2 rows.

Try It • Complete.

1.

_____ boxes in all

_____ rows

_____ rows circled

_____ ÷ _____ × _____ = _____ boxes in 3 rows

Power Practice • Evaluate.

2. $24 \div 6 \times 5$ _____

3. $64 \div 8 \times 5$ _____

4. $81 \div 9 \times 7$ _____

5. $120 \div 4 \times 3$ _____

6. $200 \div 5 \times 2$ _____

7. $144 \div 12 \times 7$ _____

8. $600 \div 20 \times 3$ _____

9. $121 \div 11 \times 6$ _____

10. $100 \div 25 \times 3$ _____

Closest Multiple

Learn

What Can I Do?
I want to find the multiple of a number that is closest to a given number.

What multiple of 9 is closest to 39?

List multiples of 9.

9, 18, 27, 36, 45, 54, …

Find the multiples of 9 that come just before and just after 39.

9, 18, 27, **36**, **45**, 54 …

Think: 36 is before 39. 45 is after 39.

Subtract to find which is closer.

$39 - 36 = 3 \qquad 45 - 39 = 6$

So, 36 is the multiple of 9 that is closest to 39.

Try It • Complete to find the multiple of 8 that is closest to 43.

1. Multiples of 8: 8, 16, 24, _____, _____, _____

Multiple of 8 before 43: _____   Multiple of 8 after 43: _____

Closest multiple of 8 to 43: _____

Power Practice • Find the closest multiple.

2. Closest multiple of 4 to 27. _____   **3.** Closest multiple of 7 to 50. _____

4. Closest multiple of 9 to 55. _____   **5.** Closest multiple of 6 to 28. _____

6. Closest multiple of 12 to 80. _____   **7.** Closest multiple of 16 to 99. _____

8. Closest multiple of 11 to 60. _____   **9.** Closest multiple of 14 to 75. _____

Properties of Multiplication

Learn

What Can I Do?
I want to multiply three factors using the properties of multiplication.

Use Multiplication Properties

Use the **Commutative Property** to change the order of the factors.

$5 \times (18 \times 2) = 5 \times (2 \times 18)$

Use the **Associative Property** to regroup the factors.

$5 \times (2 \times 18) = (5 \times 2) \times 18$

Think: Find the product of 5 and 2. Then multiply by 18.

$5 \times 2 = 10$

$10 \times 18 = 180$

So, $5 \times (18 \times 2) = 180$

Other Multiplication Properties

Use the **Identity Property** to multiply by 1. The product of any factor and 1 is the factor.

$1 \times 19 = 19$

Use the **Zero Property** to multiply by zero. The product of any number and zero is zero.

$0 \times 257 = 0$

Use the **Distributive Property** to multiply a sum by a number.

Multiply each addend by the number, then add the products.

$3 \times 54 = (3 \times 50) + (3 \times 4)$
$150 + 12 = 162$

Try It • Find each product. Identify the product used.

1. $750 \times 1 = $ _____

2. $4 \times 19 = (4 \times 10) + (4 \times 9)$

$= $ _____ $+$ _____ $= $ _____

Property: _____

Property: _____

Power Practice • Multiply using the properties of multiplication.

3. $74 \times 78 \times 0 = $ _____

4. $5 \times 24 = $ _____

5. $(6 \times 8) \times 5 = $ _____

6. $50 \times 17 \times 2 = $ _____

7. $9 \times 11 \times 1 \times 13 = $ _____

8. $87 \times 11 = $ _____

Simplest Form

Learn

Use Prime Factorization

A fraction is in **simplest form** when the numerator and denominator have no common factors other than 1.

Which fraction is in simplest form?

$$\frac{3}{6}, \quad \frac{4}{8}, \quad \frac{7}{16}$$

Write the prime factorization of the numerator and denominator of each fraction. The fraction is in simplest form if there are no common prime factors.

$\dfrac{3}{6} = \dfrac{1 \times \mathbf{3}}{2 \times \mathbf{3}}$ Think: 3 is a common factor

$\dfrac{4}{8} = \dfrac{\mathbf{2} \times \mathbf{2}}{\mathbf{2} \times \mathbf{2} \times \mathbf{2}}$ Think: 2 is a common factor

$\dfrac{7}{16} = \dfrac{1 \times 7}{2 \times 2 \times 2 \times 2}$ Think: There are no common factors.

So, $\dfrac{7}{16}$ is in simplest form.

Try It
· Complete the prime factorizations.
· Circle each fraction that is in simplest form.

1. $\dfrac{12}{18} = \dfrac{2 \times 2 \times 3}{2 \times 6 \times 3}$

2. $\dfrac{15}{16} = \dfrac{3 \times 5}{2 \times 2 \times 2 \times 2}$

3. $\dfrac{35}{39} = \dfrac{7 \times 5}{13 \times 3}$

Power Practice
· Which fraction is in simplest form?

4. $\dfrac{3}{4}, \quad \dfrac{5}{15}, \quad \dfrac{7}{14}$ $\frac{3}{4}$

5. $\dfrac{6}{9}, \quad \dfrac{8}{21}, \quad \dfrac{7}{21}$ $\frac{8}{21}$

6. $\dfrac{20}{30}, \quad \dfrac{8}{24}, \quad \dfrac{7}{15}$ $\frac{7}{15}$

7. $\dfrac{8}{14}, \quad \dfrac{16}{72}, \quad \dfrac{10}{19}$ $\frac{10}{19}$

8. $\dfrac{5}{9}, \quad \dfrac{14}{22}, \quad \dfrac{21}{33}$ $\frac{5}{9}$

9. $\dfrac{15}{20}, \quad \dfrac{8}{23}, \quad \dfrac{17}{34}$ $\frac{8}{23}$

10. $\dfrac{6}{7}, \quad \dfrac{26}{74}, \quad \dfrac{24}{33}$ $\frac{6}{7}$

11. $\dfrac{5}{60}, \quad \dfrac{13}{39}, \quad \dfrac{21}{32}$ $\frac{21}{32}$

12. $\dfrac{20}{35}, \quad \dfrac{18}{37}, \quad \dfrac{12}{40}$ $\frac{18}{37}$

Dividing by a Unit Fraction

Learn

Use Fraction Bars or a Number Line

How many $\frac{1}{2}$s are in 2?

What Can I Do?

I want to divide by a unit fraction.

1 whole	1 whole
$\frac{1}{2}$ $\frac{1}{2}$	$\frac{1}{2}$ $\frac{1}{2}$

Think: There are **2** $\frac{1}{2}$s in 1.

There are **4** $\frac{1}{2}$s in 2.

How many $\frac{1}{4}$s are in 3?

0   1 or $\frac{4}{4}$ 2 or $\frac{8}{4}$ 3 or $\frac{12}{4}$

Think: There are **4** $\frac{1}{4}$s in 1.

There are **8** $\frac{1}{4}$s in 2.

There are **12** $\frac{1}{4}$s in 3.

Try It • **Complete each sentence. Use the models.**

1.

1 whole	1 whole	1 whole
$\frac{1}{3}$ $\frac{1}{3}$ $\frac{1}{3}$	$\frac{1}{3}$ $\frac{1}{3}$ $\frac{1}{3}$	$\frac{1}{3}$ $\frac{1}{3}$ $\frac{1}{3}$

There are _____ $\frac{1}{3}$s in 3.

2.
   0   1   2

There are _____ $\frac{1}{5}$s in 2.

Power Practice • **Draw models to solve.**

3. How many $\frac{1}{2}$s are in 4? _____

4. How many $\frac{1}{9}$s are in 5? _____

5. How many $\frac{1}{4}$s are in 8? _____

6. How many $\frac{1}{5}$s are in 5? _____

7. How many $\frac{1}{6}$s are in 12? _____

8. How many $\frac{1}{7}$s are in 10? _____

Name_____

Inverse of a Fraction

Learn

What Can I Do?

I want to find the inverse of a fraction.

Use Fraction Bars

Every fraction has an inverse. When you multiply a fraction by its inverse, the product is 1.

4 $\frac{1}{4}$s is 1, or 4 × $\frac{1}{4}$ = 1.

$\frac{1}{4}$	$\frac{1}{4}$	$\frac{1}{4}$	$\frac{1}{4}$

1 whole

So, the inverse of $\frac{1}{4}$ is 4.

Inverse of a Fraction

To find the inverse of a fraction, interchange the numerator and denominator.

The inverse of $\frac{5}{3}$ is $\frac{3}{5}$.

Try It • Find each inverse.

1.

$\frac{1}{5}$	$\frac{1}{5}$	$\frac{1}{5}$	$\frac{1}{5}$	$\frac{1}{5}$

1 whole

5 $\frac{1}{5}$s is 1.

The inverse of $\frac{1}{5}$ is _____.

2.

$\frac{1}{3}$	$\frac{1}{3}$	$\frac{1}{3}$

1 whole

_____ $\frac{1}{3}$s is 1.

The inverse of $\frac{1}{3}$ is _____.

Power Practice • Find each inverse.

3. $\frac{2}{9}$ _____

4. $\frac{3}{10}$ _____

5. $\frac{1}{8}$ _____

6. 3 _____

7. $\frac{2}{3}$ _____

8. $\frac{1}{2}$ _____

9. $\frac{3}{5}$ _____

10. $\frac{7}{12}$ _____

Renaming Improper Fractions

Learn

What Can I Do?
I want to rename an improper fraction as a mixed number.

Use Division

Rename $\frac{14}{4}$ as a mixed number.

Divide the numerator by the denominator.

$\frac{14}{4} = 14 \div 4$

$$\begin{array}{r} 3 \\ 4\overline{)14} \\ -12 \\ \hline 2 \end{array}$$

Think: To continue, divide 2 by 4.

$2 \div 4 = \frac{2}{4} = \frac{1}{2}$

So, the remainder can be expressed as $\frac{2}{4}$ or $\frac{1}{2}$.

The quotient is:

$3 + \frac{1}{2} = 3\frac{1}{2}$

Try It • Divide. Then write the quotient as a whole or mixed number in simplest form.

1. $\frac{13}{5} = ?$ $5\overline{)13}$ $\frac{13}{5} = $ _____

2. $\frac{42}{9} = ?$ $9\overline{)42}$ $\frac{42}{9} = $ _____

Power Practice • Write as a whole or mixed number in simplest form.

3. $\frac{29}{8} = $ _____

4. $\frac{57}{6} = $ _____

5. $\frac{17}{3} = $ _____

6. $\frac{27}{5} = $ _____

7. $\frac{38}{6} = $ _____

8. $\frac{35}{5} = $ _____

Name_____

9. $\dfrac{44}{8}$ = _____

10. $\dfrac{75}{9}$ = _____

11. $\dfrac{63}{5}$ = _____

12. $\dfrac{81}{8}$ = _____

13. $\dfrac{36}{12}$ = _____

14. $\dfrac{51}{7}$ = _____

15. $\dfrac{25}{3}$ = _____

16. $\dfrac{69}{10}$ = _____

17. $\dfrac{72}{8}$ = _____

18. $\dfrac{46}{7}$ = _____

19. $\dfrac{53}{6}$ = _____

20. $\dfrac{80}{9}$ = _____

21. $\dfrac{37}{4}$ = _____

22. $\dfrac{65}{5}$ = _____

Learn with Partners & Parents

Renaming Game!

Use two sets of index cards numbered 1–9. Mix up the two sets of cards.

• Player 1 draws two cards and uses them to write an improper fraction. Player 2 then writes the fraction as a whole or mixed number.

• Player 2 then returns the cards to the deck and mixes them up again. The two players then change roles.

• Continue to play until each player has had ten opportunities to rename an improper fraction.

Patterns in Sums and Products

Find the sum and the product of the numbers below.

1. 3 and $\frac{3}{2}$

sum _____

product _____

2. 4 and $\frac{4}{3}$

sum _____

product _____

3. 5 and $\frac{5}{4}$

sum _____

product _____

4. 6 and $\frac{6}{5}$

sum _____

product _____

5. 7 and $\frac{7}{6}$

sum _____

product _____

6. 8 and $\frac{8}{7}$

sum _____

product _____

7. 9 and $\frac{9}{8}$

sum _____

product _____

8. 10 and $\frac{10}{9}$

sum _____

product _____

9. 11 and $\frac{11}{10}$

sum _____

product _____

10. How are the sum and product of each pair of numbers related?

_____

_____

_____

11. What pattern do you see in the sums and products as you look down the column?

_____

_____

_____

12. Compare the first and second number in each pair. What pattern do you see?

_____

_____

_____

13. Extend the pattern. Write another pair of numbers that have the same sum and product. Find the sum and product, too.

_____

_____

_____

Number Sequences with Fractions

You have found rules for whole number sequences. For example, you know that the rule for the sequence 3, 9, 27, 81 is *Multiply by 3*.

**You can also find rules for sequences that contain fractions.
Write the next three numbers in each sequence below.
Then write the rule.**

1. 81, 27, 9, 3 _____,_____,_____

   Rule:_____

2. 250, 50, 10, 2 _____,_____,_____

   Rule:_____

3. 1, 8, 64, 512 _____,_____,_____

   Rule:_____

4. 1,000, 100, 10,1 _____,_____,_____

   Rule:_____

5. $\frac{1}{8}$, $\frac{1}{2}$, 2, 8 _____,_____,_____

   Rule:_____

6. $\frac{3}{2}$, 1, $\frac{2}{3}$, $\frac{4}{9}$ _____,_____,_____

   Rule:_____

7. How could you rewrite the rule *Divide by 2* using a fraction in the rule?
   (Think: $4 \div 2 = 2$, $4 \times n = 2$)

   Rule:_____

8. Rewrite each rule for questions 1–6 above.

a. 81, 27, 9,_____

b. 250, 50, 10, _____

c. 1, 8, 64, _____

d. 1, 000, 100,10,_____

e. $\dfrac{1}{8}$, $\dfrac{1}{2}$, 2, _____

f. $\dfrac{3}{2}$, 1, $\dfrac{2}{3}$,_____

9. Draw the next figure in the pattern. Then write two rules for the pattern.

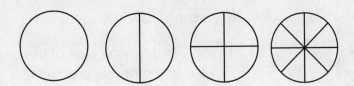

Rule:_____

10. Draw the next figure in the pattern. Then write two rules for the pattern.

Rule:_____

Name_____

Multiplying Whole Numbers

Learn

Use the Distributive Property

$24 \times 27 = ?$

You can use the distributive property to multiply by a
2-digit number.

$$24 \times 27 = (20 + 4) \times 27$$
$$= (20 \times 27) + (4 \times 27)$$
$$= 540 + 108$$
$$= 648$$

What Can I Do?
I want to multiply
by a 2-digit number.

Use these steps

Multiply by the ones digit of the multiplier.

$$
\begin{array}{r}
{}^{2} \\
27 \\
\times\ 24 \\
\hline
108 \leftarrow 4 \times 27
\end{array}
$$

Multiply by the tens digit of the multiplier
Then add the partial products.

$$
\begin{array}{r}
{}^{1} \\
{}^{2} \\
27 \\
\times\ 24 \\
\hline
108 \\
+\ 540 \leftarrow 20 \times 27 \\
\hline
648
\end{array}
$$

So, $24 \times 27 = 648$.

Try It • Complete each multiplication.

1.
$$
\begin{array}{r}
{}^{2} \\
53 \\
\times\ 28 \\
\hline
424 \\
+\ 1{,}060 \\
\hline
\end{array}
$$

2.
$$
\begin{array}{r}
{}^{3} \\
95 \\
\times\ 36 \\
\hline
570 \\
+ \\
\hline
\end{array}
$$

3.
$$
\begin{array}{r}
{}^{4} \\
66 \\
\times\ 18 \\
\hline
8 \\
+ \\
\hline
\end{array}
$$

4.
$$
\begin{array}{r}
{}^{1} \\
23 \\
\times\ 45 \\
\hline
5 \\
+ \\
\hline
\end{array}
$$

Power Practice • Multiply.

5. $\begin{array}{r} 11 \\ \times\ 12 \\ \hline \end{array}$ 6. $\begin{array}{r} 23 \\ \times\ 16 \\ \hline \end{array}$ 7. $\begin{array}{r} 31 \\ \times\ 22 \\ \hline \end{array}$ 8. $\begin{array}{r} 64 \\ \times\ 31 \\ \hline \end{array}$

9. $\begin{array}{r} 60 \\ \times\ 25 \\ \hline \end{array}$ 10. $\begin{array}{r} 45 \\ \times\ 35 \\ \hline \end{array}$ 11. $\begin{array}{r} 32 \\ \times\ 19 \\ \hline \end{array}$ 12. $\begin{array}{r} 38 \\ \times\ 90 \\ \hline \end{array}$

13. $\begin{array}{r} 13 \\ \times\ 56 \\ \hline \end{array}$ 14. $\begin{array}{r} 23 \\ \times\ 92 \\ \hline \end{array}$ 15. $\begin{array}{r} 46 \\ \times\ 29 \\ \hline \end{array}$ 16. $\begin{array}{r} 50 \\ \times\ 78 \\ \hline \end{array}$

17. $\begin{array}{r} 33 \\ \times\ 66 \\ \hline \end{array}$ 18. $\begin{array}{r} 75 \\ \times\ 74 \\ \hline \end{array}$ 19. $\begin{array}{r} 61 \\ \times\ 39 \\ \hline \end{array}$ 20. $\begin{array}{r} 89 \\ \times\ 67 \\ \hline \end{array}$

21. $12 \times 17 = $ _____

22. $13 \times 44 = $ _____

23. $18 \times 83 = $ _____

24. $25 \times 65 = $ _____

25. $47 \times 90 = $ _____

26. $64 \times 32 = $ _____

27. $91 \times 93 = $ _____

28. $58 \times 48 = $ _____

Name_____

Dividing Whole Numbers

Learn

Use These Steps to Divide

$356 \div 22 = ?$

Place the first digit of the quotient.

$22\overline{)356}$

Think: 3 < 22 Not enough hundreds.

35 > 22 The first digit will be in the tens place.

Divide the tens.

$$
\begin{array}{r}
1 \\
22\overline{)356} \\
-\ 22 \\
\hline
13
\end{array}
$$
Multiply: $1 \times 22 = 22$
Subtract: $35 - 22 = 13$
Compare: $13 < 22$

Divide the ones. Write the remainder.

$$
\begin{array}{r}
16\ \text{R4} \\
22\overline{)356} \\
-\ 22\downarrow \\
\hline
136 \\
-\ 132 \\
\hline
4
\end{array}
$$
Multiply: $6 \times 22 = 132$
Subtract: $136 - 132 = 4$
Compare: $4 < 22$
The remainder is 4.

So, $356 \div 22 = 16$ R4.

Try It • **Complete the division.**

1.
$$
\begin{array}{r}
4\ \text{R}\_\_\_ \\
13\overline{)57} \\
-\ 52
\end{array}
$$

2.
$$
\begin{array}{r}
2\ \text{R}\_\_\_ \\
14\overline{)307} \\
-\ 28 \\
\hline
\\
-\ \\
\hline
\end{array}
$$

3.
$$
\begin{array}{r}
6\ \text{R}\_\_\_ \\
14\overline{)88} \\
-\ \\
\hline
\end{array}
$$

4.
$$
\begin{array}{r}
\text{R}\_\_\_ \\
31\overline{)286} \\
-\ \\
\hline
\end{array}
$$

Power Practice • Divide. Find the quotient and remainder.

5. $13\overline{)89}$ 6. $30\overline{)265}$ 7. $52\overline{)497}$ 8. $22\overline{)673}$

9. $12\overline{)178}$ 10. $32\overline{)408}$ 11. $64\overline{)396}$ 12. $25\overline{)630}$

13. $57\overline{)177}$ 14. $60\overline{)734}$ 15. $18\overline{)563}$ 16. $36\overline{)755}$

17. $62\overline{)499}$ 18. $33\overline{)970}$ 19. $35\overline{)800}$ 20. $71\overline{)605}$

21. $82 \div 15 =$ _____   22. $99 \div 14 =$ _____

23. $820 \div 56 =$ _____   24. $375 \div 24 =$ _____

25. $712 \div 44 =$ _____   26. $900 \div 62 =$ _____

27. $954 \div 80 =$ _____   28. $763 \div 31 =$ _____

Multiplying Decimals by Powers of 10

Learn

What Can I Do?
I want to multiply a decimal by a power of 10.

Use Patterns

Use patterns to multiply 1,000 × 0.067.

$1 \times 0.067 = 0.067$

$10 \times 0.067 = 0.67$

$100 \times 0.067 = 6.7$

Think: For each power of 10, move the decimal point one place to the right.

So, $1,000 \times 0.067 = 67$.

Sometimes you will need to write zeros to place the decimal point.

$1 \times 0.28 = 0.28$

$10 \times 0.28 = 2.8$

$100 \times 0.28 = 28$

$1,000 \times 0.28 = 28\mathbf{0}$

Try It • Complete each pattern.

1. $1 \times 0.045 = 0.045$

   $10 \times 0.045 = 0.45$

   $100 \times 0.045 = $ _____

   $1,000 \times 0.045 = $ _____

2. $1 \times 0.56 = 0.56$

   $10 \times 0.56 = $ _____

   $100 \times 0.56 = $ _____

   $1,000 \times 0.56 = $ _____

3. $1 \times 1.7 = 1.7$

   $10 \times 1.7 = $ _____

   $100 \times 1.7 = $ _____

   $1,000 \times 1.7 = $ _____

Power Practice • Multiply.

4. $10 \times 0.08 = $ _____

5. $100 \times 0.07 = $ _____

6. $10 \times 2.6 = $ _____

7. $100 \times 5.13 = $ _____

8. $1,000 \times 0.25 = $ _____

9. $1,000 \times 0.079 = $ _____

10. $10 \times 8.01 = $ _____

11. $100 \times 3.004 = $ _____

12. $1,000 \times 0.456 = $ _____

Dividing Decimals by Powers of 10

Learn

What Can I Do?
I want to divide a decimal by a power of 10.

Use Patterns

Use patterns to divide 642.3 ÷ 1,000.

642.3 ÷ 1   = 642.3

642.3 ÷ 10   = 64.23

642.3 ÷ 100 = 6.423

Think: For each power of 10, move the decimal point one place to the left.

So, 642.3 ÷ 1,000 = 0.6423

Sometimes you will need to write zeros to place the decimal point.

81.9 ÷ 1   = 81.9

81.9 ÷ 10   = 8.19

81.9 ÷ 100   = 0.819

81.9 ÷ 1,000 = 0.**0**819

Try It • Complete each pattern.

1. 670.8 ÷ 1 = 670.8

670.8 ÷ 10 = 67.08

670.8 ÷ 100 = __6.708__

670.8 ÷ 1,000 = __0.6708__

2. 43.2 ÷ 1 = 43.2

43.2 ÷ 10 = __4.32__

43.2 ÷ 100 = __0.432__

43.2 ÷ 1,000 = __0.0432__

3. 7.14 ÷ 1 = 7.14

7.14 ÷ 10 = __0.714__

7.14 ÷ 100 = __0.0714__

7.14 ÷ 1,000 = __0.00714__

Power Practice • Divide.

4. 54.8 ÷ 10 = __5.48__

5. 356.1 ÷ 10 = __35.61__

6. 40.19 × 100 = __0.4019__

7. 371.4 ÷ 100 = __3.714__

8. 802.1 ÷ 1,000 = __0.8021__

9. 7.85 ÷ 10 = __0.785__

10. 3.27 ÷ 100 = __0.0327__

11. 14.03 ÷ 1,000 = __0.01403__

Multiplying Decimals

Learn

Use These Steps

When you multiply with decimals, multiply as you would whole numbers.

$$
\begin{array}{r}
12.3 \\
\times\ 0.7 \\
\hline
861
\end{array}
$$

What Can I Do?

I want to multiply decimals.

Place the decimal point in the product. Begin by counting the decimal places in each factor. Then, from the right, count the numbers of places in the product to place the decimal point.

$$
\begin{array}{rl}
12.3 & \text{1 decimal place} \\
\times\ 0.7 & +\text{ 1 decimal place} \\
\hline
8.61 & \text{2 decimal places}
\end{array}
$$

Sometimes you need to write zeros in the product to place the decimal point.

$$
\begin{array}{rl}
0.54 & \text{2 decimal places} \\
\times\ 0.12 & +\text{ 2 decimal places} \\
\hline
108 & \\
+\ 540 & \\
\hline
0.0648 & \text{4 decimal places}
\end{array}
$$

Try It • **Count the decimal places in each factor.**
Then place the decimal point in the product.

1.
$$
\begin{array}{r}
0.37 \\
\times\ 0.6 \\
\hline
222
\end{array}
$$
____ decimal places
+ ____ decimal places
____ decimal places

2.
$$
\begin{array}{r}
1.34 \\
\times\ 0.072 \\
\hline
268 \\
+\ 9380 \\
\hline
9648
\end{array}
$$
____ decimal places
+ ____ decimal places

____ decimal places

Power Practice • Multiply.

3. 0.8
  × 0.4

4. 1.2
  × 7

5. 0.55
  × 0.3

6. 7.81
  × 6

7. 3.6
  × 2.1

8. 4.3
  × 0.38

9. 0.94
  × 7.3

10. 2.6
  × 0.68

11. 31.2
  × 0.19

12. 0.853
  × 0.07

13. 1.08
  × 0.51

14. 32.5
  × 0.09

15. 24.6
  × 0.25

16. 0.407
  × 3.3

17. 0.375
  × 6

18. 1.864
  × 0.002

19. $8 \times 0.45 =$ _____

20. $20 \times 0.62 =$ _____

21. $5.9 \times 0.71 =$ _____

22. $0.047 \times 0.83 =$ _____

23. $0.36 \times 15.7 =$ _____

24. $4.8 \times 91.5 =$ _____

25. $9 \times 26.43 =$ _____

26. $3.5 \times 84.6 =$ _____

27. $0.57 \times 3.08 =$ _____

28. $16 \times 5.809 =$ _____

29. $3.7 \times 2.56 =$ _____

30. $26.3 \times 80.06 =$ _____

Dividing Decimals

Use These Steps

When you divide decimals, make the divisor a whole number. Multiply the divisor and dividend by the same power of ten.

$$0.8 \overline{)6.96} \qquad 8 \overline{)69.6}$$

Think: $0.8 \times 10 = 8.0$
$6.96 \times 10 = 69.6$

Place the decimal point in the quotient by writing it above the decimal point in the dividend. Then divide as with whole numbers.

$$
\begin{array}{r}
8.7 \\
8 \overline{)69.6} \\
-64 \\
\hline
56 \\
-56 \\
\hline
0
\end{array}
$$

Sometimes you need to round a quotient.
Find the quotient to the nearest hundredth: $4.0 \div 1.2$

$$
1.2 \overline{)4.0} \qquad
\begin{array}{r}
3.333 \\
12 \overline{)40.000} \\
-36 \\
\hline
4\ 0 \\
-3\ 6 \\
\hline
40 \\
-36 \\
\hline
40 \\
-36 \\
\hline
4
\end{array}
$$

Think: Write zeros to divide to the thousandths place.

Look at the digit in the thousandths place of the quotient. Round down if it is less than 5. Otherwise round up. $3 < 5$, so round down.

3.333 rounded to the nearest hundredth is 3.33.

Name_____

1. $0.4\overline{)5.67}$ is the same as $4\overline{)}$.

2. $0.85\overline{)46.2}$ is the same as $85\overline{)}$.

3. $2.3\overline{)0.761}$ is the same as $\overline{)}$.

4. $0.74\overline{)1.8}$ is the same as $\overline{)}$.

Power Practice • Divide. Round to the nearest hundredth, if necessary.

5. $0.6\overline{)0.96}$

6. $0.08\overline{)3.92}$

7. $0.7\overline{)0.609}$

8. $0.03\overline{)0.078}$

9. $2.1\overline{)9.03}$

10. $2.5\overline{)6.25}$

11. $0.34\overline{)0.051}$

12. $0.74\overline{)2.59}$

13. $5.7\overline{)63.4}$

14. $0.26\overline{)4.08}$

15. $0.75\overline{)0.095}$

16. $2.4\overline{)80.2}$

17. $0.84\overline{)5.46}$

18. $0.095\overline{)0.323}$

19. $0.44\overline{)2.168}$

20. $0.36\overline{)90.32}$

21. $6.57 \div 0.9 =$ _____

22. $0.0152 \div 0.04 =$ _____

23. $0.954 \div 1.3 =$ _____

24. $1.86 \div 0.72 =$ _____

25. $0.0527 \div 0.085 =$ _____

26. $1.334 \div 5.8 =$ _____

Evaluating Algebraic Expressions

Learn

Substitute and Complete

Evaluate $c - 6.43$ for $c = 8.7$.

An algebraic expression contains a variable. To evaluate an algebraic expression, substitute the value for the variable, then compute.

Substitute the value: $8.7 - 6.43$

Compute: $8.7 - 6.43 = 2.27$

So $c - 6.43 = 2.27$, for $c = 8.7$.

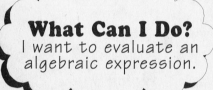

What Can I Do?
I want to evaluate an algebraic expression.

Order of Operations

Sometimes you have to perform more than one operation.

Do all the operations in Parentheses first. Multiply and Divide in order from left to right. Add and Subtract in order from left to right.

Evaluate $3(x + 5)$ for $x = 9$.

Substitute the value: $3(9 + 5)$.

Do the operation in parentheses first: $3(14)$

Multiply: 42

So $3(x + 5) = 42$, for $x = 9$.

Try It • **Complete to evaluate each expression.**

1. $x - 3.4$, for $x = 5.8$

Substitute: _____ $- 3.4$

Subtract: _____

So $x - 3.4 =$ _____, for $x = 5.8$.

2. $\dfrac{(2 + m)}{2}$, for $m = 8.4$

Substitute: $\dfrac{(2 + \text{_____})}{2}$

Add: $\dfrac{(\text{_____})}{2}$

Divide: _____

So $\dfrac{(2 + m)}{2} =$ _____, for $m = 8.4$.

Name_____

Power Practice • Evaluate each algebraic expression.

3. $x + 25$, for $x = 47$ _____

4. $1.08 - c$, for $c = 0.79$ _____

5. $8.2v$, for $v = 5$ _____

6. $\dfrac{25}{d}$, for $d = 0.2$ _____

7. $125 - 12 + a$, for $a = 25$ _____

8. $200 + 1.7k$, for $k = 20$ _____

9. $14 - (5 - x)$, for $x = 0.8$ _____

10. $4c \div 3 + 8$, for $c = 15$ _____

11. $\dfrac{(5g - 10)}{25}$, for $g = 12$ _____

12. $(19.8 \div 3f) + 8.4$, for $f = 2.2$ _____

13. $12 \times 4.5 + m \div 3$, for $m = 1.5$ _____

14. $55 - 8d + 38 \div 2$, for $d = 2$ _____

15. $75 - 25 \div a + 10$, for $a = 2.5$ _____

16. $f(17 - 8) + 3.5$, for $f = 0.2$ _____

17. $(s - 19) + 34 + 14 \div 3.5$, for $s = 70$ _____

18. $54 \div 0.6 - 4.5n$, for $n = 2$ _____

Learn with
Partners & Parents

Algebra in the Car

- A car moving at 50 miles per hour travels the distance 50t, where t is the time. Find the distance traveled in 10 hours. Choose nine other times less than 10 hours, including two times less than 1 hour. Make a table to show the distance for each time.

- What happens to the distance as you decrease the time?

- A car traveled 1,000 miles in 10 hours. Find the speed of the moving car. Repeat for nine other decreasing values for t.

- What happens to the speed as you decrease the time?

Division Patterns

Choose one number from each box to complete each division sentence.

Divisors	Dividends
16 30	3,600 842
45 40	7,962 12,030

1. _____ ÷ _____ = 90

2. _____ ÷ _____ = 52 R10

3. _____ ÷ _____ = 401

4. _____ ÷ _____ = 176 R42

5. _____ ÷ _____ = 21 R2

6. _____ ÷ _____ = 225

7. _____ ÷ _____ = 28 R2

8. _____ ÷ _____ = 267 R15

9. _____ ÷ _____ = 80

10. _____ ÷ _____ = 199 R2

Name_____

Write three other division sentences using different numbers from the box.

11. _____ ÷ _____ = _____

12. _____ ÷ _____ = _____

13. _____ ÷ _____ = _____

Complete. Then add the last line in the pattern. Describe the pattern.

14.

Dividend	Divisor	Quotient
12,663	63	
	63	202
12,789	63	203

Pattern: _____

15.

Dividend	Divisor	Quotient
17,380	79	
17,600	80	
17,820		220

Pattern: _____

16.

Dividend	Divisor	Quotient
7,210	35	
18,270	45	
33,330		606

Pattern: _____

Evaluating Expressions

1. Evaluate $n + 8$ for $n = 4$.

   _____

2. Suppose the value of the variable is doubled. Will the value of the expression double? Explain.

   _____

3. Evaluate $n \div 7$ for $n = 28$.

   _____

4. Suppose the number 7 is doubled. What happens to the value of the expression?

   _____

5. Evaluate $3(n - 6)$ for $n = 10$.

   _____

6. What must happen to the variable n for the expression to equal 24?

   _____

7. What must happen to the variable n for the expression to equal 36?

   _____

8. Evaluate $3 \times n + 5$ for $n = 4$.

   _____

9. What would be the value of n, if $3 \times n + 5 = 41$?

   _____

10. Evaluate each expression in the sequence for
$n = 5$: $n + 1$, $2n + 1$, $3n + 1$, $4n + 1$....

_____

11. Describe the pattern in Exercise 10.

_____

_____

_____

12. Write an expression for the tenth term in the sequence.

_____

13. Evaluate $n \times n + 7$ for $n = 3$.

_____

14. What would be the value of $n \times n$, if $n \times n + 7 = 88$?
What would be the value of n?

_____

15. Evaluate an expression for $n = 5$: n, $n \times n$, $n \times n \times n$, $n \times n \times n \times n$, ...

_____

16. Describe the pattern in Exercise 15.

_____

17. Write an expression for the sixth term in the sequence.

_____

Decimals on a Number Line

Learn

What Can I Do?
I want to place decimals on a number line.

Use Place Value

Place decimals on a number line the way you would place whole numbers. For decimals, first look at the whole number part of each decimal. If they are the same, look at the decimal part. Say the decimal parts in order to determine where to place the decimals on the number line.

Count by tenths.

7.0   7.1   7.2   7.3   7.4   7.5

Count by hundredths.

2.50   2.51   2.52   2.53   2.54   2.55

Think of equivalent decimals.

9.78   9.79   9.8   9.81   9.82   9.83
9.80   9.820   9.830
9.825

Try It • **Complete each number line.**

1.
0   0.1   ☐   0.3   ☐   0.5   0.6   ☐   0.8   0.9   1.0

2.
5.5   ☐   ☐   5.8   5.9   6.0   ☐   6.2   ☐   6.4   ☐

3.
3.20   3.21   ☐   3.23   ☐   3.25   ☐   3.27   ☐   ☐   3.30

4.
9.99   ☐   ☐   10.02   ☐   10.04   10.05   ☐   ☐   10.08   10.09

Name_____

5.

Name the number shown by each letter.

6.

A _____   B _____   C _____   D _____

Use the number line to answer 7 and 8.

7. Name two numbers between 4.5 and 5.0. _____

_____

8. Name two numbers between 5.0 and 5.5. _____

_____

Use the number line to answer 9–11.

9. Name three numbers between 1.7 and 1.8? Explain your thinking.

_____

10. Is 1.799 between 1.7 and 1.8? Explain your thinking. _____

_____

11. Is 1.07 the half-way point between 1.7 and 1.8? Tell how you know. _____

_____

_____

Read and Interpret Data from a Graph

Learn

What Can I Do?
I want to find information in a line graph.

Read a Line Graph to Get Information

Line graphs show change over a period of time.

This line graph shows the average monthly temperature in Minneapolis in January, April, July, and October.

This is the vertical axis

AVERAGE MONTHLY TEMPERATURE IN MINNEAPOLIS

This is the horizontal axis

To find the average temperature in Minneapolis in January:
• Find January on the horizontal axis.
• Read up from January to locate the point. Look left from the point to find the temperature. The average temperature in January is 10°F.

Try It • Use the line graph to answer 1–5.

1. What is the average monthly temperature in April? _____

2. In which month is the average temperature 49°F? _____

3. In which two months is the average monthly temperature about the same?

_____

4. Which month has the highest average monthly temperature? _____

5. What happens to the average monthly temperature between July and October?

_____

Name_____

Walter Paller's company, Baseball Plus, sells • baseball souvenirs. Use the line graph to answer each question about his company's sales.

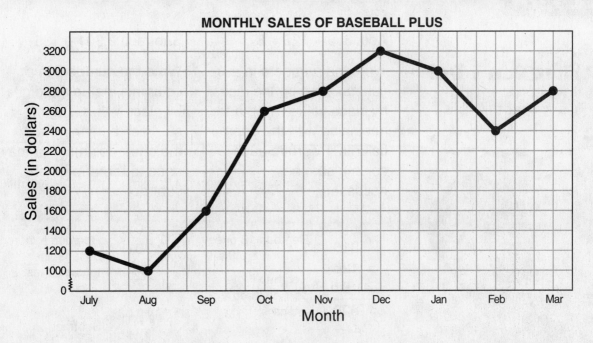

MONTHLY SALES OF BASEBALL PLUS

6. Between which two months did sales increase the most?

_____

7. Between which two months did sales increase by only $200?

_____

8. In which month did Baseball Plus sell the most items? _____

9. By how much did sales go down between December and February? _____

10. In which two months were the sales the same? _____

11. What is the difference in sales between the months with the highest and lowest

sales? _____

12. Walter believes that his company needs to sell more than $1,700 worth of baseball

souvenirs a month to be successful. What was the first month in which that

happened? _____

Add and Subtract Whole Numbers

Learn

What Can I Do?
I want to add and subtract whole numbers.

Add: 315 + 126 + 87

Write the numbers in a column. Line up the digits by place value. Then add, beginning with the ones' column. Regroup each column sum as necessary.

```
 1 1
  315
  126
+  87
  528
```

Regroup 18 ones as 1 ten 8 ones.

Regroup 12 tens as 1 hundred 2 tens

Subtract: 2,301 − 135

Write the numbers in a column. Line up the digits by place value. Then subtract, beginning with the ones' column. You may need to regroup before subtracting.

```
      9
   2 10 11
  2,301
 −  135
```

Regroup hundreds as tens, then tens as ones.

```
      9
   2 10 11
  2,301
 −  135
  2,166
```

Subtract

Try It • Complete to find each sum or difference.

1.
```
   1
  205
+ 127
    2
```

2.
```
  10 16
  316
− 128
    8
```

3.
```
   1
  416
+ 166
    2
```

4.
```
  11 15
  525
− 426
    9
```

5.
```
  1 1
  364
+ 248
    2
```

6.
```
  7 11
  681
− 237
    4
```

7.
```
   1
  532
+ 349
    1
```

8.
```
  8 10 13
  913
− 657
    6
```

Power Practice • Find each sum or difference.

9. 787
+ 309

10. 403
− 221

11. 647
+ 983

12. 353
+ 4,777

13. 487
+ 39

14. 4,103
− 685

15. 17,842
− 6,397

16. 12,345
+ 67,890

17. 10,000
− 3,482

18. 4,759
+ 98

19. 849
− 783

20. 500
− 377

21. 3,000 − 188 = _____

22. 13,021 − 7,896 = _____

23. 2,788 + 349 = _____

24. 11,110 − 379 = _____

25. 876 + 549 = _____

26. 39 + 387 + 84 = _____

27. 1,345 + 4,579 = _____

28. 5,678 − 1,349 = _____

29. 8,999 + 346 = _____

30. 678 − 99 = _____

31. 5,765 − 198 = _____

32. 5,609 + 1,189 + 57 = _____

Learn with Partners & Parents

A Close Call

Use three sets of ten index cards numbered 0-9 to make sums as close to 1,000 as possible without going over.

• For the first round, mix up the three sets of cards. Then each player draws 8 cards.

• Each player uses 6 of the 8 cards to make two 3-digit numbers that have a sum as close to 1,000 as possible.

• Each player records his or her 3-digit numbers and sums. Then each one subtracts the sum from 1,000. The player whose sum is closest to 1,000 scores 1 point.

• Repeat for a total of five rounds.

Divide Whole Numbers

Learn

Use Place Value to Divide

$891 \div 12 = ?$

Place the first digit of the quotient.

$12\overline{)891}$

Think: 12 > 8   Not enough hundreds.
12 < 89   The first digit will be in the tens place.

What Can I Do?

I want to divide whole numbers.

Divide the tens.

$$\begin{array}{r} 7 \\ 12\overline{)891} \\ -84 \\ \hline 5 \end{array}$$

Multiply: $7 \times 12 = 84$
Subtract: $89 - 84 = 5$
Compare: $5 < 12$

Divide the ones. Write the remainder.

$$\begin{array}{r} 74\text{ R}3 \\ 12\overline{)891} \\ -84 \\ \hline 51 \\ -48 \\ \hline 3 \end{array}$$

Multiply: $4 \times 12 = 48$
Subtract: $51 - 48 = 3$
Compare: $3 < 12$
The remainder is 3.

So, $891 \div 12 = 74$ R3

Try It • Tell where to place the first digit in each quotient. Then find the quotient.

1. $14\overline{)963}$ **2.** $32\overline{)275}$ **3.** $25\overline{)414}$ **4.** $42\overline{)3,901}$

_____   _____   _____   _____

Power Practice • Find each quotient.

5. $21\overline{)231}$ **6.** $64\overline{)286}$ **7.** $39\overline{)360}$ **8.** $55\overline{)353}$

9. $25\overline{)159}$ **10.** $57\overline{)402}$ **11.** $72\overline{)524}$ **12.** $19\overline{)120}$

13. $21\overline{)189}$ **14.** $27\overline{)242}$ **15.** $83\overline{)847}$ **16.** $15\overline{)120}$

17. $53\overline{)5,436}$ **18.** $24\overline{)2,169}$ **19.** $93\overline{)8,520}$ **20.** $15\overline{)4,135}$

21. $889 \div 12 =$ _____   **22.** $378 \div 62 =$ _____

23. $528 \div 88 =$ _____   **24.** $737 \div 82 =$ _____

25. $163 \div 40 =$ _____   **26.** $456 \div 82 =$ _____

27. $5,168 \div 24 =$ _____   **28.** $8,365 \div 65 =$ _____

29. $4,584 \div 83 =$ _____   **30.** $3,762 \div 75 =$ _____

Name_____

Multiply Whole Numbers

Learn

What Can I Do?
I want to multiply whole numbers.

Use the Distributive Property

Multiply: 67×98

You can use the distributive property to multiply by a 2-digit number.

$67 \times 98 = (7 + 60) \times 98$
$\qquad = (7 \times 98) + (60 \times 98)$

Multiply by 7. Regroup.	Multiply by 60. Regroup.	Add.
5	4	1 1
98	98	686
× 7	× 60	+ 5,880
686	5,880	6,566

Try It • Complete to find each product.

1. Multiply 32×86

$\begin{array}{r} 1 \\ 86 \\ \times\ 2 \\ \hline 172 \end{array}$ $\begin{array}{r} 1 \\ 86 \\ \times\ 30 \\ \hline 2580 \end{array}$

2. Multiply 78×809

$\begin{array}{r} 809 \\ \times\ 8 \\ \hline 6472 \end{array}$ $\begin{array}{r} 6 \\ 809 \\ \times\ 70 \\ \hline 000 \end{array}$

$\begin{array}{r} 1563 \\ 15630 \end{array}$

Power Practice • Find each product.

3. $\begin{array}{r} 89 \\ \times\ 19 \end{array}$ 4. $\begin{array}{r} 341 \\ \times\ 76 \end{array}$ 5. $\begin{array}{r} 605 \\ \times\ 65 \end{array}$ 6. $\begin{array}{r} 34 \\ \times\ 21 \end{array}$ 7. $\begin{array}{r} 847 \\ \times\ 35 \end{array}$

8. $\begin{array}{r} 409 \\ \times\ 27 \end{array}$ 9. $\begin{array}{r} 341 \\ \times\ 82 \end{array}$ 10. $\begin{array}{r} 55 \\ \times\ 59 \end{array}$ 11. $\begin{array}{r} 119 \\ \times\ 68 \end{array}$ 12. $\begin{array}{r} 473 \\ \times\ 99 \end{array}$

Multiply Decimals

Learn

What Can I Do?
I want to multiply decimals.

You can use what you know about multiplying whole numbers to multiply decimals.

Multiply 1.37 by 0.8.

Multiply as you would with whole numbers.	Count the number of decimal places in both factors.	Count from the left to place the point in the product.
1.37 × 0.8 ———— 1096	1.37 2 places × 0.8 1 place ———— 1096 3 decimal places	1.37 2 places × 0.8 1 place ———— 1.096 3 decimal places

So, 0.8 × 1.37 = 1.096

Try It • **Place the decimal point in each product.**

1.   81.9
× 0.03
————
2 4 5 7

2.   81.9
× 0.3
————
2 4 5 7

3.   819
× 0.3
————
2 4 5 7

4.   0.819
× 0.3
————
0 2 4 5 7

Power Practice • **Find each product.**

5.   1.3
× 0.7

6.   8.1
× 0.2

7.   5.9
× 6.7

8.   5.21
× 0.8

9.   91.4
× 0.7

10.   64.9
× 0.9

11.   37.01
× 0.2

12.   40.31
× 0.4

13.   30.91
× 0.3

14.   10.04
× 8.1

15.   71.9
× 0.91

16.   2.56
× 1.8

Add and Subtract Decimals

Learn

Add and subtract decimals as you would with whole numbers. You may need to write equivalent decimals first.

What Can I Do?
I want to add and subtract decimals.

Add: 0.5 + 0.78

Align the decimal points in the numbers. Then add as you would with whole numbers.

Think: 0.5 = 0.50
Add the hundredths.

$$\begin{array}{r} 0.50 \\ +\ 0.78 \\ \hline 8 \end{array}$$

Add the tenths.
Regroup.

$$\begin{array}{r} 1 \\ 0.50 \\ +\ 0.78 \\ \hline 28 \end{array}$$

Add the ones.
Align the decimal point in the sum.

$$\begin{array}{r} 1 \\ 0.50 \\ +\ 0.78 \\ \hline 1.28 \end{array}$$

Subtract: 0.53 − 0.28

Align the decimal points in the numbers. Then subtract.

$$\begin{array}{r} 0.53 \\ -\ 0.28 \end{array}$$

Regroup to subtract the hundredths.

$$\begin{array}{r} {}^{4\ 13} \\ 0.5\!\!\!/3\!\!\!/ \\ -\ 0.28 \\ \hline 5 \end{array}$$

Subtract the tenths.
Align the decimal point in the difference.

$$\begin{array}{r} {}^{4\ 13} \\ 0.5\!\!\!/3\!\!\!/ \\ -\ 0.28 \\ \hline 0.25 \end{array}$$

Try It
• **Find each sum or difference.**

1. $$\begin{array}{r} {}^{1} \\ 0.25 \\ +\ 0.19 \\ \hline 4 \end{array}$$

2. $$\begin{array}{r} {}^{1\ 15} \\ 0.2\!\!\!/5\!\!\!/ \\ -\ 0.19 \\ \hline 6 \end{array}$$

3. $$\begin{array}{r} {}^{1} \\ 0.54 \\ +\ 0.37 \\ \hline 1 \end{array}$$

4. $$\begin{array}{r} {}^{4\ 14} \\ 0.5\!\!\!/4\!\!\!/ \\ -\ 0.37 \\ \hline 7 \end{array}$$

5. $$\begin{array}{r} 0.64 \\ +\ 0.36 \end{array}$$

6. $$\begin{array}{r} 0.64 \\ -\ 0.36 \end{array}$$

7. $$\begin{array}{r} 0.3 \\ +\ 0.84 \end{array}$$

8. $$\begin{array}{r} 0.6 \\ -\ 0.49 \end{array}$$

Power Practice • Find each sum or difference.

9.   0.42
       + 0.78

10.   4.32
        − 1.83

11.   3.28
        + 1.37

12.   1.12
        + 3.09

13.   0.90
        + 1.24

14.   2.78
        − 1.09

15.   3.42
        + 2.99

16.   4.77
        − 0.99

17.   0.72
        + 3.66

18.   6.22
        − 2.19

19.   7.79
        + 8.11

20.   4.55
        − 3.91

21.   5.31
        + 2.45

22.   6.30
        − 0.77

23.   5.39
        + 3.49

24.   4.59
        − 3.85

25. 34.09 + 1.9 = _____

26. 139.0090 − 0.56 = _____

27. 33.999 + 23.11 + 134.11 = _____

28. 302.22 − 8.19 = _____

29. 103.47 + 0.99 = _____

30. 45.7 − 0.001 = _____

31. 94.223 + 10.64 = _____

32. 246.851 − 95.23 = _____

Divide Decimals

Learn

When you divide by a decimal, rewrite the division so that you divide by a whole number.

Divide: $7.84 \div 1.4$

Multiply the divisor and the dividend by 10.
$10 \times 1.4 = 14$
$10 \times 7.84 = 78.4$

Multiplying by 10 moves the decimal point one place to the right.

$$1.4\overline{)7.84} \rightarrow 14.\overline{)78.4}$$

Write the decimal point in the quotient above the decimal point in the dividend.

Now divide as you would with whole numbers.

$$
\begin{array}{r}
5.6 \\
14.\overline{)78.4} \\
-70\downarrow \\
\hline
84 \\
-84 \\
\hline
0
\end{array}
$$

So, $7.84 \div 1.4 = 5.6$

Sometimes you have to write an equivalent decimal before you divide.

Divide: $0.3\overline{)9}$ Think: $9 = 9.0$

$$0.3\overline{)9.0} \rightarrow 3\overline{)90} \rightarrow 90 \div 3 = 30$$

So, $9 \div 0.3 = 30$

What Can I Do?
I want to divide by a decimal.

Try It • Complete. Then rewrite the division so you can divide.

1. $4.52\overline{)5.65}$ _____ $\times 4.52 = 452$
    _____ $\times 5.65 = 565$

    ___$\overline{)}$___

2. $0.04\overline{)8}$ _____ $\times 0.04 = 4$
    _____ $\times 8 = 800$

    ___$\overline{)}$___

Name_____

Power Practice • **Find each quotient.**

3. $0.02\overline{)0.4}$ **4.** $0.05\overline{)3.9}$ **5.** $0.2\overline{)0.26}$ **6.** $0.5\overline{)2.05}$

7. $0.4\overline{)1.08}$ **8.** $0.2\overline{)0.68}$ **9.** $0.7\overline{)3.57}$ **10.** $0.6\overline{)5.88}$

11. $0.02\overline{)0.06}$ **12.** $0.09\overline{)0.108}$ **13.** $0.04\overline{)0.024}$ **14.** $0.07\overline{)0.3304}$

15. $3.2\overline{)6.592}$ **16.** $0.09\overline{)4.05}$ **17.** $0.6\overline{)0.126}$ **18.** $0.1\overline{)26.03}$

19. $29.37 \div 4.45 =$ _____   **20.** $5.04 \div 0.01 =$ _____   **21.** $0.1386 \div 6.3 =$ _____

22. $0.004 \div 0.01 =$ _____   **23.** $6.4 \div 0.1 =$ _____   **24.** $14.9 \div 0.05 =$ _____

25. $0.99 \div 0.01 =$ _____   **26.** $0.32 \div 0.002 =$ _____   **27.** $0.85 \div 0.1 =$ _____

28. $4.55 \div 0.05 =$ _____   **29.** $0.81 \div 0.09 =$ _____   **30.** $6.4 \div 0.008 =$ _____

Using a Pattern to Add

In 1787, when the German mathematician, Karl Frederich Gauss, was ten years old, he was asked by his teacher to find the sum of all the counting numbers from 1 to 100. To the teacher's surprise Gauss performed the calculations within seconds.

$$1 + 2 + 3 + 4 + \cdots + 97 + 98 + 99 + 100$$

(The "..." means that the numbers in between are there but have not been written out.)

How do you think Gauss performed the calculations so quickly? One possibility is that he noticed this pattern.

$$1 + 2 + 3 + 4 + \ldots + 97 + 98 + 99 + 100$$

101
101
101
101

1. What is the sum of each pair of numbers? _____

2. How many such pairs are there? _____

Each paired sum is 101. Since the 100 numbers are in pairs, there must be 50 pairs. Therefore, the sum of the pairs is 50×101.

3. What is the sum of all counting numbers from 1 to 100? _____

Find the sum of the counting numbers from 1 to 10.

4. Pair the first and last number. What sum do you get? _____

5. How many pairs with a sum of 11 will there be? _____

6. What is the sum? _____

Find the sum of all counting numbers within the given limits.

From 1 to 50

7. There are _____ pairs of numbers that each have a sum of _____ .

The sum of all _____ pairs is _____ × _____ = _____ .

From 3 to 12

8. There are _____ pairs of numbers that each have a sum of _____ .

The sum of all _____ pairs is _____ × _____ = _____ .

Find each sum.

9. $1 + 2 + 3 + \cdots + 198 + 199 + 200 =$ _____

10. $1 + 2 + 3 + \cdots + 998 + 999 + 1,000 =$ _____

11. $1 + 3 + 5 + 7 + 9 + 11 + 13 + 15 =$ _____

12. $1 + 6 + 11 + \cdots + 26 + 31 + 36 =$ _____

13. $2 + 4 + 6 + 8 + 10 + 12 + 14 + 16 =$ _____

14. $5 + 10 + 15 + 20 + 25 + 30 + 35 + 40 + 45 + 50 =$ _____

15. $8 + 14 + 20 + \cdots + 38 + 44 + 50 =$ _____

Name_____

CHALLENGE

CHAPTER 8

Which Costs Less?

Mr. Thomas is to travel home from a vacation. As he packs, it becomes obvious that he will not have enough room for all his packages. He decides to ship some items. Of course, he wants to ship the packages for the least amount of money. Examine the table of shipping costs for Company ABC and Company XYZ.

Shipping Cost for Two Companies

Package Size (lb)	Company ABC			Company XYZ		
	5-Day Delivery	2-Day Delivery	Overnight Delivery	5-Day Delivery	2-Day Delivery	Overnight Delivery
25.1 — 35	$10.38	$41.50	$88.25	$15.89	$23.25	$46.45
35.1 — 50	$19.51	$71.00	$129.00	$19.85	$43.05	$74.15
50.1 — 70	$21.58	$109.50	$191.50	$21.24	$58.85	$98.95

Use the information from the table to answer each question.

1. If one of the packages weighed 27.8 pounds and had to arrive in five days, which shipping company would be less expensive?

_____

2. If one of the packages weighed 62.58 pounds and had to arrive in two days, which shipping company would be less expensive?

_____

3. If one of the packages weighed 47.89 pounds and had to arrive overnight, which shipping company would be less expensive?

_____

© McGraw-Hill School Division

130 Grade 6, Chapter 8, Cluster B

4. Suppose Mr. Thomas has one 33.3-pound package that needs to be sent overnight, one 44.23-pound package that can arrive in five days, and one 9-pound package that needs to arrive in two days. Which shipping company or combination of companies should he choose so that each package is shipped at the lowest cost?

_____

_____

5. Suppose Mr. Thomas has one 68.5-pound package that needs to arrive in five days, one 30.8-pound package that can arrive in two days, and one 25.11-pound package that needs to arrive overnight. Which shipping company should he choose?

_____

6. How much more expensive is shipping a 30-pound package for 5-day delivery with Company XYZ than with Company ABC?

_____

7. How much would Mr. Thomas save by shipping a 57-pound package for 2-day delivery with Company XYZ instead of shipping the same package with Company ABC?

_____

8. Suppose you want to ship three packages for overnight delivery. One package weighs 28 pounds, one weighs 40 pounds, and one weighs 60 pounds. How much would you save if you chose Company XYZ over Company ABC?

_____

Name_____

Comparing Whole Numbers

Learn

What Can I Do?
I want to compare whole numbers.

Use place value to compare whole numbers.

Compare 14,260 and 14,306. Find which is greater.

Thousands Period			Ones Period		
hundreds	tens	ones	hundreds	tens	ones
	1	4	2	6	0
	1	4	3	0	6

Start at the left.

Compare the ten thousands. $1 = 1$

Compare the thousands. $4 = 4$

Compare the hundreds. $3 > 2$

So, 14,306 is greater than 14,260.

Write $14,306 > 14,260$.

Try It • Use a place-value chart.

1. Compare. Write >, <, or =.

52,438 _____ 52,348

2. Which place helped you decide which number was greater?

_____

Power Practice • Compare. Write >, <, or =.

3. 3,210 _____ 3,401

4. 2,319 _____ 2,391

5. 46,708 _____ 46,725

6. 30,001 _____ 29,998

7. 245,201 _____ 244,675

8. 307,602 _____ 307,620

Whole Numbers on a Number Line

Learn

What Can I Do?
I want to locate a number on a number line.

Locate 127 on the number line.

127 is between 120 and 130. Each mark stands for a number that is 1 greater than the number to its left. Count by 1 from 120 to locate 127.

Try It • Use the number line to answer each question.

1. What do you count by to get from one mark to the next? _____

2. What number does *A* stand for? _____

3. Locate 70 on the number line.

Power Practice • Use the number line to answer each question.

Write the number named by each letter.

4. *B* _____   **5.** *C* _____   **6.** *D* _____   **7.** *E* _____

Locate each number on the number line.

8. 64   **9.** 94   **10.** 76   **11.** 88

Addition Properties

Learn

What Can I Do?
I want to find an easier way to add numbers.

Use addition properties to make it easier to add.

Commutative Property of Addition	**Associative Property of Addition**

Changing the order of the addends does not change the sum.

Changing the grouping of the addends does not change the sum.

Different order
↓   ↓
6 + 7 = 7 + 6
13   =   13
↑_____↑
Same result

Different grouping
↓   ↓
(4 + 5) + 6 = 4 + (5 + 6)
9 + 6   =   4 + 11
15   =   15
↑_____↑
Same result

Sometimes you can find sums mentally when you use the addition properties.

$(3 + 6) + 7 = (6 + 3) + 7$ Use the Commutative Property.
$= 6 + (3 + 7)$ Use the Associative Property.
$= 6 + 10$ Add 3 and 7.
$= 16$ Add 10 and 6.

Try It • Tell which is different, the *order* or the *grouping*.

1. $(3 + 8) + 7 = 7 + (3 + 8)$

2. $(6 + 13) + 1 = 6 + (13 + 1)$

_____

_____

Name the property that is illustrated.

3. $3 + 6 = 6 + 3$

4. $(3 + 8) + 2 = 3 + (8 + 2)$

_____

_____

5. $(3 + 5) + 2 = (5 + 3) + 2$

6. $(3 + 9) + 7 = 3 + (9 + 7)$

_____

_____

Power Practice • Use the addition properties to complete.

7. $8 + \underline{\hspace{1cm}} = 3 + 8$

8. $16 + (9 + 8) = (16 + \underline{\hspace{1cm}}) + 8$

9. $(2 + 1) + 7 = 2 + (\underline{\hspace{1cm}} + 7)$

10. $8 + (\underline{\hspace{1cm}} + 4) = (5 + 4) + 8$

11. $(8 + \underline{\hspace{1cm}}) + 15 = 8 + (4 + 15)$

12. $(7 + 3) + \underline{\hspace{1cm}} = 7 + (\underline{\hspace{1cm}} + 4)$

13. $(8 + 6) + 9 = 9 + (8 + \underline{\hspace{1cm}})$

14. $(5 + 4) + \underline{\hspace{1cm}} = 7 + (5 + \underline{\hspace{1cm}})$

15. $19 + 6 = 6 + \underline{\hspace{1cm}}$

16. $(75 + 93) + 176 = 75 + (\underline{\hspace{1cm}} + 176)$

Use the addition properties to solve mentally.

17. $36 + 15 + 5 + 4 = \underline{\hspace{1cm}}$

18. $16 + 7 + 23 + 4 = \underline{\hspace{1cm}}$

19. $7 + 33 + 18 + 12 = \underline{\hspace{1cm}}$

20. $42 + 9 + 11 + 8 = \underline{\hspace{1cm}}$

21. $23 + 5 + 17 + 15 = \underline{\hspace{1cm}}$

22. $36 + 22 + 14 + 18 = \underline{\hspace{1cm}}$

23. $29 + 12 + 11 + 38 = \underline{\hspace{1cm}}$

24. $14 + 24 + 26 + 16 = \underline{\hspace{1cm}}$

25. $17 + 26 + 4 + 13 = \underline{\hspace{1cm}}$

26. $18 + 23 + 42 + 7 = \underline{\hspace{1cm}}$

27. $11 + 38 + 19 + 2 = \underline{\hspace{1cm}}$

28. $31 + 42 + 9 + 8 = \underline{\hspace{1cm}}$

29. $17 + 26 + 24 + 23 = \underline{\hspace{1cm}}$

30. $15 + 13 + 17 + 25 = \underline{\hspace{1cm}}$

Multiplication Properties

Learn

What Can I Do?
I want to find a way to multiply numbers easily.

You can use the properties of multiplication to find products easily.

Commutative Property

Changing the order of the factors does not change the product.

Different order
↓   ↓
$8 \times 5 = 5 \times 8$
$40 = 40$
↑_____↑
Same result

Associative Property

Changing the grouping of the factors does not change the product.

Different grouping
↓   ↓
$(4 \times 2) \times 3 = 4 \times (2 \times 3)$
$8 \times 3 = 4 \times 6$
$24 = 24$
↑_____↑
Same result

Sometimes you can use the associative and commutative properties to find products mentally.

$5 \times 7 \times 8 \times 10 = 5 \times 8 \times 7 \times 10$ Commutative Property
$= (5 \times 8) \times (7 \times 10)$ Associative Property
$= 40 \times 70$ Multiply
$= 2,800$ Multiply

Try It • Tell which is different, the *order* or the *grouping*.

1. $3 \times 8 \times 7 = 8 \times 3 \times 7$

2. $9 \times (11 \times 1) = (9 \times 11) \times 1$

_____

_____

Power Practice • Solve mentally if you can. Use the multiplication properties to complete.

3. $10 \times 7 \times 6 \times 10 =$ _____

4. $5 \times 9 \times 3 \times 2 =$ _____

5. $20 \times 4 \times 5 \times 10 =$ _____

6. $25 \times 3 \times 4 \times 12 =$ _____

7. $32 \times 25 \times 4 \times 2 =$ _____

8. $5 \times 48 \times 2 \times 4 =$ _____

The Distributive Property

Learn

What Can I Do?
I want to make multiplying easier.

You can use the distributive property to help you multiply.

The **Distributive Property** combines multiplication and addition. Here is a way to think about $3 \times (2 + 4)$.

$$3 \times (2 + 4) = (3 \times 2) + (3 \times 4)$$
$$= 6 + 12$$
$$= 18$$

You can see that there are 18 objects.

Try It • Complete. Use the distributive property.

1. $5 \times (7 + 6) = (5 \times \underline{\hspace{1cm}}) + (5 \times 6)$

2. $3 \times (6 + 8) = (\underline{\hspace{1cm}} \times 6) + (3 \times 8)$

3. $(8 \times 9) + (8 \times 5) = \underline{\hspace{0.7cm}} \times (9 + 5)$

4. $(6 \times 2) + (\underline{\hspace{0.5cm}} \times 7) = 6 \times (2 + \underline{\hspace{0.5cm}})$

Power Practice • Use the distributive property to rewrite the expression. Then simplify.

5. $8 \times (6 + 4)$ _____

6. $5 \times (10 + 3)$ _____

7. $(6 + 11) \times 7$ _____

8. $4 \times (3 + 7)$ _____

9. $5 \times (3 + 9)$ _____

10. $(8 + 9) \times 6$ _____

Solving Equations

Learn

What Can I Do?
I want to solve an equation.

Think of equations as questions in which the variable is read as "What number?" For example, $z + 5 = 7$ can be read as "What number plus 5 equals 7?"

Solve: $y - 8 = 7$

- Read as " What number minus 8 equals 7?" $y - 8 = 7$
- Solve. $15 - 8 = 7$ so, $y = 15$
- Check to see that the equation is true. $7 = 7$

Try It

• **Write a question to show how to read each equation.**

1. $a + 5 = 12$ _____

2. $3x = 18$ _____

3. $m \div 3 = 20$ _____

4. $10 - p = 4$ _____

5. $6 + n = 25$ _____

6. $\dfrac{t}{2} = 10$ _____

Power Practice • Solve each equation.

7. $y + 15 = 50$ $y =$ _____   **8.** $b - 4 = 8$ $b =$ _____

9. $\dfrac{w}{2} = 6$ $w =$ _____   **10.** $3 \times c = 27$ $c =$ _____

11. $28 - p = 19$ $p =$ _____   **12.** $t + 8 = 26$ $t =$ _____

13. $11s = 110$ $s =$ _____   **14.** $81 \div k = 9$ $k =$ _____

15. $17 + r = 40$ $r =$ _____   **16.** $h \div 3 = 12$ $h =$ _____

17. $5j = 30$ $j =$ _____   **18.** $12 + x = 18$ $x =$ _____

19. $9k = 54$ $k =$ _____   **20.** $z + 3 = 37$ $z =$ _____

21. $19 - y = 13$ $y =$ _____   **22.** $8b = 64$ $b =$ _____

23. $\dfrac{72}{n} = 9$ $n =$ _____   **24.** $z - 38 = 42$ $z =$ _____

25. $d + 14 = 47$ $d =$ _____   **26.** $\dfrac{100}{g} = 20$ $g =$ _____

27. $5p = 150$ $p =$ _____   **28.** $21 + k = 30$ $k =$ _____

29. $w - 30 = 80$ $w =$ _____   **30.** $\dfrac{r}{2} = 84$ $r =$ _____

31. $37 - x = 15$ $x =$ _____   **32.** $6x = 36$ $x =$ _____

33. $n + 13 = 30$ $n =$ _____   **34.** $\dfrac{z}{4} = 9$ $z =$ _____

35. $95 - y = 42$ $y =$ _____   **36.** $7b = 280$ $b =$ _____

Write Fractions as Decimals

Learn

Decimals and fractions both show parts of a whole. You can write a fraction as an equivalent fraction in tenths or hundredths. Then you can write the decimal.

What Can I Do?
I want to write a fraction as a decimal.

• Write $\frac{1}{2}$ as a decimal.

Find an equivalent fraction in tenths.

$$\frac{1 \times 5}{2 \times 5} = \frac{5}{10} \qquad \text{So, } \frac{1}{2} = \frac{5}{10} = \text{five tenths} = 0.5$$

• Write $\frac{1}{4}$ as a decimal.

Find an equivalent fraction in hundredths.

$$\frac{1 \times 25}{4 \times 25} = \frac{25}{100} \qquad \text{So, } \frac{1}{4} = \frac{25}{100} = \text{twenty-five hundredths} = 0.25$$

Try It
• Write each fraction as a decimal. Use equivalent fractions to help.

1. $\frac{2}{5}$

$$\frac{2 \times 2}{5 \times 2} = \frac{}{10}$$

What is $\frac{2}{5}$ as a decimal? _____

2. $\frac{9}{20}$

$$\frac{9 \times}{20 \times 5} = \frac{}{100}$$

What is $\frac{9}{20}$ as a decimal? _____

Power Practice
• Write each fraction as a decimal.

3. $\frac{3}{4} = $ _____

4. $\frac{1}{25} = $ _____

5. $\frac{4}{25} = $ _____

6. $\frac{7}{50} = $ _____

7. $\frac{9}{10} = $ _____

8. $\frac{11}{20} = $ _____

9. $\frac{4}{5} = $ _____

10. $\frac{7}{25} = $ _____

11. $\frac{5}{100} = $ _____

Write Decimals as Fractions

Learn

To write a decimal as a fraction, write the decimal as a fraction with a denominator of 10 or 100.

What Can I Do?
I want to write a decimal as a fraction.

• Write 0.7 as a fraction.

• Say the decimal name:

    seven tenths

• Write seven tenths as a fraction:

$$\frac{7}{10}$$

So, $0.7 = \frac{7}{10}$

• Write 0.05 as a fraction.

• Say the decimal name:

    five hundredths

• Write five hundredths as a fraction:

$$\frac{5}{100}$$

• Simplify the fraction.

$$\frac{5}{100} = \frac{5 \div 5}{100 \div 5} = \frac{1}{20}$$

So, $0.05 = \frac{5}{100} = \frac{1}{20}$

Try It . Complete by saying the decimal name and writing it as a fraction in simplest form.

1. 0.6

Name: six tenths

Fraction: $\frac{6}{10}$

Simplest form: $\frac{}{5}$

2. 0.35

Name: _____ hundredths

Fraction: $\frac{}{100}$

Simplest form: $\frac{}{20}$

Power Practice • Write each decimal as a fraction in simplest form.

3. 0.3 _____

4. 0.14 _____

5. 0.15 _____

6. 0.44 _____

7. 0.5 _____

8. 0.25 _____

9. 0.55 _____

10. 0.4 _____

11. 0.24 _____

12. 0.66 _____

13. 0.2 _____

14. 0.78 _____

15. 0.56 _____

16. 0.75 _____

17. 0.98 _____

18. 0.33 _____

Add Fractions

Learn

What Can I Do?
I want to add fractions.

Like Denominators

Add: $\dfrac{3}{8} + \dfrac{4}{8}$

- Both fractions have a denominator of 8. To add fractions with like denominators, add the numerators. Write the sum over the common denominator, 8.

$$\dfrac{3}{8} + \dfrac{4}{8} = \dfrac{3+4}{8} = \dfrac{7}{8}$$

Unlike Denominators

Add: $\dfrac{5}{6} + \dfrac{1}{4}$

- The denominators of these fractions are different. To add fractions with unlike denominators, use the following steps.

1. Find the least common denominator (LCD) of the fractions.

The LCD is the least common multiple of the denominator.

Multiples of 6: 6, **12**, 18, 24, 30
Multiples of 4: 4, 8, **12**, 16

The least common multiple of 6 and 4 is 12.

2. Rewrite each fraction using 12 as the denominator.

$$\dfrac{5}{6} = \dfrac{5 \times 2}{6 \times 2} = \dfrac{10}{12}
\qquad\qquad
\dfrac{1}{4} = \dfrac{1 \times 3}{4 \times 3} = \dfrac{3}{12}$$

3. Add. Write the sum in simplest form.

$$\dfrac{5}{6} + \dfrac{1}{4} = \dfrac{10}{12} + \dfrac{3}{12} = \dfrac{13}{12} = \dfrac{12}{12} + \dfrac{1}{12} = 1\dfrac{1}{12}$$

Name_____

Try It

• Add. Write the answer in simplest form.

1. $\frac{1}{7} + \frac{4}{7} =$ _____

2. $\frac{3}{4} + \frac{3}{4} =$ _____

3. $\frac{5}{12} + \frac{1}{4}$

$= \frac{5}{12} + \frac{}{12} = \frac{}{12}$

$=$ _____

4. $\frac{3}{5} + \frac{1}{2}$

$= \frac{6}{10} + \frac{5}{10} = \frac{}{10}$

$=$ _____

Power Practice

• Add. Write the sum in simplest form.

5. $\frac{1}{9} + \frac{5}{9} =$ _____

6. $\frac{1}{6} + \frac{3}{6} =$ _____

7. $\frac{1}{8} + \frac{5}{8} =$ _____

8. $\frac{2}{11} + \frac{4}{11} =$ _____

9. $\frac{2}{4} + \frac{3}{4} =$ _____

10. $\frac{3}{7} + \frac{6}{7} =$ _____

11. $\frac{2}{5} + \frac{7}{10} =$ _____

12. $\frac{5}{6} + \frac{4}{9} =$ _____

13. $\frac{1}{2} + \frac{1}{8} =$ _____

14. $\frac{3}{8} + \frac{3}{6} =$ _____

Fractions and Figures

On 20 index cards write a fraction addition problem on one side and the answer on the other.

• Stack the cards with the problem side face up. The first player thinks of a word and, on a piece of paper, draws blanks to stand for the letters in the word.

• The other player picks the top card and must solve the problem on the card before he or she can guess a letter. An incorrect solution or wrong guess allows the first player to draw one of six segments of a stick figure.

• The second player continues until he or she has guessed the word or until the stick figure has been completed. Then it is the first player's turn.

Subtract Fractions

Learn

What Can I Do?
I want to subtract fractions.

Like Denominators

Subtract: $\dfrac{7}{8} - \dfrac{3}{8}$

- Both fractions have a denominator of 8. To subtract fractions with like denominators, subtract the numerators and write the difference over the common denominator. Write the fraction in simplest form.

$$\frac{7}{8} - \frac{3}{8} = \frac{7-3}{8} = \frac{4}{8} = \frac{1}{2}$$

Unlike Denominators

Subtract: $\dfrac{4}{5} - \dfrac{1}{2}$

- The denominators of the fractions are different. To subtract fractions with unlike denominators, follow these steps.

1. Find the least common denominator (LCD) of the fractions.

   The LCD is the least common multiple of 5 and 2.
   Multiples of 5: 5, **10**, 15, 20
   Multiples of 2: 2, 4, 6, 8, **10**, 12

   The least common multiple of 5 and 2 is 10.

2. Rewrite each fraction using 10 as the denominator.

$$\frac{4}{5} = \frac{4 \times 2}{5 \times 2} = \frac{8}{10} \qquad\qquad \frac{1}{2} = \frac{1 \times 5}{2 \times 5} = \frac{5}{10}$$

3. Subtract. Simplify the difference, if possible.

$$\frac{4}{5} - \frac{1}{2} = \frac{8}{10} - \frac{5}{10} = \frac{8-5}{10} = \frac{3}{10}$$

Try It • Subtract. Write the difference in simplest form.

1. $\dfrac{7}{8} - \dfrac{3}{8} = $ __

2. $\dfrac{5}{9} - \dfrac{2}{9} = $ __

3. $\dfrac{2}{3} - \dfrac{2}{6}$

$\dfrac{}{6} - \dfrac{2}{6} = $ __

4. $\dfrac{3}{4} - \dfrac{1}{3}$

$\dfrac{}{12} - \dfrac{}{12} = \dfrac{}{12}$

Power Practice • Subtract. Write the difference in simplest form.

5.
$$\begin{array}{r} \dfrac{5}{7} \\ -\dfrac{4}{7} \\ \hline \end{array}$$

6.
$$\begin{array}{r} \dfrac{6}{8} \\ -\dfrac{1}{8} \\ \hline \end{array}$$

7.
$$\begin{array}{r} \dfrac{10}{12} \\ -\dfrac{5}{12} \\ \hline \end{array}$$

8.
$$\begin{array}{r} \dfrac{7}{10} \\ -\dfrac{3}{10} \\ \hline \end{array}$$

9.
$$\begin{array}{r} \dfrac{8}{9} \\ -\dfrac{5}{9} \\ \hline \end{array}$$

10.
$$\begin{array}{r} \dfrac{11}{15} \\ -\dfrac{6}{15} \\ \hline \end{array}$$

11. $\dfrac{21}{40} - \dfrac{15}{40} = $

12. $\dfrac{21}{30} - \dfrac{5}{30} = $

13. $\dfrac{21}{24} - \dfrac{5}{24} = $

14. $\dfrac{7}{10} - \dfrac{1}{5} = $

15. $\dfrac{5}{6} - \dfrac{2}{9} = $

16. $\dfrac{3}{4} - \dfrac{1}{3} = $

17. $\dfrac{5}{8} - \dfrac{1}{2} = $

18. $\dfrac{5}{6} - \dfrac{3}{8} = $

19. $\dfrac{3}{4} - \dfrac{2}{5} = $

20. $\dfrac{1}{2} - \dfrac{3}{10} = $

21. $\dfrac{3}{4} - \dfrac{7}{10} = $

22. $\dfrac{4}{5} - \dfrac{2}{3} = $

Multiply Fractions

Learn

Multiply: $\frac{1}{2} \times \frac{2}{3}$

What Can I Do?
I want to multiply a fraction by a fraction.

Draw a picture.

$\frac{2}{3}$ $\frac{1}{2} \times \frac{1}{3}$ $\frac{1}{2} \times \frac{2}{3} = \frac{2}{6}$

You can also use these steps to multiply fractions.

$\frac{1}{2} \times \frac{2}{3} = ?$

Multiply the numerators.
Multiply the denominators.
Simplify.

$\frac{1}{2} \times \frac{2}{3} = \frac{1 \times 2}{2 \times 3} = \frac{2}{6} = \frac{1}{3}$

Try It • Complete.

1. $\frac{3}{4} \times \frac{1}{2} = \frac{3 \times}{4 \times} = $ ____

2. $\frac{5}{6} \times \frac{3}{4} = \frac{5 \times}{6 \times} = $ ____ $= $ ____

Power Practice • Multiply. Write each product in simplest form.

3. $\frac{2}{10} \times \frac{3}{5} = $

4. $\frac{2}{3} \times \frac{7}{8} = $

5. $\frac{4}{9} \times \frac{1}{2} = $

6. $\frac{5}{6} \times \frac{2}{3} = $

7. $\frac{2}{7} \times \frac{1}{3} = $

8. $\frac{1}{9} \times \frac{3}{7} = $

9. $\frac{3}{5} \times \frac{1}{2} = $

10. $\frac{4}{7} \times \frac{3}{4} = $

11. $\frac{8}{9} \times \frac{5}{8} = $

Name_____

Divide Fractions by Fractions

Chapter 9 — Skill Builder

Learn

Find $\frac{2}{3} \div \frac{1}{12}$.

You can use fraction bars.

When you divide $\frac{2}{3}$ by $\frac{1}{12}$, you are really finding out how many $\frac{1}{12}$s are in $\frac{2}{3}$.

What Can I Do? I want to divide a fraction by a fraction.

- Show fraction bars for $\frac{2}{3}$.
- Show enough fraction bars for 12 to line up with $\frac{2}{3}$.
- Eight $\frac{1}{12}$ fraction bars is the same length as $\frac{2}{3}$.

$$\frac{2}{3} \div \frac{1}{12} = 8$$

You can also multiply by the reciprocal of the divisor to divide fractions.

reciprocals

$$\frac{2}{3} \div \frac{1}{12} = \frac{2}{3} \times \frac{12}{1} = \frac{24}{3} = 8$$

Try It • Divide.

1. $\frac{3}{6} \div \frac{1}{12} = \frac{3}{6} \times \frac{12}{1} = \frac{36}{} = $ ____

2. $\frac{1}{2} \div \frac{1}{4} = \frac{1}{2} \times \frac{}{1} = \frac{}{2} = $ ____

Power Practice • Divide. Write each quotient in simplest form.

3. $\frac{2}{3} \div \frac{5}{8} = $ ____

4. $\frac{1}{3} \div \frac{5}{6} = $ ____

5. $\frac{4}{15} \div \frac{1}{2} = $ ____

© McGraw-Hill School Division

Name _____

What's My Number?

If $\frac{2}{3}$ of my number is 18, what's my number?

- You can draw a picture to solve.

  Think: 18 objects in $\frac{2}{3}$ of rectangle.

  9 objects in $\frac{1}{3}$

  So, 27 objects in $\frac{3}{3}$

  The number is 27.

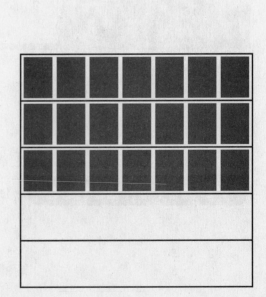

- You can write a division to solve.

  $\frac{2}{3}$ of a number is 18 → 18 ÷ $\frac{2}{3}$ = ?

  $18 \div \frac{2}{3} = 18 \times \frac{3}{2}$

  $\phantom{18 \div \frac{2}{3}} = \frac{54}{2}$

  $\phantom{18 \div \frac{2}{3}} = 27$

  The number is 27.

Solve.

$\frac{3}{5}$ of my number is 21. What's my number?

1. There are _____ objects in $\frac{3}{5}$.

2. There are _____ objects in $\frac{1}{5}$.

3. So, there are _____ objects in $\frac{5}{5}$.

4. $\frac{3}{5}$ of _____ is 21. The number is _____ .

Name_____

$\frac{2}{7}$ of my number is 14. What's my number?

5. $\frac{2}{7}$ of a number is 14, → _____ ÷ $\frac{2}{7}$ = 14 × _____ = _____

6. The number is _____.

The product of 1 $\frac{1}{2}$ and my number is 12. What's my number?

Let n represent the number.

7. The product of 1 $\frac{1}{2}$ and my number is 12 → _____ × _____ = 12

8. The number is _____.

Write an equation. Let n represent the number.

9. $\frac{1}{2}$ of the number is _____.

10. 5 is added to $\frac{1}{2}$ of the number: _____.

11. Three times the number is _____.

12. Write an equation to solve this problem. Then solve.

If 5 is added to $\frac{1}{2}$ of my number, the result is three times my number.

What's my number? _____.

© McGraw-Hill School Division

Fraction Problems

Carlos drives $\frac{9}{10}$ of a mile to work. After work, he drives $\frac{1}{2}$ of a mile back towards his house to pick up groceries. What fraction of a mile does Carlos have to go before he arrives home?

1. Write the problem as a subtraction. _____

2. What common denominator can you use? _____

3. Rewrite the subtraction problem using the common denominator. Find the answer.

$\frac{9}{10} - \frac{1}{2} = $ _____ $ = $ _____ _____

4. Did you have to simplify your answer? Explain.

_____

5. After leaving the grocery store, does Carlos have a long way to travel? Explain why or why not?

_____

The human body is made of natural elements. Its chemical make-up is approximately $\frac{3}{5}$ oxygen, $\frac{1}{4}$ carbon, and $\frac{1}{10}$ hydrogen. The rest consists of small amounts of various other elements.

6. How much of the body is made up of oxygen and hydrogen? _____

7. How much of the body is made up of oxygen and carbon? _____

8. How much of the body is made up of hydrogen and carbon? _____

A news radio show covers sports and music for $\frac{1}{2}$ of the time and weather and news for $\frac{1}{8}$ of the time. Commercials take up $\frac{3}{8}$ of the time.

9. How much of the time is spent on commercials, weather, and news?

_____

10. How much of the time is spent on weather, news, music, and sports?

_____

11. Which category do you think is most important to the station? Least important? Explain your thinking.

_____

_____

_____

Jana went shopping with a certain amount of money. She spent $\frac{3}{7}$ of that amount on food.

12. Write a subtraction expression to show what fraction of money she had left.

_____

13. Jana spent $\frac{1}{4}$ of the fraction of money she had left on gasoline. Complete

the expression to show the fraction of money she had left then.

$\frac{4}{7} - (\frac{1}{4} \times$ _____ $) =$ _____

14. She then spent $\frac{2}{3}$ of what she had left on household necessities. Complete

the expression to show the fractional amount of money she had left.

$\frac{3}{7} - (\frac{2}{3} \times$ _____ $) = \frac{3}{7} -$ _____ $=$ _____

15. If Jana started out with $84, how much did she have left at the end?

_____

16. What fraction of her money had she spent? _____.
How much money was that? _____

Customary Measurement

Learn

Use an inch-ruler to find the length of the straw.

What Can I Do?

I want to find the length in inches.

- Find the length to the nearest inch.
  The straw is between 3 and 4 inches.
  Round down. It is closer to 3 inches.

- Find the length to the nearest half inch.
  The straw is between 3 inches and $3\frac{1}{2}$ inches.
  Round up. It is closer to $3\frac{1}{2}$ inches.

- Find the length to the nearest quarter inch.
  The straw is between $3\frac{1}{4}$ and $3\frac{1}{2}$ inches.
  Round up. It is closer to $3\frac{1}{2}$ inches.

Try It • Use an inch ruler to measure the line segment.

_____

1. to the nearest inch _____

2. to the nearest half-inch _____

3. to the nearest quarter-inch _____

Power Practice • Use an inch ruler to measure each line segment to the nearest inch or fraction of an inch.

_____

4. inch   **5.** half-inch   **6.** quarter-inch

_____   _____   _____

_____

7. inch   **8.** half-inch   **9.** quarter-inch

_____   _____   _____

_____

10. inch   **11.** half-inch   **12.** quarter-inch

_____   _____   _____

_____

13. inch   **14.** half-inch   **15.** quarter-inch

_____   _____   _____

_____

16. inch   **17.** half-inch   **18.** quarter-inch

_____   _____   _____

_____

19. inch   **20.** half-inch   **21.** quarter-inch

_____   _____   _____

Addition and Subtraction Equations

Learn

Use the Inverse Operation

An equation is like a balanced scale. The quantities on both sides of the equals sign must balance, or equal each other.

To solve an equation, get the variable alone on one side of the equation. You do this by applying the inverse operation to both sides of the equation. This keeps the sides balanced.

What Can I Do?

I want to solve an equation.

Solve for n: $n + 3 = 12$

- This is an addition equation. Subtraction is the inverse of addition. Subtract 3 from both sides of the equation.

$$n + 3 = 12$$
$$n + 3 - 3 = 12 - 3$$
$$n = 9$$

Check. Substitute 9 in the original equation.
$$9 + 3 = 12$$
$$12 = 12$$

Solve for x: $x - 4 = 11$

- This is a subtraction equation. Addition is the inverse of subtraction. Add 4 to both sides of the equation.

$$x - 4 = 11$$
$$x - 4 + 4 = 11 + 4$$
$$x = 15$$

Substitute 15 in the original equation.
$$15 - 4 = 11$$
$$11 = 11$$

Try It • Complete to solve each equation. Name the inverse operation used.

1. $m + 4 = 7$

$m + 4 -$ _____ = _____

$m =$ _____

Inverse operation used:

_____

2. $y - 2 = 9$

$y - 2 +$ _____ = _____

$y =$ _____

Inverse operation used:

_____

Name_____

Power Practice • Solve each equation. Show your work.

3. $4 + n = 7$ _____

4. $n - 5 = 14$ _____

5. $16 - n = 2$ _____

6. $n + 12 = 20$ _____

7. $n + 8 = 18$ _____

8. $15 + n = 40$ _____

9. $n + 17 = 27$ _____

10. $420 - n = 419$ _____

11. $32 + x = 38$ _____

12. $x - 45 = 55$ _____

13. $x + 45 = 45$ _____

14. $n - 5 = 0$ _____

15. $x + 50 = 59$ _____

16. $x - 4 = 16$ _____

17. $x + 4 = 16$ _____

18. $15 + n = 15$ _____

19. $6 + k = 20$ _____

20. $9 = c - 19$ _____

21. $t - 7 = 21$ _____

22. $40 + s = 59$ _____

23. $g + 17 = 92$ _____

24. $77 = t - 4$ _____

Learn with Partners & Parents

Round-Robin
• Organize into a group of players.
• Take turns verbalizing equations. The first student gives a constant, the second names an operation, the third gives a variable, the fourth says "equals" and a solution, and the fifth player names a value for the variable to make a true equation.
• Players decide if the fifth player is correct. If so, the player scores 1 point. Play continues until someone has 5 points.

Name_____

Sort Shapes

 Learn

 What Can I Do?
I want to sort shapes into groups.

You can sort shapes by finding attributes they have in common.

Which shape does not belong ?

cone   **cube**   **cylinder**

The cube does not belong. It is the only figure without a circular face.

Try It • **Which shape does not belong? Tell why.**

1.

cylinder   rectangular prism   cube

cylinder because it does not have 6 sides

Power Practice • **Identify the shape that does not belong. Tell why.**

2.

rectangle   triangle   parallelogram   trapezoid

triangle only 3 sides

3.

trapezoid   square   parallelogram   pentagon

pentagon 3 sides

Polygons

Learn

What Can I Do?

I want to identify polygons.

Polygons can be named for the number of sides and angles they have.

triangle	**quadrilateral**	**pentagon**	**hexagon**	**octagon**
3 sides	4 sides	5 sides	6 sides	8 sides
3 angles	4 angles	5 angles	6 angles	8 angles

Some quadrilaterals have special names.

rectangle   **square**   **parallelogram**   **trapezoid**

Try It

• Name the polygon, or write the number of sides and angles to complete the table.

Polygon	Number of Sides	Number of Angles
1. triangle		
2.	8	
3. hexagon		
4.		5
5. quadrilateral		

Power Practice

• Put a check mark in the column if the description applies to the quadrilateral.

Quadrilateral	opposite sides are parallel	opposite sides have equal length	4 sides have equal length	4 right angles
6. rectangle				
7. square				
8. parallelogram				
9. trapezoid				

Measure Sides of Polygons

Learn

What Can I Do?

I want to find the length of a side of a polygon.

You can use an inch ruler to measure.

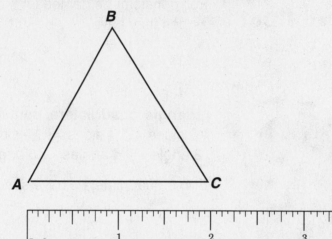

• Find the length of side *AC* of triangle *ABC*.

Side *AC* of triangle *ABC* measures 2 inches.

Try It • **Use an inch ruler to find the length of the side named.**

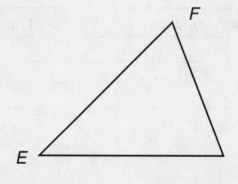

1. Side *ED* _____

2. Side *EF* _____

3. Side *DF* _____

4. Side *YZ* _____

5. Side *WX* _____

6. Side *XY* _____

7. Side *ZW* _____

Power Practice • Use an inch ruler to measure the length of the indicated side.

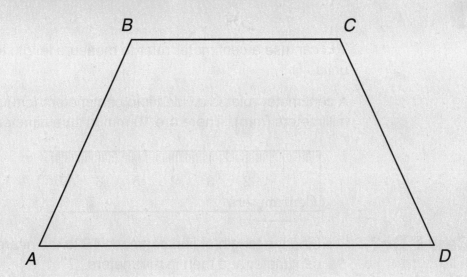

8. Side *BA* _____   **9.** Side *BC* _____

10. Side *CD* _____   **11.** Side *AD* _____

12. Side *KJ* _____ **13.** Side *KL* _____ **14.** Side *JL* _____

15. Side *BA* _____   **16.** Side *CD* _____

17. Side *AD* _____   **18.** Side *BC* _____

Metric Measurement

You can use a centimeter ruler to measure length in metric units.

A centimeter ruler is divided into centimeters (cm) and millimeters (mm). There are 10 mm in 1 centimeter.

1 2 3 4 5 6 7
Centimeters

What Can I Do?
I want to find a length in metric units.

• Find the length of line segment *AB* to the nearest centimeter and then in millimeters.

A _____ B
1 2 3 4 5 6 7
Centimeters

To the nearest centimeter, the length of line segment *AB* is 5 cm.

In millimeters, the length of line segment *AB* is 53 mm.

Try It . Use a centimeter ruler to find the length of line segment *XY* to the nearest centimeter and then in millimeters.

X _____ Y
1 2 3 4 5 6 7
Centimeters

1. nearest centimeter _____ **2.** in millimeters _____

Power Practice

Use a centimeter ruler to find the length of each line segment to the nearest centimeter and then in millimeters.

_A_____B_

3. nearest centimeter _____   **4.** in millimeters _____

_E_____F_

5. nearest centimeter _____   **6.** in millimeters _____

_M_____N_

7. nearest centimeter _____   **8.** in millimeters _____

_K_____L_

9. nearest centimeter _____   **10.** in millimeters _____

_B_____C_

11. nearest centimeter _____   **12.** in millimeters _____

_P_____Q_

13. nearest centimeter _____   **14.** in millimeters _____

Polygons in Polygons

A **polygon** is a closed, two-dimensional figure formed by joining three or more line segments at their endpoints. Polygons are named and labeled by the letters that name the vertices, or corners, where the line segments, or sides, meet.

In the figure below you can find a number of different polygons if you look carefully.

Use figure *ABCDE* to answer each question.

1. What kind of polygon is figure *ABCDE*? _____

2. What kind of polygon is formed by segments *GH*, *HI*, *IJ*, *JF*, and *FG*?

_____

3. Use letters to name the polygon in Exercise 2. _____

4. Find vertex *C*. Name four triangles that have *C* as a vertex.

_____

5. Choose a vertex other than *C*. Name three triangles that have that point as a vertex.

_____

6. Name four trapezoids.

_____

7. Name three parallelograms.

_____

8. How many triangles can you find in figure *ABCDE*? _____

Name_____

Look at the following triangle.

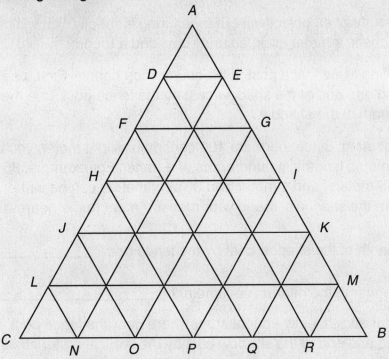

9. How many triangles have *A* as a vertex? Name them.

_____

10. How many triangles have *B* as a vertex? Name them.

_____

11. How many triangles have *D* as a vertex? _____

12. How many triangles have *E* as a vertex? _____

13. How do the numbers of triangles with *D* and with *E* as vertices compare?

_____

Measuring Shadows

You can find the height of an object without measuring it directly. You will need a piece of sidewalk chalk, a meter stick, a sunny day, and a friend.

Begin with something like a fence post, a broom, or mop handle. First, use chalk to mark the beginning and end of the shadow cast by the fence post. Use the meter stick to measure the length of the shadow.

A word about measuring: Since there are 100 centimeters in a meter, you can use decimals to write metric lengths in hundredths of a meter. For example, 85 centimeters can be written 0.85 meters, and 1 meter and 35 centimeters can be written 1.35 meters. When you measure the shadows, round your measurement to the nearest centimeter.

1. What is the length of the shadow cast by the fence post? _____

2. What is that length to the nearest centimeter? _____

Next, hold the meter stick directly upright somewhere near the fence post. Use chalk to mark the beginning and end of the shadow cast by the vertical meter stick. Use the meter stick to measure the length of the shadow.

3. What is the length of the shadow cast by the meter stick, to the nearest centimeter?

_____

4. Record your information on a chart such as the one below.

	Height of Object	Length of Shadow
Meter Stick	1m (100 cm)	_____
Fence Post	_____	_____

5. Multiply: (height of meter stick) × (length of shadow of fence post)

_____

6. Divide your answer by the length of the shadow of the meter stick. Record your result.

The quotient will be the height of the fence post.

_____

7. Now use the meter stick to measure the actual height of the fence post.

_____

8. How does the height compare with your answer to question 6?

_____

9. Use the same procedure to find the height of another object, such as a flagpole. Use a chart like this one to record the information. Round your measurements to the nearest centimeter.

	Height of Object	Length of Shadow
Meter Stick	1m (100 cm)	_____
Flag pole	_____	_____

10. Now try some other objects. Use the method to calculate the heights of other objects such as a broom, a mop handle, playground equipment, or a tree. Where possible, measure the actual length of the object to see whether your calculations agree.

	Height of Object	Length of Shadow
Meter Stick	1m (100 cm)	_____
Object: _____	_____	_____
Object: _____	_____	_____
Object: _____	_____	_____
Object: _____	_____	_____

11. Explain how the shadow method works for finding lengths or heights.

_____

_____

Multiply and Divide Decimals

Learn

What Can I Do?
I want to multiply and divide decimals.

Multiply: 6.84 × 5.3

To multiply two decimals, write the numbers and multiply as you would with whole numbers.

$$\begin{array}{r} 6.84 \\ \times\ \ 5.3 \\ \hline 2052 \\ 34200 \\ \hline 36252 \end{array}$$

Place the decimal point in the product.

$$\begin{array}{r} 6.84 \leftarrow 2\ \text{decimal places} \\ \times\ \ 5.3 \leftarrow 1\ \text{decimal place} \\ \hline 2052 \\ 34200 \\ \hline 36.252 \leftarrow 3\ \text{decimal places} \end{array}$$

So, 6.84 × 5.3 = 36.252

Divide: 0.086 ÷ 0.2

Write the problem as you would for long division.

$$0.2\overline{)0.086}$$

Move the decimal point in the divisor so that the divisor is a whole number. Move the decimal point the same number of places in the dividend.

$$0.2\overline{)0.086}$$

Divide.

$$2\overline{)0.86} = 0.43$$

So, 0.086 ÷ 0.2 = 0.43

Try It • Write the decimal point in the product.

1. 3.5 × 15.3 → __5 3 5 5__

2. 6.9 × 9.35 → __6 4 5 1 5__

Move the decimal point in the divisor and dividend until the divisor is a whole number.

3. $11.2\overline{)0.224}$ ___)___

4. $0.08\overline{)16}$ ___)___

Find each product or quotient.

5. 8.9 × 0.3 = _____

6. 0.46 × 1.2 = _____

7. 6.7 × 4.3 = _____

8. $0.5\overline{)2.75}$ _____

9. $0.9\overline{)31.5}$ _____

10. $30.6\overline{)25.704}$ _____

Name_____

11. $0.47 \times 0.8 =$ _____

12. $1.62 \times 0.26 =$ _____

13. $6.25 \times 6.5 =$ _____

14. $0.26 \times 9.58 =$ _____

15. $0.15 \times 2.4 =$ _____

16. $4.06 \times 3.51 =$ _____

17. $21.49 \times 0.8 =$ _____

18. $3.21 \times 0.04 =$ _____

19. $0.2\overline{)5} =$ _____

20. $0.7\overline{)0.77} =$ _____

21. $0.08\overline{)16} =$ _____

22. $0.4\overline{)0.004} =$ _____

23. $3.5\overline{)13.93} =$ _____

24. $6.5\overline{)340.6} =$ _____

25. $0.009\overline{)5.4} =$ _____

26. $5.1\overline{)8.976} =$ _____

Multiply and Divide Fractions

Learn

What Can I Do?
I want to multiply and divide fractions.

Multiply: $\frac{1}{2} \times \frac{5}{6}$

To multiply fractions, multiply the numerators. Write the product over the product of the denominators. Write the product in simplest form.

$$\frac{1}{2} \times \frac{5}{6} = \frac{5}{12}$$

Divide: $\frac{1}{2} \div \frac{1}{6}$

To divide fractions, multiply the dividend by the reciprocal of the divisor. Write the quotient in simplest form.

$$\frac{1}{2} \div \frac{1}{6} = \frac{1}{2} \times \frac{6}{1} = \frac{6}{2} = 3$$

Try It • Complete to find each product or quotient.

1. $\frac{2}{3} \times \frac{3}{4} = \frac{2 \times 3}{3 \times } = \frac{}{12} = \frac{}{2}$

2. $\frac{3}{8} \div \frac{1}{2} = \frac{3}{8} \times \frac{}{1} = \frac{3 \times }{8 \times 1} = \frac{}{} = \frac{}{}$

Find each product or quotient.

3. $\frac{4}{9} \times \frac{3}{5} =$ _____

4. $\frac{7}{8} \times \frac{4}{7} =$ _____

5. $\frac{2}{3} \div \frac{1}{12} =$ _____

6. $\frac{5}{14} \div \frac{10}{21} =$ _____

Name_____

7. $\dfrac{1}{5} \times \dfrac{1}{2} =$ _____

8. $\dfrac{3}{4} \times \dfrac{2}{3} =$ _____

9. $\dfrac{2}{3} \times \dfrac{1}{4} =$ _____

10. $\dfrac{5}{8} \times \dfrac{1}{2} =$ _____

11. $\dfrac{1}{3} \times \dfrac{5}{6} =$ _____

12. $\dfrac{1}{4} \times \dfrac{2}{7} =$ _____

13. $\dfrac{1}{5} \times \dfrac{3}{4} =$ _____

14. $\dfrac{4}{9} \times \dfrac{1}{3} =$ _____

15. $\dfrac{1}{3} \times \dfrac{2}{3} =$ _____

16. $\dfrac{1}{4} \times \dfrac{1}{12} =$ _____

17. $\dfrac{2}{5} \times \dfrac{1}{3} =$ _____

18. $\dfrac{2}{3} \times \dfrac{1}{6} =$ _____

19. $\dfrac{1}{5} \div \dfrac{1}{2} =$ _____

20. $\dfrac{3}{4} \div \dfrac{2}{3} =$ _____

21. $\dfrac{2}{3} \div \dfrac{1}{3} =$ _____

22. $\dfrac{5}{8} \div \dfrac{1}{2} =$ _____

23. $\dfrac{1}{3} \div \dfrac{5}{6} =$ _____

24. $\dfrac{1}{14} \div \dfrac{2}{7} =$ _____

25. $\dfrac{1}{4} \div \dfrac{1}{12} =$ _____

26. $\dfrac{2}{5} \div \dfrac{1}{10} =$ _____

27. $\dfrac{1}{2} \div \dfrac{1}{6} =$ _____

28. $\dfrac{3}{4} \div \dfrac{1}{3} =$ _____

29. $\dfrac{3}{10} \div \dfrac{1}{2} =$ _____

30. $\dfrac{2}{7} \div \dfrac{4}{5} =$ _____

31. $\dfrac{4}{5} \div \dfrac{1}{2} =$ _____

32. $\dfrac{3}{8} \div \dfrac{7}{10} =$ _____

33. $\dfrac{11}{12} \div \dfrac{2}{3} =$ _____

34. $\dfrac{7}{9} \div \dfrac{1}{3} =$ _____

35. $\dfrac{3}{5} \div \dfrac{4}{7} =$ _____

36. $\dfrac{2}{3} \div \dfrac{9}{10} =$ _____

Evaluate Expressions

Learn

What Can I Do?
I want to evaluate an algebraic expression.

You can evaluate an algebraic expression if you know the value of the variable.

To evaluate an expression, substitute the numerical value of the variable and simplify the numerical expression.

Evaluate $n - 11$ for $n = 30$.
Write the expression. $n - 11$
Substitute 30 for n. $30 - 11$
Simplify.   19

Evaluate $x + 7$ for $x = 12$.
Write the expression. $x + 7$
Substitute 12 for x. $12 + 7$
Simplify.   19

Try It • Complete to evaluate each algebraic expression for $x = 25$.

1. $x + 9$

____ + 9

_____

2. $x - 13$

____ − 13

_____

3. $x + 12$

____ + 12

_____

4. $x + 295$

____ + 295

_____

5. $x + 50$

____ + 50

_____

6. $x - 24$

____ − 24

_____

Complete each table.

7.

n	$n - 1$
20	
15	
10	
5	

8.

x	$x - 6$
12	
11	
10	
9	

Name_____

9. $n + 7$

_____

10. $n - 1$

_____

11. $n + 12$

_____

12. $n - 9$

_____

13. $n - 10$

_____

14. $n + 9$

_____

15. $n - n$

_____

16. $n + n$

_____

17. $n \div 2$

_____

Evaluate for x = 32.

18. $x + 4$

_____

19. $2x$

_____

20. $x \div 4$

_____

21. $x - 14$

_____

22. $x + 8$

_____

23. $2x - 18$

_____

24. $x + 12$

_____

25. $x - 12$

_____

26. $x + 20$

_____

Evaluate for c = 25.

27. $c + 15$

_____

28. $c - 12$

_____

29. $2c - 10$

_____

30. $c \div 5$

_____

31. $3c$

_____

32. $c - 25$

_____

33. $c + 13$

_____

34. $2c + 2$

_____

35. $c - 14$

_____

Identify Geometric Figures

Learn

What Can I Do?
I want to identify geometric figures.

A **plane** is a set of points that forms a flat surface extending in all directions without limit. Here are some geometric figures that are contained in a plane.

Line Segment	**Ray**	**Line**
The endpoints of this segment are *A* and *B*.	A ray has one endpoint and extends without end in one direction.	The arrowheads show that a line extends without end in two directions.

A———————B

R———————T→

←C———————D→

segment *AB* or $\overline{AB}$ ray *RT* or $\overrightarrow{RT}$ line *CD* or $\overleftrightarrow{CD}$

segment *BA* or $\overline{BA}$ line *DC* or $\overleftrightarrow{DC}$

Try It • Draw and label the geometric figure named.

1. ray *XY*

2. line segment *RS*

3. line *PQ*

Name each figure in two ways.

4.
C———————D→

_____

5.
E———————F

_____

6.
←O———————P→

_____

7.
S———————T→

_____

Name_____

Power Practice • Name each figure in two ways.

8.

A   R

_____

9.

A   B

_____

10.

R   Q

_____

11.

A   T

_____

12.

P   T

_____

13.

P   Q

_____

14.

L   M

_____

15.

K   L

_____

16.

C   D

_____

17.

F   G

_____

18.

R   Q

_____

19.

W   X

_____

20.

M   N

_____

Learn with Partners & Parents

Area Calculations

Use a set of 15 cards showing rectangles, triangles, or parallelograms.

• Place the cards facedown on your desk. Turn over one card at a time. Each player estimates the area of the polygon in square inches or square centimeters.

• Measure the polygon and calculate its area.

• The player whose estimate is closest to the actual answer scores a point.

Multiply Three Factors

Learn

What Can I Do?
I want to multiply three factors.

You can use the Associative Property of Multiplication to find the product of three factors.

Associative Property of Multiplication

$(9 \times 4) \times 5 = 9 \times (4 \times 5)$
$36 \times 5 = 9 \times 20$
$180 = 180$

The way the factors are grouped does not change the product.
Multiply: $7 \times 3 \times 2$

Use the Associative Property to group the factors.

$7 \times 3 \times 2 = 7 \times (3 \times 2)$

Find the product of the grouped factors.
Then multiply your answer by the third factor.

$7 \times (3 \times 2) = 7 \times 6 = 42$

Try It • **Find each product.**

1. $8 \times 2 \times 3 = 8 \times (2 \times 3)$

$= 8 \times \underline{\hspace{1cm}}$

$= \underline{\hspace{1cm}}$

2. $4 \times 5 \times 6 = (4 \times \underline{\hspace{1cm}}) \times 6$

$= \underline{\hspace{1cm}} \times 6$

$= \underline{\hspace{1cm}}$

3. $7 \times 3 \times 3 = 7 \times (3 \times \underline{\hspace{1cm}})$

$= \underline{\hspace{1cm}} \times \underline{\hspace{1cm}}$

$= \underline{\hspace{1cm}}$

4. $10 \times 3 \times 4 = \underline{\hspace{1cm}} \times (\underline{\hspace{1cm}} \times \underline{\hspace{1cm}})$

$= \underline{\hspace{1cm}} \times \underline{\hspace{1cm}}$

$= \underline{\hspace{1cm}}$

Name_____

Power Practice • Find each product.

5. $3 \times 2 \times 5 =$ _____   **6** $7 \times 2 \times 4 =$ _____   **7.** $3 \times 3 \times 8 =$ _____

8. $4 \times 3 \times 9 =$ _____   **9.** $5 \times 4 \times 5 =$ _____   **10.** $5 \times 9 \times 4 =$ _____

11. $4 \times 5 \times 7 =$ _____   **12.** $4 \times 6 \times 3 =$ _____   **13.** $8 \times 5 \times 2 =$ _____

14. $5 \times 8 \times 4 =$ _____   **15.** $7 \times 8 \times 3 =$ _____   **16.** $9 \times 3 \times 6 =$ _____

17. $20 \times 4 \times 8 =$ _____   **18.** $6 \times 4 \times 2 =$ _____   **19.** $3 \times 2 \times 10 =$ _____

20. $4 \times 6 \times 9 =$ _____   **21.** $11 \times 4 \times 10 =$ _____   **22.** $19 \times 4 \times 5 =$ _____

23. $9 \times 7 \times 3 =$ _____   **24.** $8 \times 12 \times 2 =$ _____   **25.** $12 \times 3 \times 4 =$ _____

26. $15 \times 4 \times 7 =$ _____   **27.** $11 \times 6 \times 5 =$ _____   **28.** $16 \times 3 \times 3 =$ _____

Exponents

Learn

A number that can be written as the product of equal factors is called a *power*.

$$5 \times 5 = 25$$

25 is the second power of 5.
You can write:

$$\text{power} \rightarrow 5 \times 5 = \overset{\text{base}}{\underset{\downarrow}{5}}{}^2 \leftarrow \text{exponent}$$

$$= 25 \leftarrow \text{standard form}$$

What Can I Do?

I want to use exponents to raise a number to a power

The exponent names the power of the base.
It shows how many times the factor is multiplied.

Other examples of powers:
$2^3 = 2 \times 2 \times 2 = 8$
$3^4 = 3 \times 3 \times 3 \times 3 = 81$
$6^1 = 6$

5^2 is "5 raised to the second power," or "5 squared."
2^3 is "2 raised to the third power," or "2 cubed."
3^4 is "3 raised to the fourth power."
6^1 is "6 to the first power."
A number to the first power is equal to itself.

Write the number 2^4 in standard form.

Use the Associative Property of Multiplication to multiply if the power has more than two factors. Then write the number in standard form.

$2^4 = 2 \times 2 \times 2 \times 2 = (2 \times 2) \times (2 \times 2) = 4 \times 4 = 16$

Try It • **Write each expression in standard form.**

1. $4^2 = $ _____ $\times\, 4 = $ _____

2. $6^3 = $ _____ $\times$ _____ $\times\, 6$

$= ($ _____ $\times$ _____ $) \times 6$

$= $ _____ $\times\, 6 = $ _____

3. $5^3 = $ _____ $\times\, 5 \times$ _____

$= $ _____ $\times (5 \times$ _____ $)$

$= $ _____ $\times$ _____ $= $ _____

4. $3^4 = $ _____ $\times$ _____ $\times$ _____ $\times$ _____

$= ($ _____ $\times$ _____ $) \times ($ _____ $\times$ _____ $)$

$= $ _____ $\times$ _____ $= $ _____

Name_____

Power Practice • Write each expression in standard form. Show your work.

5. $6^2 =$ _____

6. $4^3 =$ _____

7. $2^5 =$ _____

8. $5^4 =$ _____

9. $3^3 =$ _____

10. $7^2 =$ _____

11. $4^4 =$ _____

12. $2^3 =$ _____

13. $3^2 =$ _____

14. $8^2 =$ _____

15. $3^5 =$ _____

16. $2^6 =$ _____

17. $6^3 =$ _____

18. $9^2 =$ _____

19. $10^2 =$ _____

20. $3^6 =$ _____

21. $8^1 =$ _____

22. $4^5 =$ _____

23. $6^4 =$ _____

24. $1^4 =$ _____

25. $10^3 =$ _____

26. $7^3 =$ _____

27. $10^4 =$ _____

28. $2^7 =$ _____

Use Multiplication to Add and Subtract Fractions

You can use multiplication to find the sum or the difference of any two fractions.

Add: $\dfrac{3}{4} + \dfrac{1}{2}$

- First, find the cross products. To do this, multiply the numerator of each fraction by the denominator of the other fraction.

$$3 \times 2 = 6 \qquad 1 \times 4 = 4$$

- Write the sum of those products over the product of the two denominators. Simplify the fraction.

$$\frac{(3 \times 2) + (1 \times 4)}{4 \times 2} = \frac{6 + 4}{8} = \frac{10}{8}$$

- Simplify.

$$\frac{10}{8} = 1\frac{2}{8} = 1\frac{1}{4}$$

Subtract: $\dfrac{5}{6} - \dfrac{3}{4}$

- Again find the cross products.

$$5 \times 4 = 20 \qquad\qquad 6 \times 3 = 18$$

- Write the difference of those products over the product of the denominators.

$$\frac{(5 \times 4) - (6 \times 3)}{6 \times 4} = \frac{20 - 18}{24} = \frac{2}{24}$$

- Simplify.

$$\frac{2}{24} = \frac{1}{12}$$

Name_____

Use cross products to find each sum or difference.
Show your work.

1. $\dfrac{2}{8} + \dfrac{2}{3} =$ _____

2. $\dfrac{1}{4} + \dfrac{16}{25} =$ _____

3. $\dfrac{5}{6} - \dfrac{2}{5} =$ _____

4. $\dfrac{13}{15} - \dfrac{3}{4} =$ _____

5. $\dfrac{2}{3} + \dfrac{1}{5} =$ _____

6. $\dfrac{9}{10} - \dfrac{5}{8} =$ _____

7. $\dfrac{5}{9} + \dfrac{3}{7} =$ _____

8. $\dfrac{8}{9} - \dfrac{6}{7} =$ _____

9. $\dfrac{11}{12} - \dfrac{5}{6} =$ _____

10. $\dfrac{7}{12} - \dfrac{3}{8} =$ _____

11. $\dfrac{6}{7} - \dfrac{3}{5} =$ _____

12. $\dfrac{5}{9} + \dfrac{1}{10} =$ _____

13. $\dfrac{7}{8} - \dfrac{2}{9} =$ _____

14. $\dfrac{3}{14} + \dfrac{2}{5} =$ _____

Translations

A **translation**, or slide, of a geometric figure on a coordinate grid moves all the coordinates of the figure along the grid the same distance and direction. You can translate a figure on a coordinate grid by performing the same operation on each of the coordinates that are the figure's vertices, and then connecting them.

Translate figure *KLM* 8 units to the right.

You can solve this problem by adding 8 to the x-coordinate of each vertex.

1. By how much will you change each coordinate? _____

_____

2. The coordinates of the translated figure will be as follows. Plot each point on the same grid. Label the points K', L', M'.

   $K\,(^-6, \, ^-3) \rightarrow$ _____

   $L\,(^-1, ^-2) \rightarrow$ _____

   $M\,(^-4, \, ^-7) \rightarrow$ _____

3. Connect the translated points on the coordinate grid. Is the figure the same shape and size as the original figure? Explain.

_____

_____

Name_____

Translate figure *ABCD* 2 units to the right and 4 units up.

4. Since the translation is to the right 2 units and up 4 units, how will the *x*-coordinates change? How will the *y* coordinates change? _____

_____

5. Write the new coordinates. Then plot the points on the grid above. Label them *A′, B′, C′, D′.*

A (2, 0) → _____

B (3, 2) → _____

C (6, 2) → _____

D (5, 0) → _____

6. Connect the translated points on the coordinate grid. How does the new figure compare with the original?

_____

_____

Simplify Fractions

Learn

What Can I Do?
I want to simplify a fraction.

A fraction is in simplest form if the greatest common factor (GCF) of the numerator and the denominator is 1.

You can simplify $\frac{18}{24}$ in more than one way.

One Way

Divide the numerator and denominator by common factors until the GCF is 1.

$$\frac{18 \div 2}{24 \div 2} = \frac{9}{12}$$

$$\frac{9 \div 3}{12 \div 3} = \frac{3}{4}$$

Another Way

Find the GCF OF 18 and 24.

Factors of 18: 1, 2, 3, **6**, 9, 18
Factors of 24: 1, 2, 3, 4, **6**, 8, 12, 24

The GCF of 18 and 24 is 6.
Divide both numerator and denominator by GCF.

$$\frac{18 \div 6}{24 \div 6} = \frac{3}{4}$$

In simplest form, $\frac{18}{24} = \frac{3}{4}$.

Try It • Complete to simplify each fraction.

1. $\frac{16}{24} = \frac{16 \div}{24 \div 8} = \frac{2}{\underline{}}$

2. $\frac{25}{40} = \frac{25 \div}{40 \div 5} = \underline{}$

3. $\frac{12}{20} = \frac{12 \div}{20 \div} = \underline{} \frac{\underline{}}{\underline{}}$

4. $\frac{40}{50} = \frac{40 \div}{50 \div} = \underline{}$

5. $\frac{10}{12} = \underline{}$

6. $\frac{10}{20} = \underline{}$

7. $\frac{3}{5} = \underline{}$

8. $\frac{9}{24} = \underline{}$

9. $\frac{5}{6} = \underline{}$

10. $\frac{2}{8} = \underline{}$

Power Practice • Simplify each fraction.

11. $\frac{14}{16}$ = $\underline{}$

12. $\frac{15}{20}$ = $\underline{}$

13. $\frac{10}{16}$ = $\underline{}$

14. $\frac{5}{12}$ = $\underline{}$

15. $\frac{7}{14}$ = $\underline{}$

16. $\frac{8}{10}$ = $\underline{}$

17. $\frac{20}{30}$ = $\underline{}$

18. $\frac{12}{21}$ = $\underline{}$

19. $\frac{8}{12}$ = $\underline{}$

20. $\frac{10}{25}$ = $\underline{}$

21. $\frac{3}{18}$ = $\underline{}$

22. $\frac{3}{7}$ = $\underline{}$

23. $\frac{6}{10}$ = $\underline{}$

24. $\frac{15}{25}$ = $\underline{}$

25. $\frac{4}{16}$ = $\underline{}$

26. $\frac{5}{10}$ = $\underline{}$

27. $\frac{10}{35}$ = $\underline{}$

28. $\frac{14}{21}$ = $\underline{}$

29. $\frac{9}{27}$ = $\underline{}$

30. $\frac{17}{40}$ = $\underline{}$

31. $\frac{4}{10}$ = $\underline{}$

32. $\frac{5}{60}$ = $\underline{}$

33. $\frac{32}{80}$ = $\underline{}$

34. $\frac{34}{68}$ = $\underline{}$

35. $\frac{3}{24}$ = $\underline{}$

36. $\frac{25}{30}$ = $\underline{}$

37. $\frac{20}{25}$ = $\underline{}$

38. $\frac{8}{40}$ = $\underline{}$

39. $\frac{12}{16}$ = $\underline{}$

40. $\frac{25}{45}$ = $\underline{}$

Equivalent Fractions

Learn

What Can I Do?
I want to write equivalent fractions

Write a fraction equivalent to $\frac{2}{3}$.

- You can draw a picture to find an equivalent fraction.

$\frac{2}{3}$ = $\frac{8}{12}$

- You can multiply the numerator and denominator by the same number.

$$\frac{2 \times 2}{3 \times 2} = \frac{4}{6} \qquad \frac{2}{3} = \frac{4}{6}$$

- You can divide the numerator and denominator by the same number.

$$\frac{6 \div 3}{9 \div 3} = \frac{2}{3} \qquad \frac{6}{9} = \frac{2}{3}$$

$\frac{2}{3}$ is equivalent to $\frac{8}{12}$, $\frac{4}{6}$, and $\frac{6}{9}$.

Try It • Write an equivalent fraction that has the denominator shown.

1. $\frac{1}{6} = \frac{}{18}$

2. $\frac{1}{2} = \frac{}{14}$

3. $\frac{3}{4} = \frac{}{12}$

4. $\frac{1}{3} = \frac{}{30}$

5. $\frac{2}{5} = \frac{}{20}$

6. $\frac{5}{8} = \frac{}{40}$

7. $\frac{5}{6} = \frac{}{18}$

8. $\frac{3}{3} = \frac{}{15}$

9. $\frac{2}{3} = \frac{}{27}$

Power Practice • Write an equivalent fraction that has the denominator shown.

10. $\frac{3}{5} = \frac{}{15}$

11. $\frac{3}{4} = \frac{}{20}$

12. $\frac{5}{1} = \frac{}{3}$

13. $\frac{2}{6} = \frac{}{3}$

14. $\frac{8}{16} = \frac{}{2}$

15. $\frac{3}{24} = \frac{}{8}$

16. $\frac{15}{25} = \frac{}{5}$

17. $\frac{6}{10} = \frac{}{5}$

18. $\frac{28}{36} = \frac{}{9}$

Write a fraction equivalent to the given fraction.

19. $\frac{4}{6} = $ _____

20. $\frac{3}{20} = $ _____

21. $\frac{3}{12} = $ _____

22. $\frac{7}{8} = $ _____

23. $\frac{4}{5} = $ _____

24. $\frac{3}{7} = $ _____

25. $\frac{9}{10} = $ _____

26. $\frac{9}{18} = $ _____

27. $\frac{8}{12} = $ _____

28. $\frac{4}{9} = $ _____

29. $\frac{1}{2} = $ _____

30. $\frac{4}{10} = $ _____

31. $\frac{2}{9} = $ _____

32. $\frac{6}{8} = $ _____

33. $\frac{5}{6} = $ _____

34. $\frac{4}{22} = $ _____

35. $\frac{16}{56} = $ _____

36. $\frac{18}{36} = $ _____

L e a r n   w i t h
Partners & Parents

Fraction Model Roundup

You and your partner need one set of fraction models.

• Place the fraction models face up on a flat surface.

• Pick one fraction model. You have two minutes to find as many models as possible with the same amount shaded.

• Write the fraction for each fraction model for which you find a match.

• Now your partner takes a turn.

Solving Equations

Learn

What Can I Do?
I want to solve an
equation.

You can use an inverse operation to solve an equation.

Multiplication and division are inverse operations. They undo each other.

To solve an equation, use inverse operations to find the value of the variable that will make the equation true.

Multiplication Equation		**Division Equation**	
$2n = 16$	n multiplied by 2	$n \div 6 = 36$	n divided by 6
$\dfrac{2n}{2} = \dfrac{16}{2}$	Divide each side by 2 to get the variable alone on one side of the equation.	$6 \times (n \div 6) = 6 \times 36$	Multiply each side by 6.
$n = 8$	Simplify.	$n = 216$	Simplify.

Try It • **Which inverse operation is needed to solve the equation?**

1. $6y = 18$

2. $y \div 6 = 18$

3. $6 = 18y$

_____   _____   _____

Solve the equation.

4. $8m = 64$

$\dfrac{8m}{8} = \dfrac{64}{8}$

$m =$ _____

5. $\dfrac{w}{9} = 18$

$9 \times \dfrac{w}{9} =$ ___ $\times 18$

$w =$ _____

6. $9y = 90$

$\dfrac{9y}{9} = \dfrac{90}{9}$

$y =$ _____

Power Practice • Solve the equation.

7. $144 = 12x$

_____

8. $150 = \dfrac{x}{25}$

_____

9. $19a = 152$

_____

10. $5c = 85$

_____

11. $12x = 156$

_____

12. $84 = 3t$

_____

13. $\dfrac{w}{7} = 12$

_____

14. $\dfrac{p}{3} = 9$

_____

15. $8 = \dfrac{m}{4}$

_____

16. $8h = 96$

_____

17. $35r = 245$

_____

18. $88a = 792$

_____

19. $\dfrac{b}{20} = 40$

_____

20. $\dfrac{f}{56} = 4$

_____

21. $3 = \dfrac{x}{13}$

_____

22. $12x = 36$

_____

23. $\dfrac{y}{81} = 3$

_____

24. $24 = 2z$

_____

25. $3n = 72$

_____

26. $\dfrac{n}{12} = 121$

_____

27. $5 = \dfrac{m}{25}$

_____

28. $11t = 88$

_____

29. $\dfrac{s}{7} = 8$

_____

30. $\dfrac{s}{8} = 13$

_____

31. $7u = 35$

_____

32. $16x = 48$

_____

33. $15p = 105$

_____

34. $7j = 84$

_____

35. $\dfrac{t}{5} = 7$

_____

36. $\dfrac{m}{12} = 3$

_____

Name_____

CHAPTER

Skill Builder 12

Least Common Denominator

Learn

Find the least common denominator (LCD) for $\frac{1}{3}$ and $\frac{3}{4}$.

The denominator of $\frac{1}{3}$ is 3.

The denominator of $\frac{3}{4}$ is 4.

The *least common denominator* of two or more fractions is the least number that is a common multiple of the denominators.

What Can I Do?
I want to find the least common denominator for two or more fractions.

The least common multiple of 3 and 4 will be the least common denominator of $\frac{1}{3}$ and $\frac{3}{4}$.

Some multiples of 3: 3, 6, 9, **12**, 15, 18, 21, **24**
Some multiples of 4: 4, 8, **12**, 16, 20, **24**

12 and 24 are both multiples of 3 and 4. 12 is the lesser number.

So, the LCD of $\frac{1}{3}$ and $\frac{3}{4}$ is 12.

Try It • **Find the least common denominator (LCD) for $\frac{3}{5}$ and $\frac{1}{4}$.**

1. List some multiples of 5. _____

2. List some multiples of 4. _____

3. Which numbers are multiples of both 5 and 4? _____

4. What is the least common multiple of 5 and 4? _____

5. What is the LCD for $\frac{3}{5}$ and $\frac{1}{4}$? _____

Name_____

Power Practice • Find the LCD for each pair of fractions.

6. $\frac{1}{3}$; $\frac{1}{5}$ _____   **7.** $\frac{3}{4}$; $\frac{2}{5}$ _____   **8.** $\frac{5}{6}$; $\frac{1}{7}$ _____

9. $\frac{1}{8}$; $\frac{5}{12}$ _____   **10.** $\frac{4}{5}$; $\frac{1}{2}$ _____   **11.** $\frac{2}{3}$; $\frac{4}{7}$ _____

12. $\frac{5}{6}$; $\frac{2}{9}$ _____   **13.** $\frac{3}{4}$; $\frac{1}{8}$ _____   **14.** $\frac{1}{7}$; $\frac{1}{5}$ _____

15. $\frac{2}{3}$; $\frac{1}{10}$ _____   **16.** $\frac{1}{2}$; $\frac{1}{4}$ _____   **17.** $\frac{5}{8}$; $\frac{2}{3}$ _____

18. $\frac{5}{6}$; $\frac{3}{10}$ _____   **19.** $\frac{3}{4}$; $\frac{1}{10}$ _____   **20.** $\frac{2}{3}$; $\frac{4}{9}$ _____

21. $\frac{3}{8}$; $\frac{7}{12}$ _____   **22.** $\frac{3}{7}$; $\frac{4}{5}$ _____   **23.** $\frac{2}{3}$; $\frac{1}{4}$ _____

24. $\frac{3}{5}$; $\frac{2}{12}$ _____   **25.** $\frac{1}{6}$; $\frac{3}{8}$ _____   **26.** $\frac{1}{3}$; $\frac{2}{7}$ _____

27. $\frac{3}{5}$; $\frac{1}{2}$ _____   **28.** $\frac{2}{3}$; $\frac{3}{5}$ _____   **29.** $\frac{3}{7}$; $\frac{3}{14}$ _____

30. $\frac{5}{12}$; $\frac{1}{4}$ _____   **31.** $\frac{1}{3}$; $\frac{2}{9}$ _____   **32.** $\frac{1}{4}$; $\frac{3}{10}$ _____

33. $\frac{4}{9}$; $\frac{5}{12}$ _____   **34.** $\frac{3}{8}$; $\frac{5}{12}$ _____   **35.** $\frac{9}{12}$; $\frac{3}{9}$ _____

36. $\frac{3}{5}$; $\frac{3}{8}$ _____   **37.** $\frac{2}{3}$; $\frac{1}{12}$ _____   **38.** $\frac{2}{7}$; $\frac{1}{8}$ _____

39. $\frac{1}{6}$; $\frac{4}{9}$ _____   **40.** $\frac{1}{4}$; $\frac{3}{9}$ _____   **41.** $\frac{2}{6}$; $\frac{1}{8}$ _____

Measure Angles

Learn

An angle is measured in degrees (°). You can use a protractor to measure the size of an angle in degrees.

• Measure the angle shown. Place the center mark of the bottom edge of the protractor at the vertex of the angle. Be sure that one side of the angle goes through the 0° mark of the protractor.

What Can I Do?
I want to measure an angle.

Read the measure where the other side of the angle intersects the protractor.

∠ABC has a measure of 65°.

Try It • Estimate the measure of each angle. Then measure each with a protractor.

1.

_____

2.

_____

3.
G

H ——————> I

_____

Power Practice • Use a protractor to find the measure of each angle.

4.

_____

5.

_____

6.

_____

Measure Length

Learn

What Can I Do?
I want to measure length with a centimeter ruler.

The **meter (m)** is the basic unit of length in the metric system. A **centimeter (cm)** is $\frac{1}{100}$ of a meter. Centimeters are divided into tenths of a centimeter, or millimeters. A **millimeter (mm)** is $\frac{1}{1000}$ of a meter. You can measure length in centimeters or in millimeters.

To measure the length of a line segment, align the zero mark on the ruler with the left end of the line segment. Then, read the length at the other end of the segment.

You can read the measure of the line segment to the nearest tenth of a centimeter, or in millimeters.

The line segment measures 7.5 cm, or 75 mm.

Try It • Use a centimeter ruler. Measure the length of each line segment in centimeters and then in millimeters.

1. •———————————•   2. •———————•

_____   _____

Power Practice • Use a centimeter ruler. Measure the length of each line segment in centimeters and then in millimeters.

3. •———————————•   4. •————————•

_____   _____

5. •———————————•   6. •————————•

_____   _____

Name_____

Multiply Fractions and Mixed Numbers

Learn

You can multiply fractions by writing the product of the numerators over the product of the denominators. To multiply mixed numbers, first write the mixed numbers as improper fractions. Then multiply as you would for fractions.

What Can I Do?
I want to multiply fractions and mixed numbers.

Multiply: $\frac{4}{7}$ and $\frac{1}{4}$

• Multiply the numerators. Then multiply the denominators.

$$\frac{4}{7} \times \frac{1}{4} = \frac{4}{28}$$

• Simplify.

$$\frac{4}{28} = \frac{1}{7}$$

Multiply: $1\frac{1}{2} \times 3\frac{1}{2}$

• Write each mixed number as an improper fraction.

$$1\frac{1}{2} \quad \times \quad 3\frac{1}{2}$$
$$\downarrow \qquad\qquad \downarrow$$
$$\frac{3}{2} \quad \times \quad \frac{7}{2}$$

• Multiply the numerators. Then multiply the denominators.

$$\frac{3}{2} \times \frac{7}{2} = \frac{21}{4}$$

• Simplify.

$$\frac{21}{4} = 5\frac{1}{4}$$

Try It • **Complete to find each product. Write your answer in simplest form.**

Multiply: $\frac{3}{5} \times \frac{7}{12}$

1. Multiply numerators and denominators. $\frac{3}{} \times \frac{7}{} = \frac{21}{}$

2. Simplify. $\frac{21}{} = —$

Multiply: $1\frac{3}{4} \times 2\frac{1}{2}$

3. Write each mixed number as an improper fraction.

$1\frac{3}{4} = $ _____ $2\frac{1}{2} = $ _____

4. Multiply numerators and denominators. _____ × _____ = _____

5. Simplify. _____

Power Practice • Find each product.
Write your answer in simplest form.

6. $5\frac{1}{2} \times \frac{1}{2}$ _____

7. $\frac{2}{3} \times \frac{9}{10}$ _____

8. $\frac{1}{4} \times \frac{3}{5}$ _____

9. $8\frac{1}{4} \times \frac{1}{2}$ _____

10. $\frac{5}{6} \times \frac{2}{3}$ _____

11. $\frac{5}{8} \times \frac{1}{9}$ _____

12. $\frac{1}{2} \times \frac{4}{13}$ _____

13. $\frac{1}{3} \times \frac{2}{7}$ _____

14. $1\frac{13}{15} \times \frac{1}{4}$ _____

15. $2\frac{1}{4} \times \frac{4}{5}$ _____

16. $\frac{1}{11} \times \frac{2}{5}$ _____

17. $\frac{7}{9} \times \frac{2}{11}$ _____

18. $\frac{3}{4} \times \frac{1}{2}$ _____

19. $\frac{1}{2} \times \frac{14}{15}$ _____

20. $\frac{1}{5} \times \frac{5}{8}$ _____

21. $1\frac{1}{15} \times \frac{1}{20}$ _____

22. $\frac{8}{9} \times \frac{2}{7}$ _____

23. $\frac{7}{8} \times \frac{11}{14}$ _____

24. $1\frac{1}{2} \times \frac{5}{6}$ _____

25. $\frac{3}{4} \times \frac{1}{3}$ _____

26. $\frac{1}{2} \times 1\frac{7}{8}$ _____

27. $\frac{10}{11} \times \frac{5}{6}$ _____

28. $1\frac{1}{5} \times \frac{1}{2}$ _____

29. $\frac{3}{10} \times 2\frac{1}{2}$ _____

30. $\frac{12}{13} \times \frac{3}{10}$ _____

31. $\frac{2}{3} \times 1\frac{1}{3}$ _____

32. $1\frac{2}{3} \times \frac{7}{9}$ _____

33. $\frac{5}{6} \times 3\frac{7}{10}$ _____

34. $\frac{1}{6} \times \frac{2}{7}$ _____

35. $\frac{3}{5} \times \frac{7}{11}$ _____

36. $\frac{1}{2} \times \frac{9}{13}$ _____

37. $\frac{2}{3} \times \frac{3}{5}$ _____

38. $\frac{3}{7} \times \frac{1}{18}$ _____

39. $4\frac{1}{6} \times 2\frac{2}{5}$ _____

40. $3\frac{4}{9} \times 1\frac{2}{7}$ _____

41. $1\frac{1}{2} \times 3\frac{2}{3}$ _____

Writing Fractions

Use the numbers in the box to write fractions.

```
        3        1              6

    2        8        10           12

        4           5          7
```

1. Write a fraction equivalent to $\frac{1}{3}$. _____

2. How do you know that this fraction is not in simplest form?

_____

_____

3. Write 4 fractions greater than $\frac{1}{4}$ but less than 1.

_____

4. Which is the greatest fraction you can write that is greater than $\frac{1}{4}$ but less than 1? How do you know?

_____

_____

5. Write another fraction using any two-digit numbers you choose. The fraction should be greater than the fraction you wrote fro question 4 and less than 1.

_____

Use the numbers in the box to write fractions for questions 6–11

1	12	15	6
3	9	7	4
5	2	10	8

6. Use 7 as the numerator. Use other number(s) in the box to write the greatest fraction you can. Explain how you know it is the greatest fraction.

_____

_____

7. Use 8 as the numerator. Use other number(s) in the box, including 8, to write the least fraction you can with a three-digit denominator. All three digits in the denominator should be different. Explain how you know it is the least fraction.

_____

_____

_____

8. Write 4 fractions that are greater than $\frac{1}{6}$ but less than $\frac{3}{4}$.

_____

9. Write 4 fractions that are greater than $\frac{1}{5}$ but less than 1

_____

10. Write 2 fractions that are greater than $\frac{1}{3}$ but less than $\frac{3}{4}$.

_____

11. Write 3 fractions that are greater than $\frac{2}{3}$ but less than 1.

_____

Patterns in Graphs of Fractions

How do you graph a fraction? One way is to plot the numerator as an x-value and the denominator as y-value on a coordinate grid.

1. Plot the fraction $\frac{1}{3}$ on the graph. Use the coordinates (1,3).
Move one space to the right on the x–axis. Move three spaces up.
Plot the point.

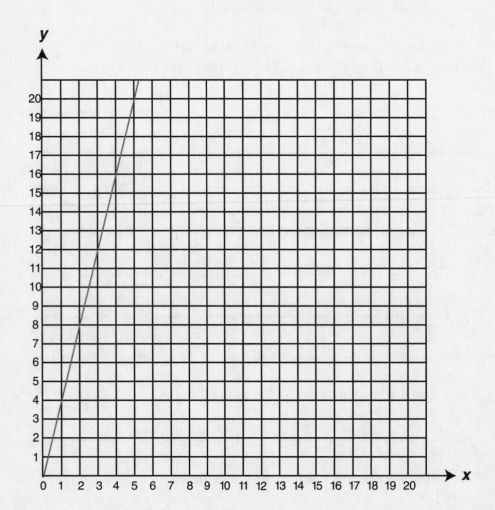

2. Write four fractions that are equivalent to $\frac{1}{3}$. _____

3. Plot those equivalent fractions.

4. Connect the points. Describe the pattern that the graph makes.

_____

_____

5. Write four fractions equivalent to $\frac{1}{2}$. _____

6. Plot the fractions on the frid you used for the other fractions.
Then connect the points.

7. What do you notice about the two graphs.

_____

_____

8. Write four fractions equivalent to $\frac{1}{4}$. _____

9. Plot the fraction on the same grid. Then connect the points.

10. What do you notice about the three graphs?

_____

_____

Writing Ratios

 Learn

A **ratio** is a pair of numbers used to compare two quantities. The order in which you show the numbers is important.

What Can I Do?
I want to compare two quantities using a ratio.

• You can find the ratio of comparing the number of hearts to the number of squares. There are 2 hearts to 3 squares. You can write the ratio as

2:3 or $\frac{2}{3}$

♥ ♥   ☐ ☐ ☐
    2   **3**

• Write the ratio of the number of triangles to the total number of figures.

• The ratio of triangles to the total number of figures is 2:6 or $\frac{2}{6}$. In simplest form, the ratio is 1:3 or $\frac{1}{3}$.

▲ ▲   ○ ○ ○ ○

Try It • Give the ratio of the figures described in two ways. Write the ratio as a fraction in simplest form when possible.

◆   ♡ ♡

1. diamonds to hearts

   1:2 or _____

2. hearts to the total number of figures

   _____ or $\frac{2}{3}$

● ● ●   ☐ ☐ ☐ ☐ ☐

3. circles to squares

   3:5 or ___

4. squares to the total number of figures

   _____ or ___

Power Practice

Give ratio of the figures described in two ways. Write the ratio as a fraction in simplest form when possible.

5. circles to triangles _____

6. triangles to the total number of figures _____

7. squares to triangles _____

8. triangles to the total number of figures _____

Give the ratio of shaded parts to the total number of parts. Use a fraction. Write the fraction in lowest terms.

9. _____

10. _____

11. _____

12. _____

13. _____

14. _____

Solve Proportions

Learn

What Can I Do?

I want to solve a proportion.

A **proportion** is an equation showing that two ratios are equal.

$$\frac{6}{8} = \frac{3}{4}$$

In a proportion, the *cross products* are equal.

$$\frac{6}{8} \diagdown\!\!\!= \!\!\!\diagup \frac{3}{4}$$

$$6 \times 4 = 8 \times 3$$
$$24 = 24$$

You can use cross products to solve a proportion.

• Solve: $\frac{4}{8} = \frac{3}{z}$.

Find the cross products. $4 \times z = 8 \times 3$

Solve the equation by using division to undo the multiplication. $\frac{4z}{4} = \frac{24}{4}$

$$z = 6$$

Try It • Solve each proportion.

1. $\frac{6}{10} = \frac{x}{20}$

    $10x = \underline{120}$

    $x = \underline{12}$

2. $\frac{5}{g} = \frac{6}{36}$

    $6g = \underline{180}$

    $g = \underline{30}$

3. $\frac{1}{4} = \frac{b}{12}$

    $\underline{4b} = \underline{12}$

    $b = \underline{3}$

4. $\frac{3}{d} = \frac{18}{27}$

    $\underline{18d} = \underline{54}$

    $d = \underline{3}$

Power Practice • Solve each proportion.

5. $\dfrac{u}{5} = \dfrac{6}{3}$

$u = 10$

6. $\dfrac{2}{8} = \dfrac{t}{20}$

$t = 5$

7. $\dfrac{15}{5} = \dfrac{6}{b}$

$b = 2$

8. $\dfrac{2}{k} = \dfrac{3}{6}$

$k = 4$

9. $\dfrac{12}{a} = \dfrac{16}{20}$

$a = 10$

10. $\dfrac{30}{a} = \dfrac{20}{18}$

11. $\dfrac{m}{8} = \dfrac{12}{16}$

12. $\dfrac{40}{y} = \dfrac{16}{2}$

13. $\dfrac{4}{9} = \dfrac{g}{45}$

14. $\dfrac{s}{28} = \dfrac{10}{7}$

15. $\dfrac{4}{5} = \dfrac{8}{d}$

16. $\dfrac{15}{5} = \dfrac{12}{c}$

17. $\dfrac{4}{7} = \dfrac{h}{56}$

18. $\dfrac{45}{x} = \dfrac{18}{8}$

19. $\dfrac{30}{3} = \dfrac{j}{2}$

20. $\dfrac{3}{r} = \dfrac{2}{8}$

21. $\dfrac{20}{8} = \dfrac{y}{2}$

22. $\dfrac{2}{20} = \dfrac{z}{10}$

23. $\dfrac{20}{d} = \dfrac{4}{5}$

24. $\dfrac{4}{x} = \dfrac{2}{7}$

25. $\dfrac{z}{10} = \dfrac{18}{6}$

26. $\dfrac{2}{3} = \dfrac{b}{6}$

27. $\dfrac{y}{2} = \dfrac{6}{4}$

28. $\dfrac{2}{5} = \dfrac{4}{n}$

29. $\dfrac{10}{m} = \dfrac{8}{4}$

30. $\dfrac{27}{6} = \dfrac{j}{8}$

31. $\dfrac{g}{35} = \dfrac{8}{7}$

32. $\dfrac{8}{36} = \dfrac{p}{9}$

33. $\dfrac{7}{8} = \dfrac{28}{r}$

34. $\dfrac{t}{24} = \dfrac{3}{8}$

Write Equivalent Fractions with a Denominator of 100

Learn

What Can I Do?
I want to write an equivalent fraction with a denominator of 100.

You can write and solve a proportion to find an equivalent fraction with a denominator of 100.

Find an equivalent fraction for $\frac{2}{5}$ with a denominator of 100.

$$\frac{2}{5} = \frac{n}{100}$$
Set up a proportion with 100 as the denominator for the equivalent fraction.

$$5 \times n = 2 \times 100$$ Write the cross products.
$$5n = 200$$ Multiply.
$$\frac{5n}{5} = \frac{200}{5}$$ Use division to undo the multiplication.

$$n = 40$$

So, $\frac{2}{5} = \frac{40}{100}$

Try It • Find an equivalent fraction with a denominator of 100.

1. $\frac{1}{2}$

$$\frac{1}{2} = \frac{n}{100}$$

$$\underline{\hspace{2cm}} = 100$$

$$\frac{2n}{} = \frac{100}{}$$

$$n = \underline{\hspace{1cm}}$$

So, $\frac{1}{2} = \underline{\hspace{2cm}}$

2. $\frac{3}{5}$

$$\frac{3}{5} = \frac{n}{5}$$

$$5n = \underline{\hspace{1.5cm}}$$

$$\frac{5n}{5} = \frac{}{5}$$

$$n = \underline{\hspace{1cm}}$$

So, $\frac{3}{5} = \underline{\hspace{2cm}}$

Power Practice • Find an equivalent fraction with a denominator of 100.

3. $\frac{3}{20} = \underline{\hspace{1.5cm}}$

4. $\frac{8}{25} = \underline{\hspace{1.5cm}}$

5. $\frac{4}{5} = \underline{\hspace{1.5cm}}$

6. $\frac{6}{50} = \underline{\hspace{1.5cm}}$

7. $\frac{8}{20} = \underline{\hspace{1.5cm}}$

8. $\frac{7}{25} = \underline{\hspace{1.5cm}}$

Write Decimals as Percents

Learn

Decimals can be expressed as percents.
A percent is a part of a hundred.

Express 0.75 as a percent. Think: 0.75 is 75 hundredths,
or 75%.

Express 0.7 as a percent. Think: 0.7 = 0.70 = 70 hundredths.
70 hundredths is 70%.

What Can I Do?

I want to write a
decimal as a
percent.

You can also multiply a decimal by 100 to express it
as a percent.

$0.75 \times 100 = 0.75$
$= 75\%$

The decimal point moves
2 places to the right.

$0.7 \times 100 = 0.70$
$= 70\%$

Try It • Write each decimal as a percent.

1. 0.29

0.29 × _____

= _____ = _____%

2. 0.13

0.13 × _____

= _____ = _____

3. 0.55

_____ × _____

= _____ = _____

4. To change a decimal to a percent, multiply the decimal by _____ and write
the % sign.

Power Practice • Write each decimal as a percent.

5. 0.44 = _____

6. 0.66 = _____

7. 0.50 = _____

8. 0.90 = _____

9. 0.35 = _____

10. 0.88 = _____

11. 1.47 = _____

12. 3.75 = _____

13. 0.005 = _____

Write Fractions as Percents

Learn

What Can I Do?
I want to write a fraction as a percent.

A percent is part of a hundred.

- A fraction with a denominator of 100 can be written as a percent.

$$\frac{14}{100} = 14\%$$

- Write $\frac{7}{25}$ as a percent.

Write an equivalent fraction with a denominator of 100. Then write the fraction as a percent.

$$\frac{7}{25} = \frac{28}{100} = 28\%$$

Try It • Express each fraction as a percent.

1. $\frac{15}{100}$ = _____

2. $\frac{32}{100}$ = _____

3. $\frac{67}{100}$ = _____

4. $\frac{9}{20}$ = $\frac{}{100}$

5. $\frac{8}{25}$ = $\frac{}{100}$

6. $\frac{7}{10}$ = $\frac{}{100}$

= _____

= _____

= _____

Power Practice • Write each fraction as a percent.

7. $\frac{27}{100}$ = _____

8. $\frac{41}{100}$ = _____

9. $\frac{95}{100}$ = _____

10. $\frac{6}{100}$ = _____

11. $\frac{29}{100}$ = _____

12. $\frac{15}{100}$ = _____

13. $\frac{11}{50}$ = $\frac{}{100}$

14. $\frac{16}{20}$ = $\frac{}{100}$

15. $\frac{12}{25}$ = $\frac{}{100}$

= _____

= _____

= _____

16. $\frac{16}{25} = \frac{}{100}$

= _____

17. $\frac{41}{50} = \frac{}{100}$

= _____

18. $\frac{11}{25} = \frac{}{100}$

= _____

19. $\frac{13}{50} = \frac{}{100}$

= _____

20. $\frac{3}{25} = \frac{}{100}$

= _____

21. $\frac{21}{50} = \frac{}{100}$

= _____

22. $\frac{7}{25} = \frac{}{100}$

= _____

23. $\frac{9}{50} = \frac{}{100}$

= _____

24. $\frac{13}{25} = \frac{}{100}$

= _____

25. $\frac{3}{4} = \frac{}{100}$

= _____

26. $\frac{9}{10} = \frac{}{100}$

= _____

27. $\frac{2}{5} = \frac{}{100}$

= _____

28. $\frac{1}{4} = \frac{}{100}$

= _____

29. $\frac{3}{10} = \frac{}{100}$

= _____

30. $\frac{4}{5} = \frac{}{100}$

= _____

L e a r n   w i t h
Partners & Parents

Guess My Percent

- To play the game, students work in pairs, each taking turns being the Game Master who selects a secret percent and writes it on a slip of paper. It must be a whole number percent between 1% and 100%. The other player must name the secret percent.

- The Game Master gives a fraction as a clue for the player, for example, "My percent equals $\frac{3}{25}$."

- The player gets one chance. If the percent name is correct, the player gets 1 point and becomes Game Master. If not, the Game Master gets 1 point and continues.

- Have pairs switch roles several times. The player with the most points wins.

Name_____

Read and Interpret a Bar Graph

Learn

A **bar graph** is a way to show data.
In a bar graph, horizontal or vertical bars are used to compare quantities. Study the bar graph below.

What Can I Do?
I want to read and interpret a bar graph.

Favorite Types of Music

Scale

Bar

- What type of music received exactly 10 votes? Find the number 10 on the vertical scale and locate the bar that ends at that number. Jazz music received exactly 10 votes.

Try It • Use the bar graph above to answer each question.

1. Which type of music received the fewest votes? _____

2. Which type received 19 votes? _____

3. Which type received about half that number of votes?

_____

4. Each person could vote for only one type of music. How many people in all were

surveyed? _____

Name_____

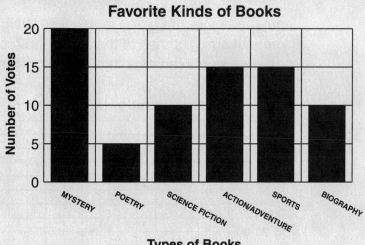

Power Practice • Use the bar graph to answer each question.

Favorite Kinds of Books

Number of Votes

20
15
10
5
0

MYSTERY · POETRY · SCIENCE FICTION · ACTION/ADVENTURE · SPORTS · BIOGRAPHY

Types of Books

5. How many people chose sports books as their favorite? _____

6. Which kind of book received the most votes? _____

7. Which kind of book received the fewest votes? _____

8. Do more people like sports books or science fiction books?
How do you know?

_____

_____

9. Which types of books received the same number of votes?

_____

_____

10. Which types of books received fewer than 12 votes?

_____

11. If each person surveyed chose only one kind of book, how many people were

surveyed? _____

Read and Interpret a Line Graph

Learn

A **line graph** shows change over time.

Janet made this line graph to show her height from birth to 8 years of age. The rise of the line in the graph shows that her height increased over that period of time.

What Can I Do?
I want to read a line graph.

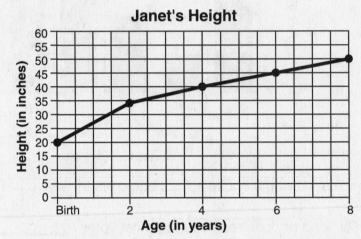

Janet's Height

About how tall was Janet when she was 2 years old?

To find the answer, locate the 2-year mark on the horizontal axis of the graph. Read up to the point on the graph. Then trace left to the vertical axis. Read the number.

Janet was about 34 inches tall when she was 2 years old.

Try It • Use the line graph above to answer each question.

1. What was Janet's height at birth? _____

2. How tall was Janet when she was 4 years old? _____

3. How many inches did Janet grow between ages 4 and 8? _____

4. Between which ages did Janet grow the most? _____

Name_____

A hot tub holds many gallons of water. Cold water is put into the tub and warmed slowly. This graph shows how long it will take the water to reach a temperature of 100 degrees Fahrenheit. A temperature warmer than that would be too hot.

5. What was the water temperature at 10:00 A.M.? _____

6. At what time did the water reach a temperature of about 74°?

_____

7. How many degrees warmer was the water at 12:00 P.M. than it had been at 10:00 A.M.? _____

8. What was the change in water temperature between 12:00 P.M. and 2:00 P.M.?

_____

9. At what time was the water about 92°? _____

10. When did the water reach 100°? _____

11. What happened to the water temperature between 6:00 P.M. and 8:00 P.M.?

_____

12. What happened to the water temperature between 8:00 P.M. and 10:00 P.M.?

_____

Addition and Subtraction Equations Skill Builder

Learn

What Can I Do?
I want to solve addition and subtraction equations.

You can add or subtract the same number from each side of an equation and the equation will still be true.

Solve: $x + 48 = 92$

Since 48 is added to x, you can isolate x by subtracting 48.

$x + 48 - 48 = 92 - 48$
$x = 44$

Subtract 48 from each side.

Solve: $y - 12 = 32$

Since 12 is subtracted from y, you can isolate y by adding 12.

$y - 12 + 12 = 32 + 12$
$y = 44$

Add 12 to each side.

Try It • Solve each equation.

1. $x - 17 = 48$

$x - 17 +$ _____ $=$ _____ $+ 17$

$x =$ _____

2. $y + 18 = 51$

$y + 18 -$ _____ $= 51 -$ _____

$y =$ _____

Power Practice • Solve each equation.

3. $x - 47 = 78$

_____

4. $y + 34.9 = 72.6$

_____

5. $w - 14.3 = 7.1$

_____

6. $z + 673 = 800$

_____

7. $13.65 = r + 8.9$

_____

8. $c - 67 = 435$

_____

9. $v + 93 = 281$

_____

10. $h + 4\frac{3}{5} = 12\frac{1}{5}$

_____

11. $6\frac{1}{3} = j - \frac{1}{2}$

_____

Multiplication and Division Equations

Learn

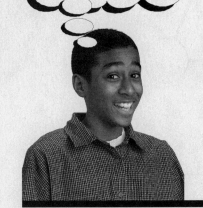

What Can I Do?
I want to solve multiplication and division equations.

You can multiply or divide both sides of an equation by the same number and the two sides will remain equal.

Solve: $\dfrac{k}{45} = 36$

$\dfrac{k}{45} \times 45 = 36 \times 45$
$k = 1{,}620$

Since k is divided by 45, we can get k alone by multiplying.
Multiply both sides of the equation by 45.

Solve: $12m = 48$

$\dfrac{12m}{12} = \dfrac{48}{12}$
$m = 4$

Since m is multiplied by 12, we can get m alone by dividing.
Divide both sides of the equation by 12.

Try It • Solve each equation.

1. $21y = 63$

$\dfrac{21y}{} = \dfrac{}{21}$

$y = \underline{}$

2. $\dfrac{r}{7.5} = 52$

$\dfrac{r}{7.5} \times \underline{} = \underline{} \times \underline{}$

$r = \underline{}$

Power Practice • Solve each equation.

3. $7f = 49$

4. $\dfrac{v}{3} = 13$

5. $34n = 170$

6. $8h = 5.04$

7. $34k = 272$

8. $24a = 96$

9. $15b = 135$

10. $\dfrac{m}{4} = 5.6$

11. $\dfrac{q}{2.3} = 7$

12. $\dfrac{x}{7} = 4.1$

13. $2.5y = 10$

14. $\dfrac{z}{8} = 3.2$

Number Fun

How can you arrange the counting
numbers from 1 to 6 in the circles at
the right so that the sum of the numbers
along each side of the triangle is 10?

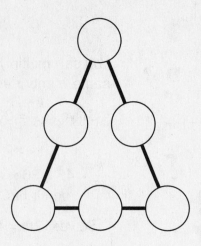

1. What are the three ways to obtain the sum of 10?

_____

2. Which numbers appear in two of these sums? _____

3. In which circles should you place those numbers? Explain.

_____

_____

4. Arrange the numbers in the circles above. How many different arrangements can you

find? _____

5. Arrange the counting numbers from 1 to 7 in the circles below so that the sum of the
numbers along each line is 10.

Name_____

6. Solve each equation.

    a. $g + 1.8 = 4.2$ _____   **b.** $h - 0.5 = 9.7$ _____

    c. $5.9 + k = 6.8$ _____   **d.** $m + 1.819 = 6.519$ _____

    e. $15.1 - r = 8.9$ _____   **f.** $s - 2.5 = 0.4$ _____

    g. $10.2 - t = 3.5$ _____   **h.** $8.1 + w = 14.5$ _____

7. Write your answers to question 6 in the circles
below so that the differences between the
numbers in the connected circles are the same.

8. What is that common difference? _____

9. Solve each equation.

    a. $x + 4.3 = 6.5$ _____   **b.** $y - 1.4 = 1.9$ _____

    c. $12.1 - a = 8$ _____   **d.** $5.6 - z = 2.8$ _____

    e. $b + 12.5 = 13.4$ _____   **f.** $c - 2.9 = 1.7$ _____

    g. $7.8 + d = 9.5$ _____   **h.** $e + 10.6 = 11.0$ _____

10. Write your answers to question 9 in the
circles below so that the sums of the
numbers in the connected circles are the
same.

11. What is that common sum? _____

Analyzing Graphs

This bar graph shows the amount of money spent on movie rentals in one year.

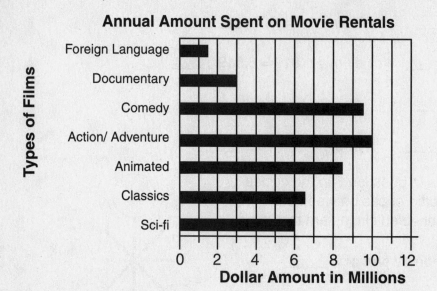

Annual Amount Spent on Movie Rentals

1. Does this graph give information about the cost of each movie rented? Explain.

_____

_____

2. Which category took in the least amount of money? _____

3. Which category was the most popular? _____

4. About how many times greater was the amount spent on documentaries than on

   foreign language films? _____

5. About how much more was spent on renting classic movies than on renting sci-fi

   films? _____

6. About how much greater was the amount spent on animated films than was spent
   on sci-fi and foreign-language film rentals together?

   _____

7. Which single category brought in an amount that is about the combined amounts
   taken in by foreign-language, documentary, and sci-fi films?

   _____

Name_____

Sandy goes jogging every day. The graph shows how far she jogged on each of 5 days last week.

8. What pattern do you see in Sandy's jogging?

_____

_____

9. If Sandy keeps to this pattern, how far will she jog on Saturday? on Sunday?

_____

10. Do you think she will continue this pattern? Why or why not?

_____

_____

11. If Sandy were to jog one extra mile on each day that she increases her distance, how far would she jog on Wednesday? on Friday? on Sunday?

_____

Simplify Fractions

Learn

What Can I Do?
I want to write a fraction in simplest form.

A fraction is in **simplest form** when the *greatest common factor* (GCF) of the numerator and denominator is 1.

To write a fraction in simplest form, divide the numerator and the denominator by the same common factors until the GCF is 1.

Method 1

$$\frac{12 \div 2}{30 \div 2} = \frac{6}{15}$$

$$\frac{6 \div 3}{15 \div 3} = \frac{2}{5}$$

Method 2

$$\frac{12 \div 6}{30 \div 6} = \frac{2}{5}$$

Try It • **Give the GCF of the numerator and the denominator.**

1. $\frac{20}{24}$ _____

2. $\frac{12}{45}$ _____

3. $\frac{21}{28}$ _____

Complete to write each fraction in simplest form.

4. $\frac{8}{12} = \frac{8 \div 4}{12 \div} = $ _____

5. $\frac{14}{35} = \frac{14 \div}{\div 7} = $ _____

6. $\frac{3}{9} = \frac{3 \div}{9 \div} = $ _____

Power Practice • **Write each fraction in simplest form.**

7. $\frac{12}{25}$ _____

8. $\frac{20}{36}$ _____

9. $\frac{28}{42}$ _____

10. $\frac{40}{48}$ _____

11. $\frac{24}{56}$ _____

12. $\frac{66}{99}$ _____

13. $\frac{28}{35}$ _____

14. $\frac{42}{49}$ _____

15. $\frac{22}{110}$ _____

Name_____

Write Fractions as Decimals and Percents

Learn

What Can I Do?
I want to write a fraction as a decimal and as a percent.

Write $\frac{3}{8}$ as a decimal.

Divide the numerator of the fraction by the denominator.

```
    0.375
8 ) 3.000
    2 4
    ───
     60
     56
    ───
     40
     40
    ───
      0
```

Write $\frac{3}{8}$ as a percent.

First, write the fraction as a decimal.

$$\frac{3}{8} = 3 \div 8 = 0.375$$

Move the decimal point two places to the right.

$$0.375 \rightarrow 37.5$$

Write the percent sign.

$$37.5 \rightarrow 37.5\%$$

So, $\frac{3}{8} = 0.375 = 37.5\%$

Try It • Write each fraction as a decimal and then as a percent.

1. $\frac{4}{5}$ = _____ = _____ %

2. $\frac{1}{2}$ = _____ = _____ %

3. $\frac{3}{4}$ = _____ = _____ %

4. $\frac{1}{8}$ = _____ = _____ %

Power Practice • Write each fraction as a decimal and as a percent. Round the decimal to the nearest thousandth if necessary.

5. $\frac{13}{20}$ = _____ = _____

6. $\frac{2}{5}$ = _____ = _____

7. $\frac{9}{10}$ = _____ = _____

8. $\frac{1}{4}$ = _____ = _____

9. $\frac{4}{25}$ = _____ = _____

10. $\frac{1}{20}$ = _____ = _____

11. $\frac{5}{12}$ = _____ = _____

12. $\frac{7}{15}$ = _____ = _____

Read and Interpret Data

Learn

The science class compiled data about how much water is used for different daily activities. The class used the data to create a table.

Activity	Average Water Use per Activity (gallons)
Showering	28
Washing Hands	2
Flushing Toilet	5
Brushing Teeth	2
Bathing	38
Washing Dishes	19

What Can I Do?
I want to read and interpret data in a table.

Find out about how much water is used each time you wash your hands.

Read down the "Activity" column until you come to "Washing Hands." Read across to find the number of gallons used.

You use about 2 gallons of water each time you wash your hands.

Try It • Use the table above to answer each question.

1. Which activities use about the same amounts of water?

_____

2. How much water is saved by taking a shower instead of a bath?

_____

3. What two activities together use about 60 gallons of water?

_____

Power Practice

Marla surveyed the sixth graders in her school about their favorite school subject. The table shows the results of her survey. Use information from the table to answer questions 4–8.

Favorite Subject	Number of Students
Language Arts	46
Social Studies	28
Science	35
Foreign Language	18
Math	40
Music	18
Art	15

4. How many students in all were surveyed? _____

5. How many more students preferred Language Arts than preferred Science?

_____

6. Which subjects had the same number of votes? _____

7. How many more students chose Science than chose Foreign Language?

_____

8. What fraction of the total number of sixth graders preferred Math? _____

The following table shows the number of students in Jonathan's school who tried out for various sports. Use the table to answer questions 9–11.

Favorite Sport	Number of Students
Touch Football	26
Softball	26
Soccer	40
Volleyball	30
Kickball	18

9. How many students in all tried out for the teams? _____

10. Which sport had the least number of students trying out? _____

11. How many more students tried out for soccer than for touch football?

_____

Multiply Fractions

Learn

What Can I Do?
I want to multiply two fractions.

Multiply: $\frac{3}{8} \times \frac{2}{3}$

Multiply the numerators. Then multiply the denominators.

$$\frac{3}{8} \times \frac{2}{3} = \frac{3 \times 2}{8 \times 3} = \frac{6}{24}$$

Write the product in simplest form.

$$\frac{6}{24} = \frac{6 \div 6}{24 \div 6} = \frac{1}{4}$$

Try It • Complete.

1. $\frac{1}{3} \times \frac{1}{2} = \frac{1 \times 1}{3 \times} = \frac{1}{\underline{}}$

2. $\frac{2}{3} \times \frac{3}{4} = \frac{2 \times}{3 \times} = \frac{6}{\underline{}} = \underline{}$

Power Practice

Multiply. Write the product in simplest form.

3. $\frac{1}{2} \times \frac{1}{4} = \underline{}$

4. $\frac{1}{5} \times \frac{1}{2} = \underline{}$

5. $\frac{2}{3} \times \frac{6}{10} = \underline{}$

6. $\frac{3}{8} \times \frac{8}{9} = \underline{}$

7. $\frac{5}{6} \times \frac{1}{5} = \underline{}$

8. $\frac{7}{9} \times \frac{3}{7} = \underline{}$

9. $\frac{2}{5} \times \frac{3}{5} = \underline{}$

10. $\frac{3}{4} \times \frac{5}{9} = \underline{}$

11. $\frac{1}{8} \times \frac{6}{7} = \underline{}$

12. $\frac{2}{7} \times \frac{7}{9} = \underline{}$

Learn with Partners & Parents

Make a Prediction

Use a bag that contains 5 blue, 5 red, and 5 white counters.

- Work with a partner. Record the number of counters as a probability of $\frac{5}{15}$ (or $\frac{1}{3}$) that any particular color will be drawn.

- Take turns. Predict which color will be drawn, then draw a counter. Revise the probabilities as you go.

- When the last counter has been drawn, start over with 1 blue counter, 5 red counters, and 5 white counters. Take turns predicting, drawing, and revising.

Add Fractions

Learn

What Can I Do?
I want to add fractions with like and unlike denominators.

If the fractions have the same denominator, add the numerators and use the same denominator.

Find $\frac{1}{5} + \frac{3}{5}$

$\frac{1}{5} + \frac{3}{5} = \frac{1+3}{5} = \frac{4}{5}$

To add fractions with unlike denominators, find equivalent fractions with a common denominator.

Find $\frac{1}{4} + \frac{5}{8}$

Rename $\frac{1}{4}$ as $\frac{2}{8}$

$\frac{1}{4} + \frac{5}{8} = \frac{2}{8} + \frac{5}{8} = \frac{7}{8}$

Try It • **Complete. Simplify if possible.**

1. $\frac{1}{2} + \frac{1}{4}$

$\frac{}{4} + \frac{1}{4} = \frac{}{4}$ _____

2. $\frac{1}{4} + \frac{3}{8}$

$\frac{}{8} + \frac{3}{8} =$ _____

3. $\frac{3}{12} + \frac{1}{4}$

$\frac{3}{12} +$ _____ $=$ _____

Power Practice • **Find each sum. Express each sum in simplest form.**

4. $\frac{1}{10} + \frac{1}{10} =$ _____

5. $\frac{4}{9} + \frac{2}{9} =$ _____

6. $\frac{2}{7} + \frac{5}{7} =$ _____

7. $\frac{1}{6} + \frac{7}{12} =$ _____

8. $\frac{7}{10} + \frac{1}{5} =$ _____

9. $\frac{2}{3} + \frac{1}{6} =$ _____

10. $\frac{3}{5} + \frac{1}{4} =$ _____

11. $\frac{1}{6} + \frac{1}{4} =$ _____

12. $\frac{3}{8} + \frac{1}{3} =$ _____

Organize Data

Learn

What Can I Do?
I want to organize data into a table.

Data includes facts such as dates, measurements, and other statistical information. There are many ways to organize data. A table is one way.

Marcel surveyed his classmates to find out if there was a birthday in each month. He recorded the birthdays on a sheet of paper.

June 3	January 15	April 1	December 9
July 30	May 9	November 27	October 14
September 29	June 3	May 17	January 22
July 6	August 10	March 20	October 25
August 13	March 7	April 7	May 30
March 16	June 19	December 26	May 5
November 27			

Then he organized the dates in a table so he could see them more easily.

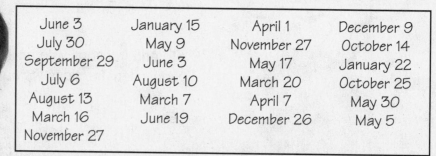

Jan	Feb	Mar	Apr	May	June	July	Aug	Sep	Oct	Nov	Dec
15		7	1	5	3	6	10	29	14	27	9
22		16	7	9	3	30	13		25	27	26
		20		17	19						
				30							

From the table, Marcel sees that no one has a birthday in February.

Try It Organize the data. The distances of the planets from the sun are shown below. Organize the data in the table according to distance, from closest to farthest.

Earth, 149,600,000 km
Saturn, 1,427,000,000 km
Mercury, 57,900,000 km
Pluto, 5,900,000,000 km
Uranus, 2,869,000,000 km
Mars, 227,900,00 km
Neptune, 4,498,000,000 km
Jupiter, 778,300,000 km
Venus, 108,200,000 km

	Planet	Distance from Sun (in kilometers)
1.		
2.		
3.		
4.		
5.		
6.		
7.		
8.		
9.		

Name_____

Power Practice • **Organize the data.**

Favorite Instrument

Instrument	Students
Violin	ЖЖ |||
Flute	ЖЖ
French horn	ЖЖ	
Clarinet	||||
Saxophone	ЖЖ ||||
Tuba	||
Trumpet	ЖЖ |||
Oboe	|||

10. Write a heading for each column of your table.

11. List the appropriate information in each column.

12. Which instrument was the favorite? _____

13. How many more students preferred trumpet to clarinet? _____

Multiply Three Factors

Learn

You can use the Associative Property of Multiplication to find the product of three factors. This property states that the way the factors are grouped does not change the product.

Associative Property of Multiplication

$(8 \times 4) \times 5 = 8 \times (4 \times 5)$

$32 \times 5 = 8 \times 20$

$160 = 160$

Multiply $4 \times 3 \times 5$

Use the Associative Property of Multiplication to group the factors.

$4 \times 3 \times 5 = 4 \times (3 \times 5)$

Find the product of the grouped factors. Then multiply that product by the third factor.

$4 \times (3 \times 5) = 4 \times 15 = 60$

Check your work by grouping another way and multiplying.

$(4 \times 3) \times 5 = 12 \times 5 = 60$

What Can I Do?
I want to multiply three factors.

Try It • **Complete to find each product.**

1. $8 \times 6 \times 2 = ($_____$\times 6) \times 2$

    $=$ _____ $\times 2$

    $=$ _____

2. $6 \times 5 \times 3 = (6 \times$ _____$) \times 3$

    $=$ _____ $\times 3$

    $=$ _____

3. $7 \times 4 \times 5 = 7 \times ($_____$\times 5)$

    $= 7 \times$ _____

    $=$ _____

4. $9 \times 4 \times 3 = 9 \times ($_____$\times$ _____$)$

    $= 9 \times$ _____

    $=$ _____

Name_____

Power Practice • Multiply. Use the Associative Property of Multiplication.

5. $3 \times 6 \times 7 =$ _____

6. $6 \times 2 \times 2 =$ _____

7. $4 \times 5 \times 2 =$ _____

8. $6 \times 3 \times 4 =$ _____

9. $2 \times 8 \times 4 =$ _____

10. $10 \times 5 \times 6 =$ _____

11. $4 \times 5 \times 8 =$ _____

12. $3 \times 12 \times 2 =$ _____

13. $2 \times 6 \times 12 =$ _____

14. $4 \times 5 \times 5 =$ _____

15. $7 \times 4 \times 3 =$ _____

16. $4 \times 9 \times 4 =$ _____

17. $4 \times 9 \times 7 =$ _____

18. $3 \times 3 \times 9 =$ _____

19. $6 \times 9 \times 2 =$ _____

20. $8 \times 9 \times 3 =$ _____

21. $5 \times 5 \times 3 =$ _____

22. $10 \times 5 \times 3 =$ _____

23. $7 \times 2 \times 49 =$ _____

24. $12 \times 3 \times 30 =$ _____

25. $14 \times 4 \times 38 =$ _____

26. $23 \times 14 \times 9 =$ _____

27. $6 \times 30 \times 15 =$ _____

28. $34 \times 8 \times 16 =$ _____

29. $50 \times 5 \times 13 =$ _____

30. $9 \times 13 \times 11 =$ _____

31. $45 \times 3 \times 25 =$ _____

32. $15 \times 12 \times 2 =$ _____

33. $40 \times 50 \times 20 =$ _____

34. $8 \times 66 \times 30 =$ _____

35. $18 \times 42 \times 56 =$ _____

36. $9 \times 100 \times 30 =$ _____

37. $20 \times 11 \times 60 =$ _____

38. $14 \times 7 \times 42 =$ _____

Name_____

Heads Up and Counting

Take a coin and flip it 50 times.

1. Before you begin, predict how many times you think you will get heads. Record your prediction.

_____

2. Each time you flip the coin, record the results of the throw. Write "H" for heads and "T" for tails.

_____

3. How did the results of your experiment compare with your prediction?

_____

4. Share your results with eight of your classmates. Use all the results to make a bar graph showing the number of times the coin landed heads up on each throw. Show one bar for each classmate and one for yourself. Use the grid below for your graph. Show the students' names on the vertical axis. Use a scale on the horizontal axis that will show the greatest number of successful throws that occurred. Give your graph a title.

5. How close did you and your classmates come to your predictions? Explain.

_____

_____

Toss a number cube 50 times.

6. Before you begin, predict what you think will be the greatest number of times a number will come up on top of the cube. Record your prediction.

_____

7. Each time you toss the cube, record which of the numbers 1–6 comes up.

_____

8. Tabulate the results for each number. Record which number came up most often.

_____

9. Share your results with eight classmates. Use all the results to make a bar graph showing the greatest number of times any of the six numbers came up. Show one bar for each classmate and one for yourself. Use the grid below for the graph. Show the students' names on the vertical axis. Use a scale on the horizontal axis that will show the greatest number of times a number came up. Give your graph a title.

10. Compare the graph your group made with the graphs of other groups. Are there any similarities in the graphs? Explain.

_____

_____

Name_____

Patterns in Multiples

You can use a calculator to discover patterns in
multiples. Look at the following multiples of 99.

$$1 \times 99 = 99$$
$$2 \times 99 = 198$$
$$3 \times 99 = 297$$
$$4 \times 99 = 396$$

1. What number pattern do you see in these products?

_____

_____

_____

2. According to the pattern, what will the fifth multiple of 99 be? Check if your
prediction is correct.

_____

3. Use the pattern to find other multiples of 99, up to 10×99. Then multiply to check.

_____

4. Does the pattern hold? Explain.

_____

_____

_____

Now look at the following multiples.

$$11 \times 99 = 1,089$$
$$12 \times 99 = 1,188$$
$$13 \times 99 = 1,287$$

5. What pattern do you see?

_____

_____

_____

_____

© McGraw-Hill School Division

6. Predict what the fourteenth multiple will be. Check if your prediction is correct.

_____

7. Use the pattern to find the fifteenth through twentieth multiples of 99. Then multiply to check. Does the pattern hold? Explain.

_____

_____

8. Now find these multiples and describe any pattern you see.

$1 \times 909 =$ _____

$2 \times 909 =$ _____

$3 \times 909 =$ _____

$4 \times 909 =$ _____

9. Describe the pattern you see.

_____

_____

_____

_____

_____

10. Find the fifth multiple of 909.

_____

11. Find the sixth through tenth multiples of 909. Does the pattern hold?

_____

_____